AF422989

"For as long as I have known Katherine, she has been able to take some of my deepest wounds, put them into words I could never find, and remind me of what God's Word says about those hurts and how He has already overcome them. For that, I could not be any more grateful. I am confident you will find *Wholehearted Trust* is just that—the testimony of a faithful friend to remind you where to look in some of life's darkest moments."

— **SAVANNAH SIMONS**

"This book is insightful in a way that makes Christianity feel less daunting. It provides a resting place for weary, anxious souls who just need to hear that you don't need to be perfect. It was encouragement—loving encouragement, may I add—and I felt understood reading it because it speaks on areas of difficulty we all struggle with."

— **CASSIE TROSINO**

"*Wholehearted Trust* is a candid, intentional blend of real-life sobering stories and godly wisdom. Katherine takes her own life experiences and utilizes them to show people the importance of abiding in the Lord. She displays how we can look at our lives as a track record of God's sovereignty and trust in His goodness despite how gut-wrenching the pain of this world may be."

— **LAUREN LUKEHART**

"Katherine takes the journey through a family tragedy and puts into words how turning to God, surrendering to Jesus, and living to tell others about the hope of the Gospel brings joy and peace in the hardest of circumstances. Her study and love of God's Word are clear throughout her writings. This book will encourage and strengthen the mature Christian and explain to the unbeliever what the Good News of Jesus Christ truly means."

— **JANA FLATTMANN**

"I never met Rebecca here, but I sure am thankful for her life and how she pointed to Jesus. I am so encouraged by Katherine's wisdom and dedication to vulnerably share her sister's story."

— **KALEY RUELAS**

"As someone prone to rely on my feelings or circumstances to determine God's nearness or goodness toward me, Katherine beautifully articulates that God's nearness and goodness are unchanging for those of us in Christ. Because of that firm truth, we can experience peace and comfort that surpass understanding. I am confident this book and the Gatti family's story woven within it will greatly encourage you and your trust in God's plans for you."

— JILL STRINGER

"You are holding a personal testimony that brings hope to us—the hope of God. This book has brought divine peace from the Holy Spirit into my heart and helped set me on His path of righteousness in this season of life that has felt so uncomfortable. It has been such a beautiful reminder of who God is."

— SIDNEY SMITH

"When we face horrific circumstances, it's difficult to believe a loving God is in control. In the midst of your grief and questions, Katherine comes alongside you and holds your hand, walking you through your pain while vulnerably sharing her own."

— HALEY ATKINS

"What a gift this book is to people in all stages of life! *Wholehearted Trust* is a testament to God's faithfulness to us and the gift His love is; we just have to choose Him. Katherine reminds us that we never have to do life alone, and when we rely on the Lord wholeheartedly, we can live in His abundant peace, joy, and purpose."

— RILEY O'CONNOR

"I have personally watched Katherine cling to Jesus through heavy trials and stay faithful even in the lowest moments of life. In *Wholehearted Trust*, Katherine beautifully displays her strength through forgiveness and teaches us how to navigate the brokenness of this world."

— REESE KELLEY

wholehearted trust

WALKING BY FAITH THROUGH FEAR, GRIEF, AND DISAPPOINTMENT

KATHERINE GATTI

To my sisters:

Being your older sister is truly the greatest honor. May you always cherish the gift of knowing Rebecca and being her sister. I wrote this with you on my heart, hoping that it will serve as a reminder of the Lord's faithfulness to our family. I pray you wholeheartedly trust God for all the days of your life and lead others to do the same. I love you and I'm always in your corner.

Contents

Foreword

Often people compliment my children and ask for my parenting secrets. My response, in truth, is the factors that cultivated their strengths are the same factors we attempt as parents to protect our children from experiencing and have little to do with me. It is the difficulties and heartaches that shape our character most deeply. It is these valleys in life that provide us the opportunities to lean on Christ and learn more about the absolute truth of His character. As a parent, I can honestly say that all that is beautiful in my girls is a direct result of the Lord working in their lives. This book is evidence of this truth.

Katherine has always stood apart, especially in how she sought the Lord and showed discipline in her Bible study and prayer as a young child consistently into becoming a young lady. As a result of her discipline, she often is credited by her mentors with a more mature faith than even the adults leading her. She engaged in countless studies with her father about spiritual maturity on the book of James and mission trips from the mere age of twelve; she was clearly set apart to be different. Life has a way of throwing us all obstacles and struggles to manage. Katherine transparently presents many of her battle wounds from relatively typical scars to deep, life–altering cuts. To help others learn from her successes and failures, she shares all these spiritual lessons which can be applied to many situations in front of us.

Our home has always prioritized sharing the Gospel with others, but Katherine has taken mentorship of others to a new level in her life. Her love for discipleship was sparked in her college years. Many of her friends and peers just slightly younger than her would consistently seek her advice. All those lessons learned from her own battles were applied to help others in the midst of their conflicts and hurts. Here is where she found her passion: teaching others about the Lord, how to be disciplined in knowing Him better, and how to apply that knowledge to daily life in the good and the bad times.

This book is primarily guided by the joy she has received by helping and loving others well. So many of her sweet friends have encouraged her to share the wisdom she has gained in her life experiences with the masses after they were changed by encountering God with Katherine. The friendships I have witnessed develop as these young ladies pursue Christ together in openness, honesty, and accountability provides hope that light continues to prevail in a world full of darkness. It is my prayer that the words so carefully laid out before you will spark light and love in your own life and draw you closer to Christ.

I have found it true that God provides you gifts through experiencing difficulties that we are unable to receive by any other means. However, it is our responsibility to share Christ and His gifts provided to us to the best of our abilities. I pray in this book you see both the intent and the message my oldest daughter has endeavored to share with you. The pages that follow carry truths that were learned, developed, and tested through experiences we would never have chosen to endure. May the words to follow equip you for the struggles of this life and prepare you for the battles ahead that can't be avoided. May this book guide you to practices that help to prevent struggles that can be avoided. It's not often the simplest path to wholeheartedly trust God, but it's always worth it.

— SUSAN GATTI, KATHERINE'S MOM

Introduction

The movie *Miss Congeniality* claims April 25th is the perfect date—not too hot, not too cold.[1] Even though I've only seen the movie once, I'll never forget this claim. I remember April 25th being called perfect because in my life it holds a different meaning. In 2007, April 25th was the day my sister, Rebecca, was born. And the day she died. And the day she came back to life. This book about my sister was released on April 25, 2023— the day that would have been her sixteenth birthday.

Even since I was a seven-year-old girl with a new baby sister named Rebecca, I knew she was special. I knew that even though her life looked different from the start, God had a plan and a purpose for her. In your hands, you are holding a testament to the impact of my little sister's short life. God used her to teach me to trust Him wholeheartedly in the midst of fear, grief, and disappointment. I've seen so much evidence of God's faithfulness throughout Rebecca's life. I'm praying this book will be an encouragement to others who are struggling to trust God.

Butterflies always make me think of Rebecca. They're delicate and beautiful. As I've been writing this book, I've seen butterflies everywhere. Even in the hurt and grief, God continues to gift me ways to see His beauty, feel His presence, and remember His promises. Butterflies don't begin their life in their most beautiful form. They're larvae first, then caterpillars, and then bundled inside a cocoon. This journey gives them nourishment and strength on the way to what they are becoming. While it's not as pretty as the end result, it's necessary for their transformation.

We want beauty without the process, but it's the process that produces and matures us into what is genuinely strong and beautiful.

Our lives often resemble this. We want beauty without the process, but it's the process that produces and matures us into what is genuinely strong and beautiful. While we may not choose the processes that form us, we can choose where we place our trust and draw our strength as we endure the difficulties.

Trials disrupt our realities, leading us to question ourselves and our beliefs. *How are you supposed to trust God in the midst of pain you didn't choose? Is peace possible when all you feel is anxiety? How do you respond to unexpected grief when you lose someone you love?* I certainly don't have all the answers, but I do have my story. I'm sharing it with you today because even though revisiting these memories is painful, I want to walk alongside you through your pain, holding your hand and reminding you that you are not alone. While I can't promise this book will solve your problems, I do hope it helps to lighten the load you are carrying by pointing you to hope that's indestructible.

When we don't understand or see the good, we have the opportunity to walk by faith and cultivate our trust in the God who promises to work all things together for our good in His timing—even if that's not until eternity. As we trust in a sovereign God and choose an eternal perspective, we can have peace, comfort, and contentment even if our circumstances don't change.

No matter your history with God or Christianity, this book will meet you where you are. If you dare to choose it, this is a roadmap of how to trust God and lead others to do the same. I can't think of anything else I could encourage you with that would be sustainable through everything life brings. As you read Rebecca's story, I hope you are encouraged to face your own hardships with courage, grace, and trust in a God who loves you.

As we trust in a sovereign God and choose an eternal perspective, we can have peace, comfort, and contentment even if our circumstances don't change.

ONE

The Birth of Fear

The black granite displays my reflection, and my eyes squint as the bright Louisiana sun bounces off the face of her tombstone. The dew on the ground soaks through my shoes; I would take them off if there weren't so many ant beds. The wind picks up the smell of the freshly cut grass covering the stone's base.

Mom pours water over the curved top, wiping away specks of dust and picking off blades of grass. The stone glistens. Flecks within the granite sparkle when the light hits. Dad picks weeds and stomps ant beds. We bought dozens of roses at the grocery store. Plucking the pink, yellow, and red petals free, we let them fall to the ground until all the grass is covered. We pray and cry. Today, she would have been sixteen years old.

Each of us, Rebecca's three sisters, created a part of the memorial. Elizabeth designed the back and Charlotte created the footstone. My handwriting loops the letters of my sister's remembrance:

Rebecca Leigh Gatti

April 25, 2007 – July 31, 2017

Beloved Daughter and Sister

Romans 5:3-5

Elizabeth, three years younger than me, created the artwork for the back of the stone. She beautifully drew flowers, roses, a lamb, and butterflies while intentionally considering the symbolism of each. Elizabeth (or "Beth") livens a room with her ability to ignite genuine laughter and bring people together. We share a strong sense of sarcasm, our identical laughs often amplifying each others.

On summer mornings in elementary school, I read beside the pool in our backyard while Elizabeth swam. She'd splash and beg me to get in until I finally conceded (mostly for the sake of my soggy book pages) and we played mermaids. We colored a concert stage on the back porch with sidewalk chalk, performing Hannah Montana songs on our purple and pink karaoke machine. One year for Christmas, she gave me a necklace with a gold heart sitting inside a silver circle, engraved with the words "chance made us sisters, hearts made us friends." Mermaids are still her favorite; she loves the beach and her room is decorated in ocean blue and covered with seashells.

Elizabeth was a freshman when I was a senior in high school, so I drove us both to school. One morning, I accidentally locked her in my car when I left for an early meeting. She set the car alarm off as everyone was passing senior row to go inside! By the time I came back to turn it off, Beth was laughing at herself with tears popping out of the corners of her eyes. While I'm easily embarrassed by small mistakes, Elizabeth's easygoing nature brings her more quickly to laughter than embarrassment.

In the first three years with her driver's license, Elizabeth was in approximately thirteen wrecks, almost all with stationary objects. Yet she is incredibly smart, now attending Vanderbilt to earn a degree in Biomedical Engineering. When we shared a room we both wished we had our own space; now we live in different states and purchase plane tickets because we want to have sleepovers.

Charlotte is an entire decade younger than me and the grand finale of the Gatti girls. She designed the footstone, drawing all five immediate family members' favorite memories with Rebecca. Mine was holding Rebecca's hand. Char and I have sister sleepovers when I'm in town, staying up late and giggling while she gives me life advice.

Our house is a second home to many, which means my friends are more like family. When these bonus big sisters come back to our hometown, they visit Charlotte even when I'm gone. My friend group from home stayed over one night the summer after I graduated from college; Charlotte stayed up playing card games and laughing with us.

Ten-year-old Charlotte stayed with me during my junior year of college. My best friends and I took her to Six Flags for "the most fun night of her entire life!" It didn't matter that she was terrified of roller coasters; she loved fighting with foam swords outside the rides and drinking 7-Eleven Slurpees at midnight.

She can carry on an intelligent conversation with anyone she meets. Our family cherishes her ability to lighten any situation with her quick and innocent humor. She lives up to the meaning of her name, which is **strong**, and her heart is kind.

Whenever there is a tragedy, whether in real life or in one of her favorite books, she is moved to tears. One summer, we watched *Wonder Woman* on the way to the beach. Charlotte sobbed over the loss of Chris Pine's character, Elizabeth and I laughed in sync with each other, and Mom told us to be sensitive to Charlotte's emotions while she struggled to contain her own laughter. Charlotte's heart breaks when she knows the hearts of others are breaking. This deep empathy is something she possesses at a young age because she has felt the depths of grief herself.

Rebecca is unapologetically everyone's favorite. She is pure and perfect, healthy and whole—the way one can only be when they are finally in the presence of God. Becca was born on April 25, 2007, when I was seven, Elizabeth was four, and Charlotte wasn't around to entertain us yet. Now I am twenty-three, Elizabeth is twenty, Charlotte is thirteen, and Rebecca has been in heaven for five years.

As soon as I learned my mom was pregnant, I dreamed about what life would look like with a new baby in the family. I tend to get ahead of myself, planning for what I desire rather than praying expectantly for where God will lead me. It's more natural for me to tell God my plans and pray for His stamp of approval than to hold my hands open to whatever God sees as best.

It often seems that the tighter I grip onto my plans, the more they hurt coming out of my hands. The more I try to hold on, the more difficult it is to be open-handed and trust God. My plans seem great, so why shouldn't they work out? If only it were that simple.

I imagined everything we would do together, from riding bikes to reading books. I wanted to teach Rebecca to swim and paint, play the piano and write in cursive, love others and love the Lord. The possibilities seemed endless. The waiting was only bearable because there was an end date approaching.

I've always seen my mom as a role model. Both my parents instilled in me a love for learning from a very young age. Just as my mom nurtured me and helped me to understand things about life and faith, I wanted to do the same for my new little sister.

THE STRENGTH OF A SERVANT

My mom, Susan, is a peacemaker, gentle and wise in the words she intentionally speaks. She has hazel brown eyes, light skin, and dark hair that I found in clumps in the bathroom trash can; the stress of the unknown regarding Rebecca's health was so great it took a physical toll on her body. We look and act similarly. We typically split meals at restaurants because we want the same thing. I run into my mom's high school friends at our hometown grocery store, and they stare as if witnessing my school-aged mother mirrored in me.

Mom loves *Pride & Prejudice*, so it's fitting she ended up with four daughters. She's the fun church camp leader, bringing all the energy and wisdom. One summer, her campers were dozing off during their small group discussion, so she cannon-balled into the pool—this woke them up! She and my dad have always taught the youth at church and hosted Bible studies in our home.

She is a wonderful mom to me and a spiritual mom to many others. In high school, she took me and my best friends to Savannah, Georgia, for our senior trip. These girls confide in my mom to this day. Mom prayed over Breanna on her wedding day, encourages Savannah when she's struggling at law school, and kindly invests in Kelci when she comes to her for wisdom. Her life is one many desire to emulate because we desire to have the same faith and strength she radiates.

Her life testifies that spiritual strength is more valuable than anything we can develop physically during our lifetime. Our pursuit of achievements, success, status, relationships, money, approval, beauty, or anything else besides God so easily distracts us and eventually disappoints us.[1] Unlike everything else, our relationship with God lasts forever.

God's complete sovereignty means He holds limitless power while also having the wisdom and ability to do all He pleases. Strength is found through acknowledging God's sovereign power, and—rather than resisting it and striving to do things our own way—we surrender to His Lordship.

One act of surrender Mom often begins her days with is spending time with God. She sits on the beige couch in our living room reading her Bible and writing in her prayer journal. By beginning her day setting her mind on God, she is able to have eyes open to see how God is working in her day ahead and a heart encouraged by the promises of His Word.

I never learned how to braid hair because she does it so perfectly. I would go to school with french fishtails, Katniss side braids, and anything else we would imagine and create. On the day of Rebecca's funeral, Mom braided Becca's hair, perfectly piecing together each delicate strand.

My mom loved her dad and served her mother every day during my grandfather's battles with cancer. As his final fight against cancer ended, our family gathered around him in the wood-paneled living room of the home he had built for his family. I witnessed my mother holding his hand, reading him Psalm 23. As she read the last line of the Psalm, "…and I shall dwell in the house of the Lord, forever," he breathed his last breath.[2]

Even as her earthly father's body passed away, her hope was rooted in the salvation she and my Pops have through Jesus. My mom lives in the absolute assurance of the hope Christians have in eternity. Even though we face heartbreak and endure grief, nothing can ultimately separate us from God's love for us.[3] Her confidence in the Gospel and constant dependence on the Lord are what give her strength.

Surrender breeds strength

I know her strength does not come from herself; it is a direct result of her intentional and constant trust in God. It is something she has cultivated over decades of pursuing Jesus. Jesus Christ is the Son of God and a solid foundation for our lives. Genuine strength can only come from the One who is good, right, and true.

My mom's strength grows with her sanctification, and it is a result of persevering through trials and seeking God through it all. Because she is filled with the Lord's strength, she points those around her to also find their strength in Him.

Surrender breeds strength—we will not develop real strength until we have surrendered our lives to the source of all strength. We will always fail on our own, but we do not have to do this life on our own. By depending on the Lord's strength, we can have the confidence to live in full obedience to Him and all He calls us to do.

LITTLE MISTAKES

This was my mom's third pregnancy. One morning at thirty-six weeks pregnant, she felt a different kind of unwell, so she stayed home from work to rest. She checked her blood pressure and saw it was a little high. After she called the doctor and told him how she was feeling, he advised her to come into the hospital as a precaution.

Their main concern was that she may have preeclampsia. When a pregnant woman has preeclampsia, her blood pressure is abnormally high; this can be dangerous for both mom and baby. Nurses confirmed her elevated blood pressure and ordered tests to see if her symptoms were truly preeclampsia.

Her doctor came in from a midday workout casually wearing tennis shoes and shorts rather than scrubs. Seeing how far along she was and her slightly heightened blood pressure, he said they might as well go ahead and induce her before receiving the test results. He wanted to get it done before the weekend because he planned to go out of town. We later learned her blood pressure was not unusually high for a woman who is eight months pregnant, and she didn't have preeclampsia.

The doctor who delivered my sister Elizabeth retired after only a few visits into my mom's third pregnancy. He recommended my parents use this doctor who was taking his place at the practice. My parents were unaware that he was not yet licensed as an OBGYN. At this point in their lives, they had no reason to distrust what a hospital or doctor recommended.

After my dad arrived, they induced my mom's labor without noticing she was in a regular hospital bed instead of one designed for delivery. To correct this mistake, they had my mom get up and move as best as she could to a proper bed after they'd already broken her water. We think this is when her placenta began to rupture.

Her ruptured placenta was only the beginning of countless things that went wrong. When recalling this traumatic night, my dad compares rehashing every little detail to rewatching a car wreck in slow motion. At each point when the doctor could have fixed a mistake or lessened the damage, Rebecca was only injured more and my mom was put further at risk.

THE WAITING ROOM

Meanwhile, our entire extended family gathered in the hospital waiting room. Since both my parents are deeply rooted in Bossier City, Louisiana, every family gathering is a party full of cousins, grandparents, great-aunts, and second cousins. This waiting room was packed with loved ones. Dad suggested I interview everyone with our handheld video camera, documenting the last moments before everything changed.

"A video of so many people who loved her before she was even born will be special to show Rebecca one day," said Dad.

I watched these videos for the first time today, fourteen years after I filmed them. It is difficult to see the sweet moments knowing what is coming. The videos begin with my dad's explanation of how to operate the camera, then I run off to interrupt conversations and overwork the zoom lens.

My family's laughter bounces off the walls and floods the room. Everyone looks happier, lighter—so blissfully unaware of the trauma and tragedy occurring in the other room. The camera-shy family members smile awkwardly, kindly pointing out someone I must have missed, sending me off in their direction.

Uncle Robbie, my dad's older brother, is dressed in his baseball coach's uniform. He coached my cousins, Hal and Hayden. When we had daddy-daughter dances when we were young, he came as our bonus date so both Elizabeth and I would have a dance partner.

"This is your new Uncle Robbie, and I wish you would hurry up and get here, my sweet little niece," he says, looking wide-eyed right into the camera. "You can come out of the oven. Attention! The bun is ready, so get here—'cause it's late! We love you, we can't wait to see you."

Granny, my dad's mom, claps and cheers, "Susan, Susan, she's our man! If she can't do it, nobody can!"

My dad's cousin Hollye-Faye sits on the floor making paper dolls with Elizabeth. No words from my four-year-old little sister; she sticks her tongue out and blows spit right into the camera. I move along.

"All right, you have to tell me when you're filming," Aunt Sharon, my dad's aunt, fluffs her blonde bob.

I giggle and say, "Oops, I already am!"

"Well, little girl, I'm up here for your birth." I can hear the smile in her voice just as clearly as I can see it on her face. "I'm with your big sisters and we can hardly wait for you to get here. Hurry up and be born. I'm Aunt Sharon, bye-bye!" She waves with both hands and I pan around the room.

I hurry over to my sweet Nana, my mom's mother, who enjoys being goofy and finding the latest life hacks on Facebook to send to her grandkids.

"We're waiting for the birth of Rebecca Leigh, and Katherine is just as happy and as excited as can be," says Nana. She has a singsong in her voice, and her short white hair frames her face.

"The whole way down in the car, Elizabeth couldn't stop saying, 'I'm gonna be the big sister!'" Nana had picked us up from dance class that afternoon before she and Pops took us to the hospital. We grew up down the street from my mom's parents, so there was rarely a week we didn't spend time with them.

"Now Katherine, where are you going to sleep tonight? Maybe we'll get to have a sleepover at my house! Do you think you will be able to contain your excitement enough to sleep?" says Nana. I don't respond to her questions because I am too distracted watching the live video on the little screen that jets out the side of the camera's body.

"You're just looking at me on that screen, aren't you? Am I just that beautiful?" Nana grins at the camera and tucks her hair behind her ears. She sends me over to Pops, my mom's dad.

"Are you going to be the big sister, or the big big sister?" my Pops asks me.

"The big big."

"We had a discussion coming up here about how long you've been a big sister, since you were two years old. And now you are five?" He furrows his eyebrows together in feigned confusion.

"Seven!" I shout and laugh.

"That's right, seven years old. And that is wonderful, and congratulations to Rebecca."

I pan the camera away from Pops and search for my next interviewee. I land on my mom's friend. Like my sister, her name is also Elizabeth.

"Miss Elizabeth, I'm taping you!" I giggle and zoom in and out.

She smiles, but keeps talking to my aunt.

"You know, it's good that it happened this way and they decided to induce her," says Miss Elizabeth. "Susan has been saying she feels so big and wants the baby to come soon!"

I return to my sister Elizabeth still making paper dolls with Hollye-Faye and beg her to look at the camera.

"Elizabeth! Beth. Beth. E-liz-a-beth!" I say her name over and over, but all I manage to get out of her was a side eye and a firm "no," then she keeps putting stickers on her paper dolls.

As I turn the camera to the right side of my Granny's face, my Aunt Jennifer comes into the frame. Her bleach blonde hair is pulled into a bump firmly cemented atop her head.

"No more visitors, Susan's blood pressure spiked. The nurses said it's not completely our fault, but the last stint of people was too much. But it was the funniest thing..." Aunt Jennifer turns her back to me as she tells the adults a story.

Unfortunately, I can't hear much of what she's saying over my yelling *Aunt Jenny-four!!* over and over. I cringe as I watch the video back, hearing fragments of her mentioning my mom starting to show signs of distress. It was brushed off as overstimulation from visitors.

Jennifer says, "I'm going to go pick up the boys, so I might be the tenth person to hold Rebecca or something like that, but that's okay."

"Oh, is it definitely going to be Rebecca?" Aunt Sharon asks.

Nana chimes in, "Rebecca Leigh, supposedly, but you know, they could still change their minds."

"Well, that's what Allison told me last week in Sunday school." Aunt Sharon taught the fifth grade girls class at our church, and Allison is the oldest of the cousins. Over the years, Aunt Sharon taught almost all of the younger girls in our family. When I was in her class, she often took Elizabeth and me to lunch after church. She was also an English teacher; she taught us how to use proper grammar and diagram sentences. Most importantly, she let us ask her all the questions we had about God and never made us feel silly for wanting to verbally process our doubts.

"You know that one," Nana points at my little sister who is still decorating her paper dolls, "was Elizabeth when they came into the hospital, and Sarah Elizabeth when they came out of the hospital, so I'm not banking on anything for certain."

Nana raises her eyebrows, and she and Sharon laugh. My parents would have too many unexpected decisions to make, so changing Rebecca Leigh's name from the original plan was never considered.

"Are you taping me?" asks Pops as I walk toward him.

"I know this good-looking little girl named Katherine," he leans in and lifts me onto his lap, "And she's going to have a baby?" I laugh at his silly comments. My Pops could always make me giggle.

"No, her mother's going to have a baby, and she's going to have a baby sister. And pretty soon she will have baby ducks walking around her yard. What do you think about that?"

I slide off his lap and Pops smiles at me. I run over to my Granny and Poppy, and Poppy sticks out his tongue.

Jennifer returns from gathering more information, telling everyone the doctor walked in and said, "Button up, let's get in here and do it."

Dad calls his brother, Robbie, with a sobering update: Mom's blood pressure has skyrocketed. On the other side of the phone, Robbie hears the beeping monitors and frazzled nurses. The first signs of concern are emerging. As soon as he hangs up, Uncle Robbie calls our pastor.

"It's not looking good. Can you gather people together to pray?" asks Robbie. He walks into another room out of the camera's reach.

"How do I turn this off?!" I ask desperately. My mom's friend takes the camera from me to help.

"Come here, my girl," says Pops. I climb into my Pops' lap, and my mom's friend turns the camera onto us.

"Hurry up, Rebecca," I sing the words, swaying back and forth. My deep dimples dig into my cheeks, and my missing front teeth are evident. My light brown hair falling right below my shoulders is wavy and parted right down the middle, tucked behind my tiny ears and a little tangled around my glasses.

"Are you going to change the first dirty diaper?" my Pops asks. "Should we tell your mom to save it for you?"

I shake my head and wrap my arms around his neck, giggling as I give him bunny ears. I clutch the ends of my fingertips, hugging his neck but leaning back enough to see his face.

He says something to make me laugh that I can't quite hear on the video. I kiss his cheek and lay my head on his shoulder, and he kisses me on the forehead, smiling and leaning his head against mine as he wraps his arms around me, lacing his fingers together.

This piece of the video with my Pops was a little treasure I didn't know existed. I'm reminded of how much my Pops always doted over his granddaughters. He loved caring for Rebecca and could usually be found rocking her in the corner of every family gathering. Watching this video now makes me miss him even more.

The video cuts abruptly from me sitting in my Pops' arms to my dad videoing my mom in the hospital bed.

"Hey baby, we're just here waiting on you. Momma, you got anything to say?" Dad asks.

Mom forces a smile, but her eyes don't leave the clock on the wall. She is timing her contractions, knowing it doesn't feel right.

Unlike the rest of their children, there is no birth video. The shock was too great, the damage too swift. The next shot is my dad skimming the camera over the fetal monitoring strips, showing how long Rebecca's heartbeat was flat.

DEATH & LIFE

Our family waited long into the night for the arrival of Rebecca Leigh Gatti. We were filled with anticipation and expectation, eager to meet and hold her. Now that the video camera was with Dad, I counted the green squares on the beige tile to help pass the time.

Hours went by, and no one told me what was happening. I mistook the heads bowed in prayer for people falling asleep. I had no reason to think anything would go wrong; hospitals are supposed to be a place where people come to be healed, not somewhere that could take your life instead of saving it.

I sat on a green cushioned chair, gripping the edge and turning my knuckles whitish-purple, staring at my feet as my brown Mary Janes swung back and forth, back and forth. The bright fluorescent lights stung my eyes and made everything around me a little out of focus. Naive and impatient, I struggled to sit still as I waited to meet my new best friend.

Eventually, our family started to leave for the night. Our mom's friend took my little sister Elizabeth and me home. Miss Elizabeth let me sit in the front seat for the first time because she did not have room for us in the back amongst a lot of clutter.

"Are you sure? I'm not allowed to ride in the front seat," I said. I've always been a rule follower.

"Yes, sweetie, it'll be safe, I promise. Just do me a favor and don't tell your mom about this part of our adventure?"

"Okay, I promise," With wide eyes and an anxious stomach, I held out my pinky and wrapped it around hers.

And I kept that promise for over ten years! I think it's the only true secret I have ever kept from my mom. She always meets my brutal honesty and raw emotions with wisdom and without judgment, teaching me how to process my feelings through the truth of God's Word and prayer. We share our faith along with our love and loss of Rebecca. She is constant and faithful, my confidant and trusted friend. At my high school graduation party, this withheld truth finally came out.

"I want to write a book about Rebecca's life, but I don't want to incriminate you by sharing the details of that night," I jokingly said to Miss Elizabeth.

"Shhh! Your mom still doesn't know?" she said, her eyes wide. "She will never let me live this down."

"I still don't know what?" asked Mom, walking up and smirking at us. Mom leaned forward and raised her eyebrows, waiting for me to share.

"She may or may not have let me ride in her front seat on the way from the hospital that night," I raised my eyebrows back at my mom, grinning at her friend.

"Katherine Lynne Gatti! You know better than to have done that." My mom laughed, completely shocked. "I seriously can not believe you kept this from me for so long."

"Susan, you know how messy my car always is—it was that or strap her on the hood!" Her friend refuted the inclination that she was an unfit babysitter, her electric laughter carrying through the room.

Our tears mixed with laughter, emotions bleeding into each other. We didn't have to explain why we were crying; it was impossible to remember that night without doing so.

I can never thank my mom's friend enough for being there that night, repeatedly allowing me to guilt her into saying yes to one more episode of *Little House on the Prairie*. She kept talking with me late into the night, letting me imagine all the fun I was going to have with my little sisters once we were finally all together.

Back at the hospital, my dad was fighting on his knees and my mom was fighting for her life. Some of the gravest mistakes made by the doctor included the heart rate monitors, which are crucial for determining the health and state of both mom and baby throughout delivery. They placed the external heart rate monitor on my mom's stomach, but thought it was broken because the reading "simply couldn't be."

Next, they placed the internal monitor on my mom's cervix instead of on Rebecca's head. Looking back over the medical records, the internal monitor's heart rate reads the exact same as my mom's. They didn't catch this until it was too late. By the time the doctor realized this mistake, Rebecca had been in distress for a long time. They missed a lot of signs and were forced to perform an emergency C-section in an attempt to save my sister's life.

My mom lost so much blood they did not think she was going to live. My dad looked down at my mom, and she was white as a sheet with an oxygen mask covering her face. Her brown hair was damp with sweat and tears, and her eyelids fluttered shut as her energy quickly faded.

He asked her, "Are you prepared for the worst-case scenario?" and she nodded, knowing he was asking if she was prepared to die, to walk into eternity with Jesus.

My dad placed his hand on my mom's rigid stomach, looked down at her, and asked, "Who are you trusting?"

Pulling the mask away from her fatigued face, she tearfully said, "God."

My dad kissed my mom's forehead, then they rolled her away to surgery. In preparation for the C-section, they draped my mom's arms straight out to the side—like she was on a cross. This reminded my mom of Jesus and what His death on the cross means for her as a Christian. Mom knew she could die, and she remained calm.

As they fought to save my mom's life, they also fought to give Rebecca a chance at life. Later, the doctors told her if she had not been so calm they would not have been able to focus on Rebecca like they needed to. She was filled with inexplicable peace because her mind was set on God, not the chaos surrounding her. Mom trusted Him with both her life and the life of her daughter.

FIFTEEN MINUTES

As soon as babies are born, they are given an Apgar score. This assesses if they are in need of further medical attention. The five components of the test are color, heart rate, reflexes, muscle tone, and respiration. Each category is scored from 0 to 2, with 0 being the worst and 2 being the best. The categories are added together to determine the baby's Apgar score.

A score of 7–10 is considered normal, with a score of 4–6 indicating the baby will likely need to go to the NICU. Rebecca was tested one minute, five minutes, ten minutes, and fifteen minutes after she came into the world. Each time, her score was 0. She was not alive.

When she came into the world, Rebecca didn't cry. My mom wrote about this moment on a blog called *Gatti Girls*. Her friend, Kristin, created this online space to keep family and friends updated on Rebecca. In the back of this book, there's a section called **Stories from Rebecca's Family**. It's where you can find this entire blog post by my mom along with a collection of some of my family's writings about Rebecca.

Mom wrote, "While I heard the physician's words, 'Oh my Lord,' and I did not hear the sound of my baby, only one thought brought me solace—GOD IS IN CONTROL." Even in the face of death, her faith was not shaken.

Because of one doctor's careless mistakes, I almost lost two of the most important people in my life. Rebecca was dead for more than fifteen minutes. Against all odds, the hospital staff was eventually able to coerce her little heart to start pumping again. She's similar to Jesus Himself in that way: dying and coming back to life. She was alive but she was also in great pain from the moment her earthly life began—her body a prison fighting against itself. She would never recover.

Sometimes I wonder what happened in those fifteen minutes. Did she go to heaven? Was she able to experience the pure joy of being in the presence of God's perfection only to have to come back to this earth and be restricted to a broken body? I wonder if God told her what His plan for her life was before she lived it, and then sent her back to fulfill what He designed her to do. This is one of the many things I will simply have to wait to know until I can join her there.

SHATTERED EXPECTATIONS

Even after my mom's friend let us stay up late watching *Little House,* I woke up before the sun. This was a rare occurrence outside of Christmas morning. I was anxious to go back to the hospital and finally meet Rebecca, and I was dreaming about what it would be like to finally hold her.

"Can you please take me to the hospital to see my sister?" I asked my mom's friend, holding her hand and giving her my saddest puppy dog face.

"Your dad will be here soon, and he will let you know more about when you can see Rebecca," my mom's friend said with sad eyes. She is someone who exudes pure happiness, but even she could not hold positivity in this moment.

When Dad walked in the door, Elizabeth and I were waiting not-so-patiently at our tan kitchen table. He joined us, reaching out and holding our hands. We were bouncing with excitement: *Was Rebecca born yet? When can we see her? Who gets to hold her first? Where is Mom? When can they come home?*

Looking back, I bet each question was a blow to my dad's breaking heart. In a matter of hours, he almost lost his wife and lost the future he'd hoped for his daughter. He slowly shared the words to explain to us what would forever change our lives.

"You know girls, sometimes babies come easy and sometimes they come and it's difficult…"

Before Dad could finish his sentence, Elizabeth said, "You mean like on *Little House* when baby Charles died?"

We'd watched that episode the week before where the family on the show lost their only son. Their faith in God was the only thing that sustained them in their grief.

I put my arm around my dad and said, "You know Dad, we're gonna spend more time in heaven with Mom and Rebecca than we could ever spend with them here on earth."

Elizabeth nodded and said, "We can make it through this."

My dad's eyes were emptied of all his tears, but still red and swollen. He said, "Y'all are absolutely right."

While the faith of others can encourage you, only your own faith in God can sustain you.

God knew those were the words from his daughters that our dad needed to hear. Dad had spent the night praying for the health of his wife and his daughter's life. They hadn't expected Rebecca to make it to the morning.

Each person in our family had to make a choice between truly believing God would carry us through this, no matter what happened next, or not. Our parents set the example of placing their faith in God, but each of us had to make our own choice if we were going to trust Him for ourselves. While the faith of others can encourage you, only your own faith in God can sustain you.

"Your little sister has something wrong with her brain." Dad shared the few details he knew at that point. "They had to cut open mommy's tummy to get the baby out. Your mom is still in a lot of pain, but she is okay now. Mom and Rebecca will have to stay in the hospital for a while. Rebecca is going to be sick when she comes home," he kept his gaze on Elizabeth and me, shifting eye contact between the two of us.

My mom's friend stood quietly in the doorway that led to our living room with tears in her eyes. She watched the three of us hold hands while Elizabeth prayed for Rebecca and Mom. Dad left so he could see Mom before going to see Rebecca again when the NICU reopened.

I went to school, but I was distracted by thoughts of Rebecca all day. My first grade teacher showed my class a picture of her laying in a NICU bed connected to countless tubes. I was so proud to be her big sister and happy that my class got to see how precious she was. My chest ached in anticipation of seeing her in real life and holding her in my arms.

Neither Elizabeth nor I really understood what my dad meant by Rebecca being sick. *How is Rebecca sick if she is barely even alive? How did Mom get hurt when she was surrounded by doctors?* To us, sick meant a cold you would get over or a stomach virus that only lasted the night.

In our minds, sickness was temporary, and the worst result was taking some awfully disgusting cherry medicine.

I did not understand Rebecca's sickness was actually a brain injury. I did not know my mom and sister came close to death. I did not know my sister's brain injury could have been avoided if the doctor had not been so careless.

I soon realized my plans for Rebecca were never going to happen the way I'd hoped. My expectations were shattered unexpectedly and I was overcome with fear, grief, and disappointment. I was fearful about what her life would look like and when it would end. I grieved what I hoped her life would be. I was disappointed as I wrestled with the difference between what I'd dreamed for her and what our present reality was. The more I learned, the more scared I was. I wanted to trust God was in control, but I didn't know how He could be when nothing made sense or felt fair. With every detail learned and hope deferred, my faith in God and trust in Him were tested.

Where do you turn when the plans you've made and dreams you've hoped for are suddenly ripped away? The person you are investing in becoming now is who will live through your most difficult tomorrows. While you can't avoid future hardships, you can choose to invest your time now in what will hold you steady in the midst of them.

The person you are investing in becoming now is who will live through your most difficult tomorrows.

TWO

The Reality of the Gospel

Dad always says people spell love T-I-M-E, and he proves his love to us by the time he spends with each of his daughters. He likes to say quality time emerges from quantity time. The very first of Rebecca's time was spent in the NICU, so that's where my dad was. He spent the night kneeling next to Rebecca and crying out to God for help.

My dad always encourages me to do the hard thing and to leverage every part of my life for the sake of God's kingdom. We started a Bible study together for my close friends in high school. We met every Tuesday morning for four years at our local Chick-fil-A. We picked a book of the Bible to study together, then designated someone each week to prepare questions beforehand and lead the discussion. The names of my friends are still written above their assigned sections in my Bible. We wrote down our prayer requests and prayed for each other. In these early morning gatherings, I learned how to study the Bible and discovered a passion for teaching the Word of God to young ladies around me.

When Dad has the opportunity to teach a group of people, I can almost guarantee it will include Bible verses from the book of James or Romans. Dad says people learn by repetition. For three years, he taught my middle school's morning Bible class. We repeatedly learned about living as a Christian through studying the book of James, why everyone in the world has a sin problem from Genesis 3:1-6, and presenting ourselves as living sacrifices from Romans 12:1-2.[1] Dad loves creating memorable illustrations. My favorite one came after a late-night Target trip.

"C'mon, we're going to get a couple of things," said Dad. "You grab pudding—the JELL-O brand. See if you can find some plastic containers we could store it in."

"And what are you getting?" I asked.

"Play-Doh," he said. "Ready, break!"

A few minutes later, I met him at the front of the store with JELL-O, plastic containers, and a pink journal that caught my eye from the edge of an aisle.

Dad placed his items on the counter next to mine. "Well, isn't that a pretty notebook?"

"I just filled mine up so it's time for a new one. Is that okay?" I asked.

"Of course, as long as you promise to fill this one up, too." All my life, he's been the biggest encourager of my writing.

"So what are we using this stuff for?" I asked.

"You'll just have to wait and see," said Dad.

The next morning at Bible class, Dad pulled a table to the front of the room. He placed the yellow tubs of Play-Doh on the tabletop along with the clear plastic container filled with chocolate pudding. Next to this, he put two empty plastic containers like the one holding the pudding.

Dad tossed the Play-Doh to a boy on the front row. "Make something for us, please sir—whatever you want."

The boy opened up the red Play-Doh and squeezed it before rolling it into a ball.

"Alright, can somebody read Romans 12:1-2 for me?" Dad asked. Most of us had these verses memorized because Dad taught them often.

A girl with round glasses and a ribbon around her ponytail flipped open her Bible and read the passage: "I appeal to you therefore, brothers, by the mercies of God, to present your bodies as a living sacrifice, holy and acceptable to God, which is your spiritual worship. Do not be conformed to this world, but be transformed by the renewal of your mind, that by testing you may discern what is the will of God, what is good and acceptable and perfect."[2]

"Thank you. Today we are going to talk about the difference between living transformed and living conformed. When we live conformed, we mold into our surroundings." Dad began to pour the pudding into one of the empty containers.

"Like this pudding takes on the shape of whatever container it's in. If I put it in a star-shaped container, it would look like a star. If it was in a tall, skinny container instead, then it would take on that shape. Its surroundings determine its shape."

Dad held his hands up to the boy with the Play-Doh, and the boy tossed it to Dad. It's a heart.

"Perfect. Thank you, sir." He held up the heart. "Now, what do you think will happen when we place this heart in a container like the container the pudding is in?"

"Nothing," said the girl who read earlier. "It will stay the same."

"Yes ma'am," Dad nodded. "This is what it means to live transformed. No matter what situation you are in, you have been shaped by God to look like Him. Even when it is tempting to conform to the culture and people around you, you can be transformed by renewing your mind with the truth of God's Word. Then when we are in situations that tempt us to shapeshift, we have done the work to help us to stand firm."

"Mr. Gatti?" asked Play-Doh boy, "Can I eat that pudding? I haven't had breakfast."

And with that, the focus of every middle schooler was gone for the rest of class.

To be transformed like Play-Doh, we present our lives to God as living sacrifices and renew our minds with God's Word. In the Old Testament, followers of God sacrificed animals to atone for their sins. This represented the spotless Lamb (Jesus!) who was to come. Now that Jesus is the perfect atonement for our sins, God doesn't ask us to sacrifice animals but to place our faith and trust in Jesus. As a result, we present ourselves and our lives to Him sacrificially.

Every moment after our salvation, we have the opportunity to know God more and make Him known.

Once we place our faith in Jesus and believe His death and resurrection cover all of our sins, our eternity is forever changed. Jesus saves us from an eternity of suffering and separation from our Creator. Every moment after our salvation, we have the opportunity to know God more and make Him known. One of the ways we can do this is by seeking transformation to look more like Jesus. This includes growing in our knowledge of God and reflecting on the character of Christ. While we will never attain perfection, God doesn't ask that of us. He wants our hearts and devotion. He grows us in wisdom and discernment, guiding us through this life until we are finally with Him.

Because my parents spent time transforming their lives to look like Christ and renewing their minds with truth, they did not conform to the situation around them when they were in the hospital with Rebecca. Everything around them told them to panic, but the truth they built their lives upon told them to trust in God and believe that He had a bigger purpose than what they could see. Knowing these truths doesn't take away the pain of the present tragedies, but it does give hope beyond them.

During my junior year at Texas Christian University, my college pastor announced he would be preaching on my dad's favorite passage the next week: Romans 12:1-2. Immediately, I texted my dad and asked him if he wanted to come. He quickly and joyfully rearranged his schedule to spend the weekend full of daddy-daughter dates and go to church with me. I'm thankful for a dad who says yes when I ask him to go to church with me, even when it's over three hours away.

While I can't imagine my dad's relationship with God not being at the center of all he does, his faith didn't become his foundation until I was almost two years old. One Saturday night, I kept my parents awake because I was sick. When Sunday morning came, my dad offered to stay home with me so I could rest while my mom (who was pregnant with Elizabeth) went to church alone.

While my mom was gone, I woke up my dad. I somehow managed to put on my church dress and velcro on my own shoes. "I want to go to church," I said.

"Honey, it's way too late," said Dad.

When Dad looked at the clock, however, he realized we had time to make it to the second service. He says I begged him to take me, so he got dressed and we went. I wanted to sit in the front row, but my dad wanted to sit in the back row. We compromised and sat in the third row of green-carpeted pews. The pastor taught from the book of Nehemiah about everyone needing to do their part to build the wall of Jericho.

"Everyone must do their part in the church to build the kingdom of God. Even children can lead people to Christ!" he exclaimed.

My dad loves to put his most heartfelt sentiments on Facebook, so he posted this story for my 21st birthday, saying, "I knew it was my day to do business with Jesus because my child woke me up to lead me to church. She did her part. My life has never been the same, I'll never be good enough. But I'm so glad God worked through her that day."

God allows us to be a part of sharing His Gospel with those around us. The power is not simply in the words we say, but in the Spirit within us. That Sunday morning, my dad wholeheartedly surrendered his life to Christ. I am so grateful He changed not only my dad's eternity that day, but also shifted his priorities for how he was going to live his life and lead his family.

MY TESTIMONY

Dad kept taking me to church, and would even let me sit in "big church" (what we called the adult services in the main sanctuary) with him and my mom sometimes. I wanted to take notes like my parents, but would mostly just scribble in my pink spiral notebook.

I always loved church: the songs, the people, the summer camps. I loved the idea of this God I was learning about, this Father who loved me and wanted to be my friend. One morning in big church, our pastor taught about the life of John the Baptist. He was Jesus' cousin who gained quite a following. Instead of focusing on himself or taking any credit for his effectiveness, he pointed everyone that looked to him to look to Jesus. When I learned how John did everything in his life to point people to Jesus and not himself, my understanding of what it means to be a follower of God shifted. I liked God but I was not living my life for Him; I was a fan, but not a follower.

At six years old, my perfectionism and inner self-critic already made me well aware of my shortcomings. I wanted to be a good enough person to earn God's love, but it's impossible to earn what's freely given.

Sin is anything less than perfection, especially things in opposition to God's perfect and holy design for His creation. God never asks us to strive to be perfect on our own accord; the entire point of God sending Jesus to be the perfect, complete sacrifice for our sins is that there was no other way.

God knew we could never completely remove our shortcomings and sins that keep us from the perfection required to be in His presence. That is why He sent Jesus to live a perfect life then die as the just punishment and full payment for the sins of all those who place their faith in Christ. Nothing we do could ever be good enough to earn God's affection; apart from Him we can do no good thing.[3] Our worth is not in what we do or achieve but in what Jesus has already done for us.

Christianity is described as childlike faith because although surrender is not easy, it is simple. If you want to become a Christian, the starting point is to acknowledge your unavoidable sin against God that separates you from Him. Then, choose to trust in His Son for the forgiveness of those sins. This faith in Jesus for the forgiveness of your sins is what leads you to an eternal relationship with God Himself. By placing your trust in Jesus and believing that His sacrifice covered all your sins, you can walk in freedom from the brokenness surrounding us.

While Jesus is indeed our Savior, He is also our Lord. Lordship means deserving of complete surrender. We surrender our lives to Jesus, living for Him instead of ourselves. Our life is no longer considered our own

I wanted to be a good enough person to earn God's love, but it's impossible to earn what's freely given.

and about doing whatever we want; we belong to God who purchased and redeemed us through the blood of His Son.[4]

On October 1, 2006, I chose to wholeheartedly place my trust in Jesus. A week later, I was baptized, publicly declaring my personal decision for Jesus to truly be both my Savior and my Lord. Baptism is an outward expression of our inward devotion to God and salvation through Jesus. Representing burial with Christ and death to our sins, we are submerged under the water. Showing how we are completely washed clean of our sins, we are raised out of the water. This act of baptism itself doesn't save you; it simply represents the salvation of your soul that has already occurred. It is a public act of obedience following our trust in Jesus. In the Bible, Jesus Himself sets the example of baptism. In fact, He was baptized by His cousin, John.[5]

When I surrendered my life to Jesus, I committed to live a life focused on eternity. Even if I looked a little different or silly like John the Baptist did, I knew in the depths of my soul it would be worth it. Jesus gifted me forever, so it just made sense to live my life for Him by obeying what He has called His people to do in His Word.

As I have grown up, my understanding of God has deepened along with my gratitude for the Gospel. I am no more saved now than I was then, but I do know God better than before, and pray I continue knowing Him more and more. Being a Christian hasn't made life easy; there are always hardships and I am always making mistakes. He is gracious to forgive me when I keep messing up and gracious to allow me to come to Him when I am tired and broken by my circumstances or my sin.

I see now how God revealed Himself to me in His perfect timing, just six months before I would need a firm foundation of faith and eternal security to process Rebecca's brain injury. Because God allowed me to have confidence in a relationship with Him at a young age, this faith has carried me through each season of my life. I can't comprehend why God graciously gifted me with growing up in a relationship with Him, but I am eternally grateful. He knew the hard times were coming, and they haven't stopped coming. But God is faithful, and He is the firm foundation where I wholeheartedly place my trust.

LEAVE EVERYTHING IN GOD'S HANDS

Elizabeth and I waited three long days before meeting our little sister. We finally arrived at her hospital room, and there she was: the most beautiful baby I have ever seen held by the strongest woman I know.

I gasped, giddy with excitement, covering my mouth with my hands and pushing my purple-rimmed glasses up with my fingertips. My mom and I smiled at each other, showing the dimples she passed along to Rebecca and me. When Charlotte came along in 2010, she undeniably resembled Elizabeth. Rebecca and I favored each other, with our pale skin and light hair. Her beautiful blue eyes were uniquely hers, standing out from the brown and hazel of the rest of the family. Although she would never see through her eyes, they followed the sound of our voices.

Holding her for the first time was a gift, just like every time I held her after that. In the video of this first moment, I lean in and rub our noses together and smile. Each time she was in my arms from the first to the last, I was filled with so much peace.

One of my cherished mentors and dear friends, Miss Jana, shared this precious thought with me one day as I was pouring out my hurting heart to her: "You know Katherine, I bet you never felt more loved and held by the Father than when you were holding your sweet Rebecca."

What truth that is! While I held Becca in hopes of bringing her some peace and comfort, I always felt more peace and comfort with her in my arms than when I was anywhere else. Rebecca is a constant reminder of the goodness and faithfulness of God, even and especially during the hardest of times. After all, Rebecca is by far the greatest gift the Lord has ever given me.

I remember looking down at her, holding her tiny hand, and telling her repeatedly, "I love you so much, pretty girl. I'm so happy I am your big sister."

I was obsessed with baby Rebecca Leigh. A few months after she was born, a friend pointed out that her middle name is also an acronym: **L**eave **E**verything **I**n **G**od's **H**ands. Unintentionally on my parents' part, her name included a reminder of the only way we would be able to endure her short life. We must trust in the One who holds her in His hands.

Rebecca is by far the greatest gift the Lord has ever given me.

From the moment I first held her, she was never defined in my heart by her disabilities but by the fact that I loved her more than life and could not be more honored to be her sister. There was a long road ahead, but the Lord had already been preparing our hearts. Over the ten years of her life, God would prove Himself faithful to walk with us through each moment.

WALK BY FAITH

Rebecca was perfectly pure and wholly unique, capturing all of our hearts completely. From the first day Rebecca was born, our family had no idea what her future would look like. We were told it was a miracle she was even alive, and each day we continued to learn how to best love her as her family.

Rebecca showed slow progress as a baby, but we were hopeful for her healing and expectant for the Lord to continue to work miracles through her. A pressing issue for baby Rebecca was her head's lack of growth. Her brain was not developing. During her birth, Rebecca suffered a lack of oxygen to her brain for an extended period of time. This caused her lack of brain development, which led to her brain's inability to communicate correctly with the rest of her body. No matter how much time passed, her little brain simply did not continue to grow.

The seizures began a few months after her birth. Watching her tiny body twitch and hearing her cry in pain was torture. Doctors performed an electroencephalogram (EEG) on her little brain; the results could not have been worse.

It took time to find the right combination of medication to put a dent in the pain she was experiencing. She took medication multiple

Leave everything in God's hands

times throughout the day. We gave her Pediasure (which we called "milk") to provide her body with necessary nutrients since she was unable to keep down any solid food. Because it was so difficult to get her to ingest her milk and medicine on her own, a G-tube was put in her stomach at fifteen months old. This allowed everything to go straight into her stomach without her having to swallow or taste the nasty medicine.

She spent her life confined to a wheelchair. Because she was hypertonic, her muscles were extremely tight. As a baby, she received multiple botox injections in her arms and legs in an attempt to relax these muscles. Because she never walked, her hips were never in a socket. Despite physical therapy, the grooves couldn't form. They could have surgically created sockets for her hips, but the pain was guaranteed to be excruciating while the likelihood of success was low. My parents decided it was not worth the pain of the surgery to fix her hips since she would never be able to walk.

She was unable to see, speak, or have any voluntary muscle movements. I loved holding her, letting her head rest against me as I ran my thumb over her hand. One of her most common seizures would cause her to straighten out her entire body and lock her knees, which is when I would see the dimples we share.

Our family developed our new normal. Apart from my relationship with God, being Rebecca's sister has impacted who I am the most. Often, the unimaginable hardships yield the most spiritual fruit and experiential wisdom. She gives us all perspective, reminding us of what is truly important and strengthening our faith.

When Rebecca was two months old, I told Mom, "We do not deserve such a wonderful gift. We make so many mistakes and sin so much, and it is amazing that God would give us a beautiful baby girl."

As a child, God blessed me with this mindset to carry me through this trial. Whenever I am weighed down by the pain of seeing someone

I love suffer, He always draws me back to Himself and reminds me to have a spirit of gratitude. Rather than focusing on what our family lost because of Rebecca's brain injury, I want to live in appreciation for all the ways He has blessed us. Not ignoring the pain, but enduring it because my God is a steady foundation.

When we walk by sight, we are focused on what we see. We make our decisions and form our perspective solely on our prominent surroundings and personal experiences. Walking by faith requires focusing on the promises of God and putting our trust in them—even if we do not see the fulfillment of these promises yet. As we live out wholehearted trust in God, we walk by faith, not by sight.[6] This means we place our hope in God Himself, not solely in what He can do. We don't have to see the good to walk by faith and trust that He is working to bring about good.

THE POSSIBILITY OF HOPE

Because of the Gospel, there is a possibility for light in the darkest situations. God has given us hope beyond our present realities. In Christ, we can see purpose in the present and have perspective for eternity. As the truth transforms our minds, we have the ability to shift our perspective in the midst of the pain and place our hope in the reality of eternity.

This means whatever pain we are facing today doesn't hold complete power over us. While we are still affected by the sin and circumstances surrounding us, they do not define us. When you are in Christ, God defines who you are. He declared your worth by Jesus paying your sin debt on the cross. No matter what feels defeating now, we can rest knowing Christ has already won the ultimate victory.[7]

The pain today may feel excruciating and have no end in sight. I fervently pray and hope that your pain will be removed and a miracle will occur soon. Know if you believe in God a miracle is guaranteed, if not in this life then the next. God is the giver of all good gifts, and He is deserving of all praise when the good does come!

But even when the good doesn't come in this lifetime and your worst fears occur, I pray you still trust in the goodness of God and cling to

In Christ, we can see purpose in the present and have perspective for eternity.

Him in the midst of the pain. Without Jesus, this would not be possible. In Him, all things are possible. He bridges the gap our sin causes between us and God. As Christians, we can approach our God with confidence.[8] While this path to wholehearted trust in God is not easy or natural, it is the way to live a life marked by a peace that surpasses all understanding.

I've experienced pain, both the deep kinds that still linger and flare up when my wounds are brushed against and the daily kinds that unexpectedly throw my emotions for a loop. We are human, and hurt is going to happen. Hardships will take their toll on our hearts. But because of Jesus, we can confidently know this agony will not be our ending. In this world we will face trouble, but we can have courage because He has overcome the world.[9] Jesus' life, death, and resurrection have secured eternity; nothing on this earth can take that away. When our present realities are wearing us down, the Holy Spirit is always with us; He is our comforter. In Christ, we have hope for eternity and comfort in our hardships.

The reality of the Gospel has the power to shift how you interact with your present reality. When we trust in our sovereign God and have an eternal perspective, we can have peace, comfort, and contentment even if our circumstances don't change.

Without the Lord and our faith in Him, my family would not see the good in this hardship or in anything else. Just because we don't see good doesn't mean there isn't any. There is power in learning the truth and shifting our perspective.

God can take our fear and give us peace, our grief and give us comfort, and our disappointment and give us contentment. These are gifts that come from drawing near to God and cultivating our trust in Him, not a result of our circumstances changing. The hope is in knowing God, not in changing what is out of our control.

God can take our fear
and give us peace,
our grief and give
us comfort, and our
disappointment and
give us contentment.

This book is not a roadmap on how to avoid the pain, but on how to trust God even in the midst of the worst pain you will encounter. The Gospel is evidence that God has a greater picture in mind; He is looking out for our purpose on earth and destination for eternity. He is working all things together for our good and His glory. My prayer is that through these pages, God moves in your heart to help you take steps toward trusting Him more and believing not only that He is capable of good, but that good is what He will do.

THREE

This Doesn't Feel Good

Because Rebecca was unable to go to school, teachers for children with special needs would occasionally come to our house. They attempted to teach her cause and effect through touch and noise. The exercises to help her muscle development and tone were painful for Rebecca and for anyone watching. I was usually at school when they came, but one day in fourth grade I was home sick. I listened from my room as they showed her light-up toys and asked her questions.

"Rebecca, what color is this?"

"Look at the light and tap it."

"Rebecca, can you touch the flower for me?"

"Can you squeeze my hand?"

Listening to them ask her to do things I knew she couldn't do made me frustrated. *No, she can't tell you what color it is. No, she can't see the light. No, she can't lift her hand. No, she can't.* It was a reminder she wasn't getting better. There was nothing specialists could do to help her gain normal motor skills. Short of a miracle, this was going to be Rebecca's life.

I desperately wanted answers for how my sister could get better. Her life was bookended by her traumatic birth and the ultimate end, but for the decade in between I did not know how her story on earth would unfold. Her brain injury's effects were unpredictable.

The best predictions we received were wide nets of ways she would most likely die. If she got pneumonia, accumulating fluid in her lungs could be deadly. Knowing this, we protected her from colds and viruses as best as we could. It was also likely for her to pass away in her sleep simply because of the uncontrolled nature of her seizures. Rebecca sleeping quietly was rare, so when she was completely silent, it was terrifying.

No one could tell us how long they anticipated her to live or what her life would look like. Some predicted just a few years while others hoped it could be a decade based on the high quality of care she received. There was constant, dreaded anticipation of what could happen because so much was unknown. I felt helpless.

What I knew to be true about God and what I saw as the reality of my sister's brain injury led me to ask a lot of questions. *If God is good and in complete control, why does this feel anything but good? If God really cares about me, why isn't He doing the good He is capable of in my life right now?* These are natural questions to wrestle with when we are enduring painful circumstances.

One of the primary authors of the New Testament of the Bible is Paul. He experienced intense trials and pain in his lifetime, yet he remained faithful to God and joyful in Him. In the book of Philippians, Paul wrote that he had learned the secret to being content regardless of his circumstances or possessions.[1] Passages like this in the Bible can sound beautiful but feel unattainable. *Is this steadiness really possible? To have peace and find joy, even in the midst of suffering?* Because I believe the Bible is true, I asked God to help me see how this could be true. My head believed it, but my heart didn't feel it. I begged God to fill me with His peace and joy, and to strengthen my faith when I wasn't feeling strong.

CONTENTMENT IN WAITING

Sometimes a situation just stinks. There is no bright side in sight, and the horrible circumstances show no signs of changing. Some hurts can't be revoked and certain pain has permanent repercussions. How do we not let this define us? How can we find contentment in these uncomfortable times of in-between?

Discontentment can grow when we are waiting for something we don't yet have or wanting God to remove something we don't desire. In times of waiting, it is natural to grow impatient and irritated that things aren't playing out in the way or timing we'd hoped. Unfulfilled desires for a spouse, children, career, or recognition can feel like gaping holes. Seasons of waiting can feel excruciatingly slow, leaving us feeling frustrated or even hopeless.

Discontentment comes from a feeling of lack; we feel like we deserve something better than what we have. We interpret so much of our reality based on how we feel. Discontentment feels bad, so we attribute not having what we want as being bad. We are convinced we know best, and that it's wrong we don't have these good things and good outcomes.

What do you believe will fulfill you? The answer to this lies in where you spend your time, energy, and thoughts. What we are devoted to is revealed by where we turn when we feel discontent.

The truth is, discontentment is unavoidable. We should not be surprised when we feel an ache in our chest for something more. This inevitable longing is there to draw us to God; He alone can satisfy the deepest desires of our souls. Until we find satisfaction in God, we are doomed to be dissatisfied and discontent. Even if we receive everything in this life we could ever want, it's all meaningless apart from God. Everything but Him comes to an end.

Discontentment is natural, but it is meant to be the launching pad toward contentment and satisfaction. By recognizing our feeling of lack, we find the motivation to turn to the source of satisfaction to fill the emptiness in our souls. Feeling our need for God and what only He can give us is a gift because it draws us closer to Him.

EXPERIENCING CONTENTMENT

Contentment is experienced when we are completely satisfied. Knowing God will sustain us and supply our every need allows for rest without worry. When our spirit is in a state of contentment, it affects how we view everything around us. This lens of contentment positively alters how we experience even the grimmest realities.

The secret to contentment is trusting there is a purpose to where God has you.

When I was little, Dad took Elizabeth and me to our elementary school parking lot to teach us how to ride bikes. It was a big open area with smooth concrete, so it should have been the easiest and safest place to learn. Aside from three light poles, the parking lot was fully open.

"Katherine, keep pedaling and I'll be right behind you," my dad promised. "Just don't go near the poles."

Staring at the poles in an effort not to hit them led to me repeatedly crashing straight into them. I focused on the poles I wanted to avoid rather than where I wanted my bike to go. We drift where we focus, even if it's to our own detriment.

Shifting from discontentment to contentment begins with something we choose: our thoughts. While we can't control every thought that pops into our minds, we do have a general ability to choose what stays. We just need to know how to use it.

Our thoughts and where we direct them are crucial to finding contentment. When we feel anything from disappointment to joy, our feelings can help us understand what we have been setting our minds on.

We don't have to hide our emotions from God; He already knows. When we are feeling discontent, the first step is to bring these emotions to God and pray He would help us discern the root of why we are feeling this way. Invite Him into the conversation you're having in your head with yourself. Ask Him to help the spiraling thoughts settle.

That day when the teachers came to the house, I initially thought I was upset because they were asking her to do things she couldn't do. Then when I spent time with God and prayerfully processed what I was feeling, He helped me to see that at the root of my frustration was actually a grieving of the life Rebecca will never have. Through discerning what was truly leading me to feel bad, I was able to process those emotions and focus on what was true. While she will never have the life I'd hoped she would on this earth, we will have a life of health, joy, and peace together for all eternity. This truth didn't take away all the pain, but it allowed me to not be hopelessly crushed by it.

The secret to contentment is trusting there is a purpose to where God has you. To see a reason, we choose to set our minds on God and ask Him to show us. Sometimes, He shows us His purpose in our present placement. Other times, we have the opportunity to exercise our trust in Him and place our hope in what's to come rather than what we can see. Even when we can't see it, we can confidently trust God is working. This is why it's called faith.

Faith without sight can be scary. Trust without knowledge about who you're trusting feels unsafe. We aren't destined as Christians to blindly follow God; we are invited into relationship with Him and given the Bible to grow our understanding of what we are trusting in. Jesus, our Savior and friend, is the object of our faith.[2] The more we know Him, the less fear we have in who we are following because we know the One leading us.

FAITH OVER FEELINGS

When we face disappointments and anxieties, our emotions can run rampant and our thoughts can quickly spiral. The Bible talks about taking "every thought captive and making it obedient to the law of Christ" (2 Corinthians 10:5b).[3] If we want to reign over our thoughts and emotions, we must know the truth to filter them through. We must learn to trust God more than our emotions, especially the despairing ones.

It is possible to learn the truth so our feelings are not dominated by our circumstances. Rather than passively reacting to our circumstances, we can actively respond. While we can't control our circumstances, we can affect our thoughts and emotions. Paul instructs believers in the book of Philippians on what to think, how to think about it, and the benefits of thinking this way:

"Rejoice in the Lord always; again I will say, rejoice. Let your reasonableness be known to everyone. The Lord is at hand; do not be anxious about anything, but in everything by prayer and supplication with thanksgiving let your requests be made known to God. And the peace of God, which surpasses all understanding, will guard your hearts and your minds in Christ Jesus.

Finally, brothers, whatever is true, whatever is honorable, whatever is just, whatever is pure, whatever is lovely, whatever is commendable, if there is any excellence, if there is anything worthy of praise, think about these things. What you have learned and received and heard and seen in me—practice these things, and the God of peace will be with you." (Philippians 4:4-9)[4]

The foundation of peace is joyful trust in the Lord. Through knowing and trusting in Him, we bring all things to Him in prayer while expressing gratitude for who He is and what He has already done. In this honest communication with God, His peace will guard our hearts and minds. I'm a journaler, and here is a prompt I often work through when I'm feeling anxious, unsteady, or discontent:

What am I burdened by?

What am I grateful for?

What is true? Honorable? Just? Pure? Lovely?
Commendable? Excellent? Praiseworthy?

What are specific ways I can practice the
things I have learned in the Bible?

Whether you want to process through these with a friend, in your head, or on paper, I would encourage you to take the time to be honest with yourself and God about what you are feeling. Invite Him in and give these instructions from Philippians for finding peace a try.

Through knowing God and knowing His Word, you can stand firm in situations that threaten to crush you. Your feelings are real, but they are not always reliable. Invest in knowing what is true so you can take captive the thoughts that are not. When you walk by faith, your feelings don't have the final say.

The foundation of peace is joyful trust in the Lord.

Our hope isn't dependent on a circumstance we can't control, but in Christ who is the same yesterday, today, and forever.

As I initially processed what happened to Rebecca, my feelings and faith didn't align. Feelings say a good God who loves me would not allow this to happen. Faith tells me that "for those who love God all things work together for good, for those who are called according to His purpose" (Romans 8:28).[5] This is a difficult truth—one that I often struggle to truly believe in a way that impacts my emotions and actions. But the more I see God bring good out of even the most horrific situations, the more my faith is strengthened and my perseverance is lengthened. I pray for God to allow my faith to inform my feelings, directing my emotions to be most impacted by what is true and trustworthy.

God has shifted what I view as good. The more I study the Bible and seek to know God, the more I am focused on God's purposes for my life rather than my own plans and preferences. As my mind is focused on God and I trust that He is in control, I am filled with His perfect peace that does not make sense in the midst of chaotic and tragic circumstances.[6]

My parents chose to cling to Christ from the moment this long journey began; this led my sister Elizabeth and me to do the same. Throughout this journey, I've resonated with these verses:

"I would have lost heart, unless I had believed that I would see the goodness of the LORD in the land of the living. Wait on the LORD; be of good courage, and He shall strengthen your heart; wait, I say, on the LORD!" (Psalm 27:13-14)[7]

Waiting on the Lord means to hope in Him and trust in Him. Through the most difficult times, waiting on the Lord is the key to hopeful perseverance. Hoping in the Lord fixes our eyes on Jesus, lifting our focus above what we can see.

Patience and hopeful perseverance are crucial when someone we love is suffering. There's a balance of hopes in it all, and we hold these hopes with an open hand in trust. We pray for them to be healed and for our time with them on earth to be lengthened. We also have peace knowing that even if their earthly body isn't healed, Christians have a secure and sure final destination in eternity, no matter what happens in this lifetime. Our hope isn't dependent on a circumstance we can't control, but in Christ who is "the same yesterday, today, and forever."[8]

The only reason Christians can push through the hardships of this life like the loss of a loved one is because of the assurance we have that if they have a relationship with Jesus, we will see them again. This is possible because God sent Jesus to be the perfect sacrifice to pay for our imperfections. Jesus made a way for us to choose an eternal relationship with a perfect God who couldn't be in a relationship with us in our imperfections. His Word constantly reminds me to wait on His timing and His ways rather than my own, and He promises to strengthen my heart. And my heart can feel so weary. Being strengthened by the Lord is the only way I have been able to walk through the valleys victoriously, for Jesus has already won the ultimate victory over death.

When I am struggling to allow my faith to overrule my feelings, I pray for Him to align the desires of my heart with His. One of my favorite Scriptures to pray over myself and others is Psalm 19:14, which says: "May the words of my mouth and the meditation of my heart be pleasing to Your sight, O LORD, my Rock and my Redeemer."[9] I desire for everything from the inside out to glorify Him. Rather than putting on the show of living a moral and religious life, I want to genuinely serve God with all that I am.

When we are broken by our sins or circumstances, these cracks reveal what is on the inside. I never seek out these shattering moments, but they have a way of occurring within this broken world. The times that break us are opportunities to strengthen our faith through steadfastly persevering and relying fully on Him.

Now when I am broken, I want to fall to my knees in surrender and turn expectantly to God, holding my broken heart up to Him in desperation. I cry out to Him through my tears, knowing with complete assurance that He will carry me through this. Our trust in God brings about stability because He never changes. Placing our trust in anything else would not allow us the same firm foundation and hope.

Even if I don't see the good until I am finally united with Jesus in eternity, I choose today to trust in what I know to be true: that God is good and He is bringing together goodness I never would have been bold enough to ask for.

FIX YOUR FOCUS

One day during His three years of ministry, Jesus miraculously fed thousands of people with five loaves of bread and two fish. Afterward, He told His followers to go ahead in the boat across the water to the next town. He stayed behind alone and spent time praying to God.

After dark, a storm came and the disciples were tossed back and forth in the boat. They were terrified the waves were going to overtake them.

In the middle of the night, Jesus came to meet them. He didn't take a boat—He walked on top of the stormy waters. When they saw Jesus, His friends did not recognize Him.

"It's a ghost!" the disciples screamed.

"Don't be afraid; it's Me," said Jesus.

Peter, one of Jesus' closest friends and disciples, called out, "Lord if it is You, command me to come to You on the water."

Jesus told Peter to come, and Peter climbed out of the boat. As he looked at Jesus, Peter walked on top of the waves toward Him.

Peter began to look around at the wind and waves, and he was afraid. He started to sink into the water. "Lord," cried Peter, "save me!"

As soon as Peter cried out to Him, Jesus immediately reached out His hand to Peter and held him up.

"Oh, you of little faith," said Jesus to Peter, "why did you doubt?"

When Jesus climbed into the boat, the winds stopped and the waves calmed. They all declared that Jesus truly is the Son of God.[10]

Of all the disciples there, Peter was the only one who took the steps out of the boat toward Jesus. His faith in Jesus led him to action. When Peter started to doubt Jesus and focus more on what he feared, he began to sink. By focusing on Jesus and calling out to Him, Peter survived the storm he feared would engulf him.

When Peter was on the water, whether he sank or hovered over the water wasn't completely determined by the state of the storm. Even in the calmest of waters, Peter could not have walked on water without supernatural help. More than the waters or the storm surrounding him, what mattered was where Peter was placing his focus. Both in the storms and the stillness, fixing our focus on Jesus is how we survive.

Peter was able to walk on water when he was walking by faith, not by sight. Making decisions based solely on what we see stifles boldness. Faith is the confidence and hope in things unseen.[11] The more your focus is on God, the more you will walk by faith.

After the chaos of Rebecca's birth, my dad was unsure if my mom or Rebecca would survive. Dad read and meditated on this story of Peter walking on water, and it reminded him to set his mind on Jesus, not the storm surrounding him. He fell to his knees in prayer and begged God to help him navigate this storm.

When you face hard times, you see what is sitting on the throne of your heart. Where are you finding your identity? What are you focusing on? Where are you placing your hope? The answers to these questions reveal where you are placing your trust. In the midst of deep sorrow, it is crucial to remind ourselves of who God is and all He has done. This is why knowing and abiding in His Word is so important; we will be able to remember and rely on it when we don't have the energy to do much else.

When my circumstances or the unknown so easily distract me, my heart and mind are unsettled. When my mind is focused on God and my heart is captivated by Him, I find genuine joy and rest. The key to having joy in trials is not pretending to love the horrible situation you are in; it is focusing on Christ instead of the storm surrounding you.

Problems arise even when we have the best intentions because we are so easily distracted. Then we are robbed of peace because our mind

We can have peace in the middle of the unknowns because our hope is in Who holds our future, not in what our future holds.

is not set on the only One who can give us perfect peace. A mentor of mine described the distractions of life as pulling our focus down.

I can still picture her turning her head desperately back and forth, saying, "When we are distracted by everything that is pulling on us, we think God isn't there and He isn't working. As I pray and ask, 'God where are you, what are you doing?' I feel Him nudging me and saying, 'Look up, child.'" She lifted her own chin delicately with her pointer finger, which shifted her gaze upward.

Life is full of times when our focus shifts to what is pulling us down. We must intentionally lift our gaze and set it back on God. Through daily deciding to fix our focus on God and His Word, He can shift our perspective and comfort our hearts. Rather than focusing so much on doing the right thing, it is more important to fix our eyes on Jesus as He leads us toward His righteousness in all things.

Walking by faith and trust in God leads to confidence in each step. The closer you are to God, the more you understand what it looks like when He nudges you into acts of faith. I pray when you are given opportunities to cultivate your faith in God, you choose to trust Him. Faith is a muscle you grow over time; what is one step of trust you can take today to walk by faith?

HOW DO WE WAIT WELL?

I don't know about you, but I don't like feeling like I don't have a plan. When it seems like I'm behind or I don't know the right thing to do, I am unsettled. Senior year of college, everyone around me was attempting to make decisions on next steps after graduation. There were many things to be decided such as where to live, who to live with, and what job to take. All this must be decided in the midst of everything in your life shifting. It's easy to be overwhelmed when trying to make decisions that feel so significant.

I've always been the person who plans ahead and likes to be prepared. When taking a next step, I want a clear answer and certain confirmation that I am making the right choice. Despite an effort to make postgrad plans, I graduated without clarity on my next steps. All throughout my senior year, I was constantly asked what I was doing next and where I was going. I shared hopes and prayers for where I felt God directing me, but was honest about not truly knowing what was in store.

Having to constantly say "I don't know" was humbling. God taught me in this season of unknowns to place my security in Him alone, not in my plans. I was seeking Him and working diligently to find the obedient next step, but ultimately trusted that God was the one in control and would place me where He wanted me.

No matter how well I plan, I will never be in control. I can make my plans, but it is the Lord who establishes my steps.[12] We can have peace in the middle of the unknowns because our hope is in Who holds our future, not in what our future holds. In times of waiting and making decisions, we have a choice. We can depend on ourselves and strive for control which will lead to anxiety, or we can work diligently at what the Lord places in front of us in His timing and experience the peace that comes from trusting Him.

Today, we can choose to faithfully do what God has in front of us until He leads us somewhere else. There's life to be lived today, and we don't have to wait for our circumstances to change. We can live purposefully right where we are.

God used my situation of not yet knowing my postgrad plans to allow me to be a safe place for others who didn't have it figured out either. By showing our weaknesses or being honest about what we are waiting on, we can be an empathetic source of encouragement for others. We don't need to wait for the outcome to have peace; we can find genuine rest in the middle of unfortunate situations because we are placing our trust in

Rather than focusing so much on doing the right thing, it is more important to fix our eyes on Jesus as He leads us toward His righteousness in all things.

the One who is over it all. Rather than wishing the waiting away, pray for God to show you how He can use you in the midst of it.

When God did provide job offers, an opportunity to live with two of my best friends, and peace about all of it in one afternoon, I knew it was nothing short of a gift from Him. He provided the next step in His way and timing, and all I could do was be grateful. The details fell together better than anything I could have planned and it made me excited for the next season to unfold.

My peace and security didn't arrive when I had a job and signed a lease; my peace and security were constantly accessible when my eyes were fixed on my God who never changes, not on my circumstances that are always shifting. When we find our stability in our God who is constant, we are able to be content in shifting circumstances.

Some resolutions won't occur on this side of heaven, but there are always ways we can partner with God wherever we are. Just as my parents had peace despite the unknown the night Rebecca was born, peace is accessible to us when we fix our eyes on Jesus. Pray for Him to open your eyes to what He is doing now, and lead you to trust Him even though you can't yet fully see what He is doing.

While waiting in the unknown feels terrifying to us because of our limited perspective, God isn't phased. He has prepared good works for us to do in our lifetime before we were even born.[13] All of our days are written in His book.[14] He goes before us to prepare the way and walks beside us as our companion.[15] In Colossians 1:17, Paul says Jesus "is before all things, and in Him all things hold together."[16] God is able and faithful to fulfill all of the promises He has made in Scripture.[17] In times of waiting, I find comfort knowing I can't mess up God's will. His plans are set and His ways are certain. Even when nothing else in my life makes sense, these truths remain constant and steady my nervous heart.

Regardless of our situation, believers have access to joy in Christ and the ability to genuinely appreciate and even enjoy these times of in-between. Whether waiting for a prayer to be answered, a job opportunity to come, the cancer to go away, or a relationship to be healed, waiting well matters more than the outcome. Each season of waiting is an opportunity to grow in patience and grow closer to God, learning to trust Him at all times. Even when we are crippled by fear of what could happen next.

PRAISING GOD IN THE STORM

When there seems to be nothing to be grateful for, gratitude is of utmost importance. Being intentionally grateful is a spiritual discipline. Whether it is something we think to ourselves, say to others, or list on paper, acknowledging what we are grateful for helps to reframe our perspective. When the heaviness feels consuming, gratitude reminds us there are still things that are good and praiseworthy. Most of life is a combination of both the good and the hard. Expressing our gratitude to God and all the good He has done and will do is crucial to being content.

When I don't have the words to express what I am feeling, worship music is one of my favorite places to turn. These songs express real and raw emotions, but point listeners back to the truth and help shift our focus back on Jesus. A song I listened to growing up is *Blessings* by Laura Story.[18] I first heard it at a funeral for a young girl in our hometown who'd unexpectedly passed away. The lyrics contain truths that help reframe my perspective:

> *What if Your blessings come through raindrops?*
> *What if Your healing comes through tears?*
> *What if a thousand sleepless nights are what it takes to know You're near?*
> *What if trials of this life are Your mercies in disguise?*
> *What if my greatest disappointments*
> *Or the aching of this life*
> *Is the revealing of a greater thirst this world can't satisfy?*
> *What if trials of this life*
> *The rain, the storms, the hardest nights*
> *Are Your mercies in disguise?*

Waiting well matters more than the outcome.

On the surface, the pain we experience seems more like a curse than a blessing. When we look beyond what we can see, sometimes these difficulties hold God's greatest mercies to us. I am not discounting the pain or tragedy of these situations but highlighting how God uses the worst of what can happen to us in this world as a catalyst for His mercy. While watching Rebecca suffer is the most painful experience I have ever endured, it has also proven to be God's greatest mercy to me. Only God can take our most broken places and turn them into something beautiful.

While what we feel during these times is so real, it's not always true. Learning to filter our emotions through truth can keep us from spiraling into devastation. When we surrender our raw emotions to God and then search His Word for what is true, His Spirit in us works to align our hearts with His. Jesus Himself is truth, and He never changes. It's impossible to confidently rest and experience peace in something that is always changing. To have peace, we must trust in our unchanging God. And to trust in Him, we must know Him. The more we read His Word, spend time with His people, and speak to Him in prayer, the more we will know Him.

Jesus' brother writes to Christians about how we should respond to trials:

> "Count it all joy, my brothers, when you meet trials of various kinds, for you know that the testing of your faith produces steadfastness. And let steadfastness have its full effect, that you may be perfect and complete, lacking in nothing." (James 1:2-4)[19]

Steadfast means to be resolutely or dutifully firm and unwavering. Knowing He works all things together for good leads you to look at all things expecting to see His goodness—and you will see it when you are looking for it. But when we passively wait out trials, complaining our way through them and blaming God for the pain, we are wasting an opportunity to grow in steadfastness.

The difficulties you are facing are testimonies you are stewarding.

Looking back at my prayer journals from the years of Rebecca's life, I often wrote out these verses from James and prayed for God to help me see this trial as a joyful blessing. Praise God for how He changed my heart and led me to see the joy in this trial, even as I continued to feel the pain. The outcome of Rebecca's life was out of my control, but I did have a choice of whether or not I would seek to honor God through this trial. I can't undo the death of my sister, but I can steward her testimony well and share it in an effort to point people to the only One able to carry us through these trials. The difficulties you are facing are testimonies you are stewarding; are you stewarding them well? How are you sharing what God has done in your life to point others to trust in Him?

We can often learn much more through the waiting than if we'd received what we desired immediately. Through Rebecca's life, I learned how to trust God even when I could not see what He was doing or like how things were playing out. God has slowly revealed ways He has brought about good from Rebecca's suffering. I am sure there are ways He's working through it that I won't see this side of heaven. I've grown to be grateful to serve a God who sees beyond what I can see and works beyond what I can fathom.[20] God is truly greater than anything else, and He still chooses to love His children and have a personal relationship with us through Jesus. Although there are many things I am still learning and seeking to understand, it is enough for me to rest in knowing God and the gift of being known by Him.

CULTIVATING CONTENTMENT

Looking back on my life, there are already many things I have changed my mind about, plans that seemed perfect back then that I am now overjoyed never came to pass. God proved Himself trustworthy, time and time again. *Why am I so quick to doubt and pridefully think I could do better?* I've learned the hard way that making plans does not change the fact that only God is in complete control and I'm not. I used to think if only I was in control, then unfair pain and excruciating heartbreak could be avoided. God has patiently shown me how it is a gift not to bear the burden of being in control, but rather to surrender the weight I carry to Him because He cares for me. There is great value to growing in godliness while cultivating contentment.[21] Rather than anxiously fighting for an illusion of control, finding rest in knowing His purposes always prevail brings me peace.

I'm now grateful for the moments I would not have survived if He was not carrying me because of the daily dependence I learned to have on the Lord. Such deep comfort and contentment come with knowing in my mind and believing in my heart that "God is my refuge and strength, my very present help in trouble" (Psalm 46:1).[22] For me, the knowledge of God's character came through reading and being taught from the Bible, but the belief came undeniably through having no other way to face life than total dependence on His strength.

As Corrie ten Boom said, "You don't realize Jesus is all you need until Jesus is all you have."[23] Even when the losses feel hopeless, we can use these feelings of lack to remind us that we have access to complete and eternal satisfaction in Jesus. When our mind is fully and constantly fixed on God, we can live a life of contentment. Each day when our gaze is tempted to drift from Him, we have a choice. I pray He gives you the strength each day to choose Him and to find contentment.

FOUR

Does Pain Have a Purpose?

Rebecca's eyes were tracking light. She sometimes lifted her head when we placed her on her stomach, slightly pushing up for a second or two. We hoped she would gain fine motor skills and develop like most newborns, even if the trauma her brain experienced slowed this process. It was difficult to have her enter this world immediately suffering, but there was hope that her entire life didn't have to be this way.

Unfortunately, this hope quickly faded. Rebecca's vision never improved beyond squinting at harsh lights. She could not hold up her head or control her muscles, and all the progress we initially saw quickly regressed. The large wheelchair she spent a lot of her time in had a strong support system, wrapping in a c-shape around the back of her head. She was secured by straps across her waist, chest, and legs. If she wasn't strapped in, the movement from her seizures could have tossed her out of her chair.

Rebecca's seizures were powerful. Grand mal seizures were a normal, daily occurrence. These are the most intense type of seizures where she'd lose consciousness while enduring violent muscle contractions. She would convulse and cry. Her head would sometimes be flung out of her headrest. Rebecca would scream in discomfort as soon as she came out of her seizure until we were able to carefully lift her head.

As soon as an intense seizure like this was complete, we would quickly unstrap her and hold her close as she cried in pain. There was nothing worse. Her medication wouldn't stop the seizures, and all we could do was comfort her when they inevitably came.

From being Rebecca's sister, I've learned the power of simply extending comfort and love to someone in pain, even when there is nothing you can do to fix the pain. While we don't hold the power to fix all painful situations, we do have the ability to love and comfort others while they are in pain. It may not remove it, but it can lighten the weight of their pain.

Our whole family could recognize the difference in Rebecca's cries. There was the painful cry we heard after terrible seizures like the ones I described. Sometimes she wanted to be held, and she had a cry that let us know she wanted attention. There was a cry that felt like she was talking to us, delicate and calm. She even sounded like she said "ma-ma-ma" sometimes, calling out for our mom. We learned to understand her, and words weren't needed. I long for the day when I get to see her in heaven and speak with her, finally hearing all she has to say.

As more years passed, every hope we had for Rebecca's healing and progress turned into another disappointment. *Will there ever be an end to her pain?* I would have given anything to alleviate the pain, but I don't have that power. God does, and seeing her in pain made me question why God wasn't using this power to help her.

My black-and-white thinking as a child rationalized that good people deserve a good life, and bad things happen to people who do bad things. Rebecca was pure and incapable of wrong. I couldn't think of anyone that exemplified goodness more than Rebecca. Watching her in pain, this logic was already proving faulty.

I still prayed for my sister's healing. We have the freedom and gift to pray, but we lack the knowledge or perspective of how prayers will be answered. When Rebecca didn't get better, it was hard to believe God was actually listening or that He cared. I understand the pain from prayers not being answered in the way or time you'd hoped.

I have no way to know what God's plan is for you or your current situation. However, you can talk to God who knows your future and your heart. I prayerfully hope you are able to find healing from whatever is bringing you pain or disappointment. Even if you don't see what you perceive as good, could there still be a purpose to your pain?

When we're experiencing pain, life doesn't stop. We still have places to be and responsibilities to tend to. We must learn how to live with the pain. Our family never stopped hoping and praying for Becca's healing, but we also developed new norms around our painful reality.

In the busyness of the daily shuffle, I didn't see the good in her pain. When I slowed down and spent time refocusing my mind on God, He graciously and repeatedly reminded me that what I see isn't the end of the story. Even in the messy middle, God's perspective revealed redemption that's unlimited by this lifetime. While today may look hopeless, we can have faith in the promised hope. We can endure today, no matter how painful, by placing our trust in the One who holds all our tomorrows.

SUNDAY MORNINGS

Getting our family to church on a typical Sunday morning required a team effort, especially after Charlotte was born. Dad would come into my room where Elizabeth and I shared a bunk bed and turn on the lights.

Dad would sing, "Get your butt outta bed—brush your teeth and comb your head!"

I went down the hall to the bathroom all the sisters shared. I squeezed past Mom, then splashed cold water on my face and brushed my teeth. Mom was changing either Rebecca's or Charlotte's diaper on the light green changing table on the counter across from the sinks. Cabinets and doors constantly opened and closed. We inevitably bumped into each other. Everyone helped everyone. One Sunday morning, Dad took a picture of Rebecca strapped in her chair while I gave her a breathing treatment and Mom braided my hair.

Rebecca's daily regimen was strictly scheduled: 8:00 a.m. meds and milk, 11:00 a.m. meds, 2:00 p.m. meds and milk, 5:00 p.m. meds, 8:00 p.m. meds and milk. This schedule became the basis of our family's schedule. Her pills were crushed until their sand-like consistency easily dissolved into water. All the medications were carefully measured into syringes. Rebecca's G-tube went straight to her stomach so she didn't have to taste the medication. The smaller side opening of the extension of her G-tube had a tiny hole that fit the mouth of the syringes. We'd give her medicine then flush it down with two syringes of water.

I learned how to help feed her by age seven: Pop open the can of Pediasure. Pour eight ounces into a bottle. Warm up the bottle for thirty seconds. Dip my pointer finger in to check the temperature. Grab a funnel. Go to Becca. Pop open her G-tube extension. Twist and lock in the tube. Put the funnel in the top opening of the tube. Pour an ounce or two into the funnel. Unlock the tube. Elevate it so the milk can flow into her stomach. Lock the tube. Give her a break. Hold her for several minutes before the next ounce so she had time to digest the milk. Repeat.

We finished giving Becca her morning medication and milk before we left for church. Her medicine is difficult to set up on the go, so Mom would prepare her later morning medicine while she put together the morning doses. If we wanted to eat lunch with other families after church, we made sure to be back home in time for her 2:00 p.m. meds and milk.

We'd load up her medicine and diaper bag into the car, folding her wheelchair down and lifting it into the back of my mom's gray-blue minivan. The day she bought this car, Mom rolled Rebecca's chair around the lot while I held Rebecca inside the dealership. The first place she looked in each car was the trunk. She'd open it, then fold down Rebecca's chair and lift it into the trunk. The minivan was the winner because it had a lower trunk that dipped to perfectly hold her chair. The trunk would close automatically over the wheelchair, not having to be pushed closed like all the other cars she'd seen. When my parents found a car for me for my sixteenth birthday, they also made sure Rebecca's chair would fit in the trunk easily.

Charlotte and Rebecca had matching car seats. Elizabeth and I would strap them in. If Rebecca's muscles were especially tight or she was having a seizure, it was a slower process. Holding her in my arms like you'd cradle a baby, I'd bend my right arm beneath her knees, coaxing them to bend and get her body closer to a seated position. Once her body

We can endure today, no matter how painful, by placing our trust in the One who holds all our tomorrows.

wasn't fully extended, I would lift her into her seat. Slowly pulling her arms through the straps, I moved her frail body delicately. She would cry and fidget, not enjoying the restraint of the car seat. As soon as she settled, I clicked the straps across her body and between her legs.

Depending on Charlotte's mood, she would let Elizabeth and I climb into the third row from her side. If not, we squeezed past Becca. Charlotte's three years younger than Rebecca, but it didn't take long for her to start caring for and loving on Rebecca, too. Rebecca was not a fan of car rides. She would cry, and one of us sisters would hold her hand.

Our friends at church would volunteer to watch Rebecca on Sunday mornings and give the 11:00 a.m. doses of her medication. They kindly took care of Rebecca and others with special needs while my parents taught Sunday school classes and went to the later service. If no one at church was able to watch Rebecca that day, we would drop her off at my Nana and Pops' house.

Dad would drive the minivan under the overhang by the children's area. Our joyful friend Mr. Paul would slide open the minivan doors and extend a hand to help us out of the car, greeting us each with a smile and hug.

As soon as we unloaded, we would divide and conquer. I typically took Charlotte to get checked in and brought her to her class. Elizabeth took herself to class, and Mom met whoever was watching Rebecca. Dad parked the car before meeting me upstairs in the kindergarten class we taught together.

Beginning when I was in seventh grade, my dad and I had the privilege of teaching the same students for five years. During that time, we experienced the gift of seeing many of them learn what it means to trust in Jesus and surrender their lives to Him.

Sometimes our friend taking care of five-year-old Rebecca rolled her around the children's ministry in her pink wheelchair. She stopped by our class of kindergartners, and I thought about how they were the same age.

One of the girls I was closest to is named Ava. She always wanted to sit next to me and drew me the most beautiful pictures. We talked

The pain we experience can be God setting us up to be used by Him in a specific way.

about dance and her trips to visit her grandparents. I went to her birthday party at the skating rink and helped teach her dance classes at the studio we both attended. She asked me questions about God and the Bible stories we read.

Over the years of being one of her Sunday school teachers, I saw Ava grow in her understanding of God and His love for her. It was the greatest gift to witness her surrendering her life to Jesus! I've loved watching her continue living her life for Him. I've always thought she and Rebecca would have been friends.

I'd had many hopes and dreams for how I could love and teach Rebecca, and being a good big sister to her looked different than I anticipated. God took the painful disappointment I felt through not being able to teach and lead Rebecca in these ways and allowed me to appreciate my ability to care for these children even more. It was impossible to love and teach these children without thinking about what it would be like for Rebecca to be in the classroom with us. Witnessing their childlike faith and teaching them about Jesus was a joy, even though it was bittersweet.

The pain we experience can be God setting us up to be used by Him in a specific way. Our trials become part of our testimony, which is the story we tell as followers of Jesus to proclaim how God has radically worked in and through our lives. One of the ways I have found purpose in the pain of loving and losing Rebecca is when I share her story. By telling everyone from these kindergartners to my coworkers about Rebecca, others are able to see a glimpse of God's goodness through the story of her life.

While it is tempting to bury the pain, not addressing or sharing it won't make it go away. Instead, it could increase the grip your pain has on you. When you bring what holds tight to you in the darkness to light, God uses the most painful things to bring about good.

Through trust and over time, He will show you how He has a plan and a purpose for your life, even now.

THE ROLE OF THE CHURCH: A COMMUNITY OF COMFORTERS

My parents prioritized church. Not just going on Sundays, although you saw a glimpse into how much effort that alone took each week. They volunteered, were in small groups, taught classes, let us volunteer and teach classes, and were there almost every time the doors were open. We didn't do church things to earn our faith or prove its validity to others; obedience and being in Christian community is an overflow of genuine faith.

I remember going to conferences on nights and weekends with my Dad and singing in Christmas choirs with Elizabeth. We went to every camp and were in the children's ministry plays. Rebecca's first stop after she left the NICU was to watch us in one of our plays; she came to church before she even went home. I truly love church, and it has always been a place of comfort and like a second home to me.

When telling His disciples who He came for, Jesus said, "Those who are well have no need of a physician, but those who are sick. I came not to call the righteous, but sinners" (Mark 2:17).[1] Jesus did not come for the people with the cleanest track record and perfect church attendance; He came for those who are hurting and hurting others.

Church is designed to be a gathering of the sick seeking the Physician, living in community and confessing our sins. It's not a place to come and act like we have it all together. Church is where we can let the facade fall away and admit that the only good in us is Jesus Christ. When we fight to be a church that looks like this, it's a much healthier place to be.

The church is more than the building where we gather. The church is the body of believers, made up of everyone who has placed their faith in Jesus. We gather together as a church in a building we refer to as church, but believers ourselves are the church.

Paul describes the church as one body with many parts, all working together to serve a common purpose.[2] Eyes and legs serve different purposes and look very different, but they each fulfill a unique purpose for a body. Just as God designed different body parts to work together, the body of believers is designed to live in unity and service to God and the world together.

The body of believers is composed of many individual parts with different gifts working together for the glory of God. When we remove ourselves from the body, we are removing our gifts that are meant to be a blessing to others. We are taking away our perspective and testimony that could comfort someone who is hurting. We are missing out on the blessing that the gifts of others can be to us and the comfort they could provide in our times of desperation.

The church as God designed can be one place where we see purpose in our pain. Both in the everyday disappointments and life-altering tragedies, all pain is best processed with other believers who are living surrendered to God. Our trials and what God teaches us through them are not just for our own edification and benefit; they are to be shared with other believers and used to build them up during their times of need. Paul writes about how God comforts us in our trials so we are able to extend that comfort to others:

"Blessed be the God and Father of our Lord Jesus Christ, the Father of mercies and God of all comfort, who comforts us in all our affliction, so that we may be able to comfort those who are in any affliction, with the comfort with which we ourselves are comforted by God." (2 Corinthians 1:3-4)[3]

Christ comforts us in our afflictions so we can comfort others in theirs. Some of the kindest ways God has brought me comfort are through friends who sit with me in the hurt. A few of my friends even understand what it is like to have a sister with special needs or a sibling pass away, and I am grateful for the ways we are able to use this shared experience to love each other better.

I met one of my dearest friends, Kaley, on a summer retreat through TCU Greek Life in Waxahachie, Texas. One afternoon, our group's lunchtime conversation drifted to religion. Everyone was sharing what we believed and asking each other questions.

Both in the everyday disappointments and life-altering tragedies, all pain is best processed with other believers who are living surrendered to God.

I shared what I believe about God. Kaley also shared, and we smiled at each other when we realized we're both Christians. Others around the table asked questions like how we can believe God is good and what happens when we die. Kaley and I shared what the Bible says and parts of our own stories.

After that cafeteria conversation, we were inseparable for the rest of the week. We stayed up late into the night sharing our testimonies, learning about our families, and praying for each other. While our lives had their own paths, there was one remarkable detail that was the same.

"Katherine, I have a sister with special needs, too," said Kaley. "Her name is Rebecca."

We both teared up and sat in awe of how God brought the two of us together, two sisters to precious girls named Rebecca. Kaley is a steadfast friend who isn't afraid of messy emotions like grief. She comforts me, understands me, loves me, and points me to Jesus.

I had the privilege of being a bridesmaid in Kaley's wedding, and I loved spending the celebrations with her family. As I danced with Kaley's sister, Rebecca, at the wedding, I was reminded of how God Himself not only understands and loves me, but He has surrounded me with others who understand and love me in ways I never thought possible. I am so grateful God allows me and Kaley to be friends that empathize with and encourage each other.

There is power in Christian community. My brothers and sisters in Christ comfort me in my pain and remind me of the truth. They point me back to God and help me to keep an eternal perspective. Then, when they are the ones hurting or drifting, I can encourage and comfort them.

We are not made to do this life alone. Community is a gracious gift from God. It is worth being vulnerable to bring someone into the messiness of your pain because God didn't design us to endure hardships in isolation. When we are alone, it's easy to forget the truth and to believe lies.

Often we pray for God to help and comfort us, and He frequently answers those prayers through His people. This should help us to be open to care from others, and be willing to extend that care as well. I encourage you to find a church that teaches the Bible and invest your time there. Expect to be hurt and to hurt others, but remember the greater purpose and fight for unity. Darkness would love for us to give up on the church, for it is one of the most powerful ways God displays His light and goodness.

As I have grown up, I've seen deep brokenness within the walls of the church where I used to naively think that kind of deception and sin couldn't exist. I've learned that the people sitting in church are sinners too, and we are all in need of the same grace. I healed from a lot of pain inflicted by those within the church walls, and this pain has taught me more about God's grace than a perfect church ever could.

I am in no way discounting the deep pain that can occur within churches; some of my deepest pain was inflicted by people in the church. However, I am encouraging you not to give up on the church because people are broken. There likely needs to be forgiveness, healing, and reconciliation, but don't give up on the bride of Christ, which is what God calls the church.

We aren't designed to do this life alone, and the church is God's design for how His people live together in community. I'm so sorry for any hurt you may have experienced within the church walls or with church people. Keep believing for God's best; I promise it's worth it.

GOD IS OUR SHELTER

Every summer growing up, Mom's side of the family went to Hot Springs, Arkansas, together for a week. We all loved the lake, especially my Pops. On the water, Dad would sling us around on the tube behind the boat. The adults attempted to teach us how to water ski. I loved riding with the wind blowing in my face.

Rebecca didn't like being wet or jolted on the boat so my Nana or

Pops would stay inside with her on our boat days. From the lake, we could see them on the balcony cheering us on as the cousins tried to ski.

On days when we didn't go on the lake, we did puzzles, played board games, swam in the pool, and had family dinners. In the condo's living room, there were glass sliding doors that opened to the patio. One night, Elizabeth and I started watching *Mamma Mia*. When Pops came out to join us, we could tell it wasn't his favorite even though he tried to get into it for us. We switched it over to *Shark Week*, and I soon fell asleep on the couch. A loud thunderstorm woke me up in the middle of the night, and I looked around and realized I was alone.

I was about to hurry to the room Elizabeth and I shared when I looked out the window. The lightning struck over the lake and momentarily illuminated the sky and its reflection in the water. The branches slammed into each other, and the rustling leaves made a melody. The raindrops pittered off the railing of the patio. All the sights and sounds together were almost peaceful. I wrapped my blanket around myself and laid back on the couch. Facing the window, I watched the storm until I fell back asleep.

The next morning, my family complained that they got no rest last night because of the loud storm. Someone mentioned the branches scraping across their window, and another said the thunderclaps kept jolting them back awake.

This memory reminds me of how the Bible describes God as our shelter and dwelling place. He is our protector and sustainer, our shield from the storm. From the shelter of inside the condo, I was able to remain untouched by the storm and even see the beauty in it. While I could not stop the storm from raging outside, I did not have to fear because I was safe and sheltered.

Even though my family was in the same shelter from the storm as me, they did not have the same perspective on the storm. Irritation because a loud storm robbed them of sleep is natural. It's unnatural to see the good in something like a storm when the negative effects are so prominent. However, when we are intentional to slow down enough to notice, our perspective can be shifted to see the beauty in the storms.

Through seeking God and setting our focus on Him, He reframes our perspective. He renews our minds and allows us to rightly view the pain in our lives. The storms will still rage and the pain will still ache, but our souls can find comfort when we set our minds on things that are above, not on things that are on earth.[4]

When we experience storms that shake us, it's okay to acknowledge that these circumstances are jarring. But we must also remember the One providing us shelter. No matter what hardships we endure in this life, nothing can separate us from God. In Him, we are eternally secure. He doesn't protect us from all pain, but He does take the pain that is a result of living in a broken world and somehow work it together for good. The storms will come, but we have an unshakeable shelter. Take refuge in Him.

OUR RESPONSE TO THE STORMS

My family has kept the summer tradition of spending quality time together near the water, sometimes at a beach instead of a lake. The summer after my sophomore year of college was the longest summer of my life due to COVID-19. Our family drove to Florida, deciding if we had to be cooped up in a house it might as well be next to a beach.

Sitting next to the ocean, the salty air around me felt sticky. I turned the page in my book and leaned back into my chair, stretching out my legs and pushing my toes deeper into the sand.

"Kat, will you go on a walk with me?" Elizabeth laid her head on the sand next to my chair and stuck out her bottom lip. It felt like when we were little and she wanted me to play mermaids in the pool with her but I wanted to sit and read.

"Yes, just let me finish this chapter."

"Aight, bet. Come tap me when you're ready."

I finished the chapter then closed my book, tucking it in the back of the chair. Elizabeth managed to fall asleep in those five minutes, so I woke her up, "Hey, I'm ready!"

When we are intentional to slow down enough to notice, our perspective can be shifted to see the beauty in the storms.

She jumped up and we started walking along the beach. Every tent we passed seemed to be blaring Thomas Rhett. We talked about his concert we went to together a few years ago and tried to avoid the flying frisbees.

Sand kept hitting our legs. We thought it was flying up from the kids sliding on boogie boards around us. Or maybe because of the wind; it picked up and my short hair kept blowing into my face. We noticed people starting to pack up for the day, which was unusual because it was only midafternoon.

"Do you want to turn around up there?" I glanced at my Apple watch. "We've gone about two miles, so it'll be another two miles back."

As soon as she agreed on the midpoint, the sky turned a blue only a shade above black. The rain wasn't an increasing drizzle but an immediate downpour. The combination of the rain and the swirling sand felt like bullets.

Elizabeth laughed and yelled, "Oh my lanta—run!"

We stuck our phones in our swimsuits, turned around, and sprinted back. We ran past the condo to our family's spot, thinking there was no way Mom could have carried everything on her own.

By the time we reached where our family was, they were gone. The beach was empty other than a single metal tent. Two ladies tried to hold down the tent that threatened to fly away with every gust of wind. Elizabeth and I grabbed the unattended two poles. It started to lightning, and Elizabeth and I exchanged a glance that said *we need to let go of this metal lightning rod and get upstairs.* We waited for their husbands to get back, then we left.

"This is crazy, that came out of nowhere!" Elizabeth giggled and shaded her eyes from the pelting rain as we ran in the wet sand. I wondered if my book in the back of the chair was soaked.

"Mom's going to be so upset she had to carry all of that stuff on her own!" I yelled over the storm, thinking about the chair holding my book along with everything else. It had taken all five of us to get everything to the beach that morning.

I was running a lot slower than Elizabeth. I watched where I was stepping, scared of accidentally landing on something sharp. We went up the wooden stairs down the long deck to our condo entrance. I held onto the railing because the steps were a little slippery. We saw all the guests gathered under the overhang, cheering for us.

Elizabeth, still running, turned back to me and yelled, "Katherine, my goodness, hurry up!"

She whipped her head around, and her momentum caused her feet to fly into the air. She landed right on her back.

I rushed to her, and she was already laughing. All the people who were watching from the overhang saw her bust it. A few concerned men started running toward us.

"Are you okay? You need to get up before these men hurt themselves trying to help you," I said, holding out my hand to help her.

"I'm all good!" She got up and started running again, "See that wouldn't have happened if you had been going faster, Kat."

They were all cheering for her when we reached the overhang. They started laughing once they saw she was okay. Dad was laughing harder than anyone.

"See, I was laughing as soon as you went down, but decided I should see if you were okay once I saw other guys were concerned for you," he slapped Beth's back.

"Also your mom is pretty irritated, she had to carry it all back on her own," said Dad.

"We tried to go back and find her!" I said, "How did she get the umbrella, four chairs, bag, and all our shoes?"

Dad was right about Mom being upset that we weren't there and that she had to carry it all back up in the rain and wind. As soon as we came in laughing uncontrollably and told her about how Elizabeth busted it, she forgot her frustration and laughed along with us.

No matter what hardships we endure in this life, nothing can separate us from God. In Him, we are eternally secure.

The storm stopped, and Elizabeth came into our room and closed the door. "Katherine, have you seen my sapphire ring? I put it on my towel because I didn't want to wear it into the ocean because I was scared I would lose it."

"Oh no, I haven't. I'm so sorry." This is bad. Elizabeth had already lost this ring once. It was a gift from our parents, and this was the replacement. "Have you told Dad?"

"I'm about to. I don't know what we're going to do about it though in the middle of a tropical storm."

She told our parents and we looked through everything from the beach again. The ring was nowhere to be found. The downpour slowed to a drizzle. Dad looked out the glass doors to the balcony and saw people on the beach with metal detectors.

"I'm going to go find it, see y'all later." He went down to the beach and started searching in the sand. Elizabeth felt horrible, and Mom was disappointed that she even brought it down to the beach in the first place. She said Beth should have left it in the room.

"Well I didn't anticipate the towel being tossed around frantically as you fled the beach in the middle of a tropical storm," Beth said back. "But I'm sorry, I feel horrible. I don't know what to do."

"Just pray your dad finds it." So that's what we did. We prayed that against all odds and without a metal detector, he would find it. Mom talked with him on the phone as she stood on the balcony, guiding him where to look from her perspective.

Dad came back up thirty minutes later and didn't say anything. We all looked at each other quietly. No one wanted to know what the rest of our night would be like if the mood was brought down by losing her replacement ring. Dad pulled something out of his pocket and put it on the counter.

"My ring! You found it!" Elizabeth squealed and gave him the biggest hug.

"I'll take that," Mom picked it up and put it in her room with her jewelry.

There were so many different emotions and circumstances in that three-hour stretch. When the storms came, Elizabeth and I chose to laugh as we ran and were hit with pellets of sand. When Elizabeth fell on her back in front of an audience of strangers, she got back up and kept going. The thing she valued was lost, but we came alongside her to help her find it and prayed for God to provide, and it was found.

While the storms and circumstances were unexpected, we had a choice in how we responded to them. If you invest time in growing in trust and dependence on God now, you are preparing for how you are going to respond when unexpected storms come.

The best time to seek the Lord is right now. He will bring intentionality to the waiting and purpose to the pain. He's not done with you yet, and God is going to bring the works He's set before you to completion before you see Him in heaven.[5] God has a plan, and all we need to do is trust in Him and His leading. While the storms may be unexpected for us, He is never surprised. He is stronger than any storm we might face and sovereign over everything. When the storms hit, I hope we choose to remember these truths.

As Christians, we are the hands and feet of Jesus. By sharing our stories and pointing out how God has worked in our lives, we love those around us and show them there is hope in a dark and painful world. I've found so much purpose and peace in the midst of my deepest pains by sharing them with others who are also hurting. Through this book, I am sharing Rebecca's story and how God used it in my family with you. As others have comforted me through these trials, I want to be a source of God's comfort and encouragement for you in whatever you may be facing. And in turn, I pray you can serve as an encouragement and source of God's comfort to those who are hurting around you.

FIVE

The Sovereignty of God

At three months old Rebecca's seizures intensified. During seizures, her left arm stiffly bent upward while her right arm tightly extended by her side. Her head twitched to the left toward her lifted hand. Both eyes gazed up and to the left; she didn't blink. The motions repeated, the seizing lasting longer than usual. When this seizure was finally complete, she cried in pain. It was only moments before the next one began.

Despite medication and Mom's attempts to comfort her, the cycle of seizures was unbroken. Because her seizures showed no signs of stopping, my parents took her to the hospital. This was the fourth time in two weeks they'd taken her to the ER because her seizures couldn't be tamed.

As Rebecca laid on the little hospital bed, the white sheets barely contrasted with her sickly skin color. The nurses attached her to monitors and examined her brain activity.

"Are you sure you have been administering her seizure medication?" The nurse doubted they gave Rebecca the meds as prescribed if the seizures were this rampant.

My mom is actually Dr. Gatti; she received her Ph.D. in Psychology. She cares for children with learning and behavioral disabilities by crafting their specialized learning plans. Not only is she intelligent, but she is an extremely qualified caregiver.

When Rebecca was born, my mom paused practicing as a School Psychologist. Caring for Rebecca was a full-time job. We were lucky Mom was able to care for Rebecca and we did not have to send her somewhere outside of our home. Caring for a child to this extent is often too much for families to do on their own. My mom's top priority was ensuring Becca had everything she needed and was cared for in the best possible way. Despite the emotional and physical strain, my mom cared for her with all that she had. And she did it well.

"No," said Mom, "she has never missed a dosage." The nurses continued doubting this and asking questions.

"This is ridiculous," said Dad, "We're leaving."

My dad was filling out the discharge paperwork when someone knocked on the door. It was a hospital administrator checking on my mom because she used to be a faculty member at the hospital's university.

"How are you guys, really?" he asked.

"Terrible. Susan's constantly trying to help her seizures stop, and nothing is working. We're exhausted," said Dad.

"You know, Ryan, I have a grandson with special needs," he shared. "Without the help of his sitter, the family wouldn't be making it. I'll be praying you guys can get some help. If you ever need absolutely anything from me, do not hesitate to call."

As they left the hospital, my dad called a friend who was a pediatric intensivist (a doctor who cares for extremely sick children). When Dad told him about the medication they were giving Rebecca, he said, "That will metabolize way too quickly for someone of her size. It is dissolving into her bloodstream before having the chance to affect her seizures. You need to get her to Dallas Children's Hospital as soon as possible."

My parents loaded Rebecca into the minivan and immediately drove three hours to Dallas. Nurses were waiting for Rebecca when they pulled into the ER deck to bring her into a patient room at once. Rebecca was still having nonstop seizures. As the nurses looked at Rebecca's EEG, they said it was one of the worst they'd ever seen.

"Nothing has helped her seizures, we don't know what else to do," said Dad. "Can you help her?"

A pediatric pharmacist crushed some pills and mixed them with water. With my parents' permission, she pushed it down the IV and Rebecca's seizures stopped immediately. Finally, she was at peace.

The peace, however, was temporary, and her seizures intensified with age. There was no way to stop them, but the right medication kept them from becoming constant again.

Our brain is essentially an electrical being, with neurons firing back and forth to create brain activity. The thinner-than-hair strings sending messages from one neuron to another are called axons. Like any electrical current, a barrier between raw electrical cords is necessary for safe transmission. Without it, the interaction of the exposed cords leads to electrical misfires. During the first two years of life, a baby's brain myelinates. This process is what coats the brain's wiring like rubber insulation surrounding an electrical cord. This coating over the brain's axons allows for correct and safe electrical action.

When the medical staff helped Rebecca's heart start beating again, she suffered a reperfusion injury. This means the blood rushing from her heart to her brain essentially fried all the brain's pathways. Because Rebecca's brain was unable to myelinate, the result of unprotected electrical currents in her brain was her seizures. That's the technical way of saying her brain was fried and the damage was irreversible.

When neurosurgeon Ben Carson came to speak in Louisiana, my dad bought ten of his books so he would have a few minutes to talk to him while he signed them. Dad pulled out his laptop and showed Dr. Carson Rebecca's brain scans, MRIs, and EEG.

Shaking his head, Ben Carson said, "Just love that baby, there's nothing you can do."

And love her we did. With all our hearts for all her days, we loved her the best we knew how. We cherished our time together, bonding as a family in the midst of our pain.

MEETING MISS CATHY

A few months after my parents returned from their first of many visits to Dallas Children's Hospital, they began looking for someone to help care for Rebecca. They looked for months and interviewed several people. It seemed like they'd never find someone; everyone said her seizures were too severe and they couldn't handle it.

Elizabeth and I played on the same softball team in elementary school, and Dad was our coach. On the way home from one of our games, we stopped at the gas station to get celebratory ICEEs. As he was checking out, my dad noticed a picture of a young boy on the bottom corner of our local newspaper. He reached down to grab the paper, flipping it open to the page with his story on it.

It was the young boy's obituary. As Dad read the obituary, he realized this was the grandson of the hospital administrator who talked to him right before they first went to Dallas Children's.

"We'd like to give thanks to Mason's very special nanny, Cathy Jacks," Dad read.

Remembering how the grandfather had called this sitter a gift from God and the only reason the family was making it, Dad asked my mom to call her colleague and ask about Miss Cathy. Both personally and professionally, Miss Cathy had nothing but glowing recommendations for how to care for children. My parents knew they would do whatever was necessary for her to be the one caring for our Rebecca.

Later, Miss Cathy told my parents she wasn't sure if she would take the interview. After Mason, Miss Cathy didn't think she could take another job like this. It is excruciatingly painful to love and care for a terminally ill child, spending all of her time with them knowing she would lose them. The night before the interview, she wasn't able to sleep. She couldn't stop thinking about Mason, and she pictured Mason there with her. Miss Cathy felt like if Mason were there, he would want her to take the interview and care for another baby. These thoughts of Mason gave her the peace to take the interview and meet our family. Before she came to the interview, she knew with Rebecca was where she needed to be.

Through her interview, my parents learned more about Miss Cathy's decades of experience caring for children with special needs. She was highly qualified to provide the best care for our sweet Becca. After only a few moments with Rebecca, Cathy completely understood Rebecca's injuries and needs.

"Oh my, what a strong little girl," Miss Cathy said as she held Rebecca in her arms for the first time. She wasn't scared of Rebecca's injuries and was immediately compassionate toward her.

Elizabeth and I sat in the hallways outside our room listening to the interview. We hadn't thought anyone else they'd interviewed was good enough to take care of our sister, but this one felt different.

"Isn't your son Robbie?" we heard Dad ask. "We played football together at Airline!"

"Dad literally knows everyone," whispered Elizabeth.

"Girls, come in here!" said Mom.

We walked out and met Miss Cathy. She wore silver wire glasses and had short white hair. She is tough, but has a kind smile. Everyone in our family had complete peace about entrusting her to help care for our Becca.

Miss Cathy came to our house most days for over nine years. She was a companion and best friend to Rebecca. She took care of us sisters, too. She taught us how to knit and gave us monogrammed laundry bags to keep our socks from losing their matches, although Beth still purposefully mismatched hers. Miss Cathy was at every birthday party and joined our family on Christmas mornings. She cross stitched me an angel for my 10th birthday, choosing that pattern because she thought her golden-brown hair looked like mine.

Not only did God decide to bless our family with Rebecca, but we also received the gift of being loved and protected by Miss Cathy. While this storm did threaten to overtake our family, God surrounded us with support from people who loved Him, loved us, and loved Rebecca. In His perfect timing, He always provided our family with His strength to get through each day and His comfort to endure every sorrow.

GOD IS IN CONTROL

In both the big things like bringing our family Miss Cathy and in the small things, God is in control. He sees the bigger picture, and He is orchestrating the details both for the ultimate good of His people and for His glory. One of the ways I see God's intentionality in my life is not only through placing Rebecca as my sister but also through my sisters Elizabeth and Charlotte. Even though we've faced so much heartbreak together, they always help me to laugh and find joy in all situations.

Charlotte and I went to the post office together to purchase stamps for my college graduation announcements. The only stamps they had were patterned with blue and orange sea animals. I looked at the post-cards I'd carefully designed and imagined a sea animal on the corner.

"Are you sure you don't have any normal stamps?" I asked the postal worker.

"Normal? I'm not sure what you mean," she said.

"Like American flags? Or flowers?" I suggested.

Charlotte explained, "She's kinda a perfectionist, and she wants her graduation announcements to look pretty and these just clash with what she has going on."

As usual, Charlotte was right and unafraid to call me out in public. I wanted them to look the best they could, and those stamps were not a part of what I had imagined. I can get so attached to how I planned for things to be and to my perception of good that I make myself disappointed if the reality is anything different than that.

My desire to be in control plays out in my perfectionism. In my brain, I see it as my responsibility to do my best to bring about as much good as possible. The extreme of this plays out when I want the details of everything to be perfect, which can irritate everyone around me. I've slowly learned to let the details go and focus more on pursuing righteousness for the sake of the kingdom, not just righteousness because I want to be right.

Being as perfect as possible is one of the ways I try to avoid pain. After all, Rebecca's brain injury happened as a result of a mistake. Somewhere along the way, I began to believe that mistakes are not to be tolerated. By God's grace, He has shown me that this exhausting way of living is not His design. He is the one holding all things together, not me.[1] I've learned there can also be good in owning up to mistakes, not just avoiding them.

I've slowly learned to let the details go and focus more on pursuing righteousness for the sake of the kingdom, not just righteousness because I want to be right.

To truly trust God, we must know Him first.

God never asked me to bear the burden of ultimate responsibility or complete control. The more I learn about how God is in control and sovereign over everything, the less weighed down I feel by the pressure to be perfect. While I still like things to be the best they can be, God has taught me how to daily interact with His grace for me and those around me.

We are not in control, and that is a good thing. Only God can bear the weight of being in control, perfectly balancing His love, wisdom, and sovereignty for the ultimate good of His people and the glory of Himself. While we may desire to be in control temporarily to change a diagnosis or get our dream job, we don't have the necessary perspective to bring about genuine good from all we would decide to do.

We are able to be in a relationship with the God of the universe who fully knows and loves us. While we don't have sovereignty over the trials we face, God does. And we are free to approach Him in prayer and talk to Him anytime we please. Unlike people, we don't need to explain ourselves to God; He already knows us completely. We can trust that in His love for us and perspective of eternity, He is the most qualified sovereign ruler of His creation.

Without knowing God personally through a relationship with Him, it would be a little scary to think about the kind of power He holds over our lives and this world. This is why to truly trust God, **we must know Him first**. While He is an almighty ruler, He is also a loving Father and faithful friend. He has given us His Word to learn more about Him and prayer to talk to Him. I would encourage you to take the time to talk to God, asking Him to help you trust Him more and help you to develop a greater understanding of His sovereignty. He cares about you.[2]

GOD IS SOVEREIGN

Not only does God care for you, but He also is completely sovereign. I like this description of God's sovereignty interacting with His character:

"God in His love always wills what is best for us. In His wisdom, He always knows what is best, and in His sovereignty, He has the power to bring it about."[3]

To be sovereign means to have complete control and power. If this were anyone but God, we should be scared. Think about the plot to any superhero movie ever: there is typically someone with evil intent that the good guys are trying to keep from gaining power. When evil reigns sovereign, there is fear. When goodness reigns, we can have peace.

While I know in my head God has a different perspective than me, it can be difficult for me to grasp what that truly means for my everyday life. My perspective is often limited by what I can see, and that can be frustrating.

I was very frustrated by what I saw when Miss Cathy tried to teach me how to knit. After constantly having to unknot the yarn in the scarves I attempted to make, she taught me how to cross stitch. This has a pattern to it that I like. Using different colors to create the pattern, basic cross stitching is simply making little Xs over and over again. It's like paint-by-number; the hardest part is making sure you are putting the right color in the right place.

Miss Cathy would sit in a brown leather chair with Rebecca in our living room, and I would sit in the chair next to hers making little Xs over and over. When I laid my cross stitching down on its face, the back looked like a knotted mess. It was impossible to tell what I was creating. But when I flipped it over, the design was beautiful and I could see the picture emerging. This reminds me of what Paul wrote in the book of Romans about the good that God brings about for His people.

"And we know that for those who love God all things work together for good, for those who are called according to His purpose." (Romans 8:28)[4]

Like the back of my cross stitching, sometimes our perspective affects what we can see. From God's perspective above, He sees the beautiful picture being formed and His perfect plan unfolding. Over time, He is weaving all the details together for good. Just because our perspective

> *Just because our perspective limits the good we can see does not mean the good does not exist.*

limits the good we can see does not mean the good does not exist. That is why we can find comfort knowing the One we are trusting has a perspective high above our own.

God's sovereignty encompasses everything, the good and the bad. In Lamentations, the Bible says, "Who can speak and have it happen if the Lord has not decreed it? Is it not from both the mouth of the Most High that both calamities and good things come?" (Lamentations 3:37-38).[5] While this can feel conflicting to understand how a good God can rule over calamities, we must view God's sovereignty in light of His character. He is powerful enough to use even the bad for His ultimate good. God's loving, gracious, and kind character is affirmed all throughout Scripture. David, the shepherd boy turned king who wrote the majority of the book of Psalms, wrote about God's character: "The Lord is merciful and gracious, slow to anger and abounding in steadfast love" (Psalm 103:8).[6]

He is also just, righteous, and sovereign. His love is ultimately shown through His overarching power. Even on the darkest day in history (literally, the sun went dark when Jesus died on the cross),[7] God used this to bring about the greatest potential for good. What the enemy means for evil, God uses for good.[8]

I've heard the saying, "If it's not good, God is not done." While I agree overall with the sentiment, I think it is often misunderstood. First, we must ask the Holy Spirit to help us reframe what we believe to be good and renew our minds to understand good as God does. Second, know the ultimate good God is working toward may not happen during our lifetime.

God's purpose is not to lead us into a life of earthly prosperity, filled with good things and an abundance of material possessions. His ultimate goal is to redeem the world to Himself, leading us to a life of wholehearted surrender. Because He created us to be worshippers of

As we work and rest and live our lives, we can do it all for the glory of God. This is how He designed us to live.

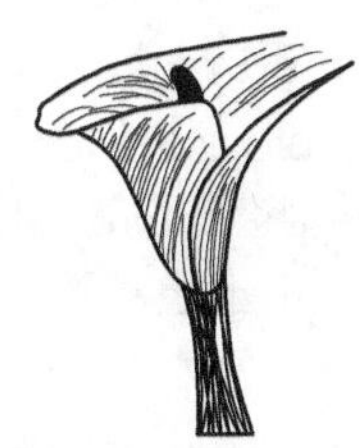

Him, this is also where we will feel most fulfilled and joyful. We are filled with His peace when we participate in His plan through walking in obedience. As we work and rest and live our lives, we can do it all for the glory of God. This is how He designed us to live.

God's good may not look good while we are on earth, but His good is not limited to what the world deems as successful. We can completely trust that God will bring about good in the lives of all His people for eternity. This may not look like relational success or earthly possessions because that is not what holds value in the kingdom of God.

The plans God has and the ways He brings about good are often far beyond what we can comprehend. As we grow to know Him personally and deepen our understanding of His heart, we are able to trust Him even when we don't understand what He is doing.

For those who love the Lord, Scripture says, "All the paths of the Lord are steadfast love and faithfulness" (Psalm 25:10).[9] God is in control, and He loves His people immeasurably. For those who are in Christ, all things are working together for good. Walk by faith in Him, trusting that He is working even when you can't see.[10]

GOD IN THE DETAILS

For the first years following Rebecca's death, Miss Cathy still came to our house most days. She continued finding ways to be helpful, and none of us could imagine her not being there. She's truly a part of our family.

Coming home from high school senior year, it was jarring to see Miss Cathy but not see Rebecca. I'd smile and tell Miss Cathy about my day, but my heart was aching. I would make it to my room right before the tears came. Even through my closed door, I could hear her humming in the living room and singing the lullaby she'd always sing to my sister.

"Go to sleep, sweet baby of mine. No more tears, no more fears, sweet baby of mine."

Over time, I stopped being surprised when Rebecca wasn't there. Instead, I was just sad. There's an emptiness in our home and our family. It's not something I wanted to fill or forget. We keep up the last family portraits we took all together on the walls in frames. A blanket Miss Cathy knit for her is draped over the chair in what was her room. It's all a reminder that everything on earth is incomplete and broken, and true wholeness and eternal life are only found in Jesus after we leave this earth. I see Rebecca in all things beautiful, especially flowers and butterflies. These reminders of Rebecca became part of my new normal.

My sophomore year of college, my hometown best friend Savannah FaceTimed me. She was walking on her treadmill, her head bobbing up and down.

"I'm coming to Dallas for the Jonas Brothers concert tomorrow! Mom, Heather, Peets, and I are going for Heather's birthday," said Savannah.

Heather is Savannah's older sister. She has special needs and is very high functioning—Heather gives the best hugs! Having sisters with special needs has bonded us deeply. Peets is her family's nickname for Patsy, who had been helping take care of Heather for Savannah's entire life. Like Miss Cathy for us, Peets was a part of their family.

"Maybe I can come to Dallas and see you! It's not that far from Fort Worth. Let me know if you want to meet for dinner," I said. We tentatively made some plans, then hung up.

I woke up early the next morning to a call from Savannah.

"She's gone," Savannah cried. "Peets is gone. She died."

There is nothing to prepare you for the sudden loss of a loved one. You wake up expecting them to be there, but instead find them laying lifeless. It's traumatizing. My heart was breaking for Savannah, for Heather, and for their entire family. Peets was Heather's best friend and constant companion—who would do life with Heather now?

As I prayed for Savannah and her family during this time, God placed something on my heart. We had been blessed beyond measure by Miss Cathy and the way she loved Rebecca. Could Miss Cathy now be the one who loves Heather in that way?

It was difficult to imagine Miss Cathy becoming a part of any family besides ours, but we knew Savannah's family would love and care for her the way they did for Peets. Heather needed a caretaker, and Miss Cathy is too gifted not to use her abilities to care for someone in need.

Now, Miss Cathy spends her days with Heather. Savannah's family lives in the neighborhood across from our house, so we are still able to see Miss Cathy. There is nothing that can fill the gap of Rebecca or Patsy for either of our families, but knowing Miss Cathy and Heather now have each other comforts me.

There is deep pain in not being with the ones we love anymore on this earth. I am grieving alongside you if you have ever lost someone you love; you understand this pain all too well. Like my sister's tragic death now separates her from me, our sin separates us from God. Now that I know what it feels like to be completely separated from a loved one, I have a better understanding of the severity of our sin and the gap it causes between us and God. I can't do anything to bring my sister back to life, and we can't do anything to heal our own brokenness.

Because of Jesus, this separation our sin causes does not have to be final. By placing our trust in Jesus as the perfect payment for our sins, the gap between us and a holy God can be closed. It's not about what you can do to earn forgiveness; it's about placing your faith in what Jesus has already done on the cross.

Not only do those who wholeheartedly place their trust in Jesus have eternal unity with God, but also with all others who have placed their hope in Him. No more sorrow or separation forever—this is the hope of the Gospel!

Apart from trusting in Jesus, there is no hope for me to offer you in the midst of your grief. Even when we trust in Jesus and know we have hope in eternity, there is still the present pain we must endure. But with Christ, there is hope beyond whatever pain you are facing. God sees you and He cares for you, and He has not abandoned you. He is both our hope for eternity and our comfort in our present.

God cares deeply for you, and experiencing pain on this earth doesn't disprove that. Rather than putting a bandaid on your bullet wound, God gives us a solution that will last forever. His perspective is so much greater than what we can see, and that is why we can confidently and wholeheartedly trust Him. He promises to bring about good eventually in His sovereign timing—even if that means we don't feel relief until we are with Him in eternity.

The way that details fall into place sometimes is evidence there is a greater perspective we don't have. This was certainly the case with how we found Miss Cathy. And how Mason's family found her before that. And how Miss Cathy found Heather.

Looking back over a decade of events surrounding Miss Cathy, it's now obvious how God was working through each loss to bring about good. In the midst of grief, however, it's difficult to see the possibility of good. When I am feeling weighed down, I try to remember ways that God has already been faithful. I look in His Word and see how He has always cared for and protected His people. I reflect on my own life, on situations I've witnessed like these with Miss Cathy, and remember how He has been good to me and those around me. I am in awe of how God can take even the most painful circumstances and bring about something beautiful.

God is high above it all, and He is making all things beautiful in their time.[11] God never changes.[12] When everything else feels like it is falling apart, these truths bring me comfort. He is always with us, and He has given all believers His Spirit to live in us.[13] Even if I do not see how God is working, I can trust that He is. He has been faithful before, and I trust He will be faithful again.[14]

The more we reflect on how God has been faithful through past situations, the greater our confidence becomes that He will also be faithful in the midst of whatever we are facing today. What are some of the ways God has been faithful in your life? I encourage you to write these down and reflect on these, thanking God for His faithfulness to you.

SIX

Trustworthy Wisdom

"In the beginning, God created the heavens and the earth," I read out loud from the Bible to Rebecca.[1] We started at the very beginning of the book together. When I was done reading each day, I put a blue piece of cardstock in between the pages to mark it for the next time.

There is a different blue piece of cardstock on the dashboard of my car. It says, "So do not throw away this confident trust in the Lord. Remember the great reward it brings you! - Hebrews 10:35."[2] Much of my life has changed since I put that paper in my car when I was sixteen. I thought I wanted to go to Baylor for undergrad and then go to law school. Instead, six years later I graduated from TCU (Baylor's rival and ironically my dream school!) with a business degree. I always thought I would be like my parents: marry my high school sweetheart and live in Louisiana forever. Instead, I've stayed in Fort Worth after college and love the life I am building here. In just a few short years, so much of what I thought my life would be has changed. I can't even trust what I believe about my own future. Because I change, I am not perfectly reliable over time. Perfect trustworthiness can't exist where there is change.

The only one who will never change is God. He is the same yesterday, today, and forever.[3] Because God never changes, neither does His Word. The little blue card with the Bible verse has stayed in my car for years because each day, it is true and applicable. As the card says, my confident trust in the Lord brings a great reward because He never changes and He will never let me down. When I see this card, I am encouraged to remember all the ways it has been worth it to trust God. Long after my car is no longer mine and this card is nowhere to be seen, the power of God's Word will remain. The words of God are as reliable today as they were a hundred years ago and as they will be a hundred years from now.

What makes God's Word different from other writings or historical accounts? I've read more books in my life than I can recall, and only one of them has changed my life. While the entertainment provided or lessons learned from most books eventually fade away, the Word of the Lord remains forever.[4] It's God-breathed, which means God inspired and directed the writing and collection of His Word through His people.[5] It has withstood the test of time and remains remarkably consistent with original texts. The more archaeologists uncover the more trustworthy the Bible has proven to be.

God's Word is full of His promises, and He is faithful to fulfill them.[6] We can't base what it looks like to trust God on our experiences with people who inevitably let us down. Unlike God, people will change, leave, hurt, and misunderstand us. God is not like people since He never changes and always keeps His Word.[7] God's Word is trustworthy because He is trustworthy. Through studying Scripture and reflecting on our own lives, there is an evident track record of God's faithfulness. There is no firmer foundation for your life than the Word of God.

WHOLEHEARTED TRUST

Bright notecards covered the wall behind the door to my room in my sorority house. Pink, orange, green, and yellow—the neon color pack from Target. The word I chose to focus on that year as a sophomore in college was **wholehearted**. Our heart is the center of our emotions, motivations, and desires. When the heart is mentioned in the Bible, it represents our innermost being. The heart is the lens through which we filter and perceive the world. Our heart can only be made whole when it's focused on the One who created it.

Our heart can only be made whole when it's focused on the One who created it.

I felt brokenhearted, and I trusted God could continue healing and making my heart whole again. I was scared of feeling overwhelmed because I had a lot on my plate, and I wanted to do it all well in a way that honored Him. Rather than rushing through it all, I wanted to be present and obedient in each moment. My prayer all year was to intentionally live a life of complete and wholehearted devotion to God in every friendship, class, and organization.

On a pink notecard, I wrote the definition of wholehearted: "completely and sincerely devoted and determined and enthusiastic; marked by complete earnest commitment; free from all reserve or hesitation."[8] After taping this card in the middle of the wall, I began hand-lettering Bible verses on other notecards that were encouragements and instructions on how to live wholeheartedly. I taped them around the pink card until the entire area was covered. Here are some of my favorites:

"Teach me Your way, O Lord, that I may walk in Your truth; unite my heart to fear Your name." (Psalm 86:11)[9]

"Trust in the Lord with all your heart, and do not lean on your own understanding. In all your ways acknowledge Him, and He will make straight your paths." (Proverbs 3:5-6)[10]

"Having purified your souls by your obedience to the truth for a sincere brotherly love, love one another earnestly from a pure heart." (1 Peter 1:22)[11]

"I therefore, a prisoner for the Lord, urge you to walk in a manner worthy of the calling to which you have been called, with all humility and gentleness, with patience, bearing with one another in love, eager to maintain the unity of the Spirit in the bond of peace." (Ephesians 4:1-3)[12]

"Therefore, my beloved brothers, be steadfast, immovable, always abounding in the work of the Lord, knowing that in the Lord your labor is not in vain." (1 Corinthians 15:58)[13]

As I meditated on these verses and prayed for wholehearted faith and devotion to the Lord, my mindset began to shift in all that I was doing. I learned as much about what it means to do things wholeheartedly as I learned about what it looks like to do things halfheartedly.

When we do things halfheartedly, we're just going through the motions. The focus of work is simply completing the task quickly so we can move on to the next one. Living halfheartedly shows a lack of drive and a misunderstanding of purpose. We keep ourselves busy to fill our time, but the work we are doing is not fulfilling our purpose.

God created us to work diligently and cultivate the earth that He created. He designed us in His image and has called us to emulate Him in this world. The work He has set before us to do is important, but He cares most about our heart behind all we do. While people focus on what we can see when we are making decisions, God looks at our hearts.[14]

Colossians 3:17 sums up well what it means to do all things wholeheartedly: we work as if we are working for the Lord in all we do, not for people.[15] As God aligns the desires of our hearts with His desires for us, obedience can joyfully flow from a devoted heart. When we have a proper understanding of God and what He has called us to do, we are able to do all things wholeheartedly.

That is a little of what the Lord has taught me about what it looks like to do things wholeheartedly. But what does it mean to wholeheartedly **trust** Him? In the same way, wholehearted trust means trusting without reserve or hesitation. To wholeheartedly trust means to trust completely.

Trust is a firm belief, and belief is confidence in the truth of something. To begin to trust God, we must know Him. One of the greatest ways of knowing God is knowing His Word. It teaches us about His consistent heart, character, and faithfulness. As we deepen our knowledge of God, we can trust Him more. There comes the point where wholehearted trust requires faith. There is a reason the apostle Paul wrote that we "walk by faith, not by sight" (2 Corinthians 5:7).[16]

Until we know God, we can't expect to trust Him. And there is no better way to begin getting to know Him than through His Word.

Two of my friends from college, Haley and Riley, came home to Louisiana with me for Easter while we were at TCU together. The chickens roaming free in our backyard didn't phase Riley, who was a part of Future Farmers of America in high school and raised livestock for years. On the other hand, Haley was not used to seeing animals outside of a zoo. When the chicken ran up to her as she approached our backdoor, she was terrified.

"Katherine!" Haley ran inside and slammed the French door. "You didn't tell me you lived on a farm!"

While where we live is far from what can be described as a farm, seeing a chicken was so abnormal for Haley that she did not have anything else to compare it to. Haley has since been home with me many times, each time a little less tense as she passes the black hen sitting by our back door.

The last time she visited, I heard her calling my name from across the yard.

"Katherine, look!" Haley smiled big as she held the chicken above her head.

Because she'd spent more time around the chicken, she learned that it wasn't going to hurt her. My sister Charlotte loves to pick up the chickens and hold them, and she showed Haley how to do the same. The more information Haley gained about the chickens and the experience she had around them, the less afraid she was of this animal.

At first, everything seems intimidating when you don't know much about it. It can be dangerous to approach what is unknown, especially animals. It makes logical sense why we are hesitant to fully embrace the unknown. The same is true of God when He feels unknown to us.

Some are less fearful of the unknown and jump in with blind faith. If you feel ready to take that leap of faith, do it! There is no better time than now to begin wholeheartedly trusting God with all that you are.

If you are on the fence about trusting God, I completely understand where you are coming from. Wholehearted trust does not come without time and intentionality. While it makes sense why you are hesitant to jump right in, I hope you don't stay on the fence. Spend some time around people who have been walking with God and can show you what it has looked like in their lives. Go to a church where they are teaching God's Word and can help answer the questions you have. Even when Christians hurt you and churches offend you, give God another chance. He's perfect, but His people aren't. I'm so sorry for the hurt you may have experienced. Pray for God to open your mind and heart to understand what is true and to help you trust Him.

God is patient, and He is able to handle your doubts and questions. When you have these doubts and questions, bring them to Him and His people. I pray that as you seek to understand, you are filled with His understanding and led to a place of surrender and wholehearted trust.

Charlotte, Elizabeth, and I have watched many Marvel movies together. I remember in *Captain America: Winter Soldier*, Steve Rogers tells Natasha Romanoff, "You know it's kind of hard to trust someone when you don't know who that someone really is."[17] This sentiment is just as true for people in our lives as it is with God. Until we know God, we can't expect to trust Him. And there is no better way to begin getting to know Him than through His Word.

Through studying His Word and learning His character, you learn why He is trustworthy. The Bible is filled with hundreds of promises God has made and kept. He is in complete control, and all of His ways are perfect and purposeful. Does this seem too good to be true? Pray for God to reveal Himself to you through His Word, and spend time reading it for yourself. His Word is "living and active, sharper than any two-edged sword, piercing to the division of soul and of spirit, of joints and of marrow, and discerning the thoughts and intentions of the heart" (Hebrews 4:12).[18] As I've said, no other book I've read has changed my heart and life like the Bible. There is an abundance of evidence and information available at our fingertips, but there will come a point where trust requires faith.

We can not change what happens to us in this life, but we do choose how we respond to it. God's Word is a lamp to our feet, showing us the next wise step even when the whole path isn't known.[19] A life of peace and meaning is found in wholeheartedly believing His truth. We can know we are steady and secure in God regardless of how we feel or what we believe. Find rest not in the calmness of your current situation or the blessings God has given you, but in the unchanging fact that He is in complete control and He will never leave you.[20]

WHY SHOULD I READ THE BIBLE?

Every summer, college students give their time to be camp counselors. At most camps, the counselors aren't allowed to have their phones, but they can receive mail. A friend of mine had been dating her boyfriend all of junior year. While she was excited about how he was using his summer to serve God and others, she was sad about being apart since he was going to training in May to be a camp counselor all of June.

Every day in June, my friend wrote her boyfriend a letter. She filled it with prayers, encouragement, funny memories, and printed pictures. Each Saturday, she sent care packages with his favorite snacks and little gifts she thought he would like. My friend missed him but was happy to think about the joy he must feel receiving all of her mail.

Toward the end of June, her phone rang. To her surprise, it was her boyfriend.

She answered excitedly, "Hi, I'm so happy you called! How are you? When will you be home?"

"Hi, yeah, I was just letting you know I decided to stay for July. So I won't be coming home until August."

"Oh, okay. Well— " he cut her off before she could finish.

"I'm sorry but this is all the time I had with the phone, but it was good to hear your voice and I will see you in a few more weeks!" And with that, he hung up.

As God aligns the
desires of our hearts
with His desires
for us, obedience can
joyfully flow from
a devoted heart.

She was obviously sad and disappointed, but tried to reason away the brevity of the conversation and why he didn't mention anything she'd sent him.

For the month of July, she sent the same daily letters and weekly care packages. The last week of July, she received a letter from the camp. Based on who had been sending the counselors mail, they were inviting friends and family to surprise the full-summer staffers at their end-of-summer banquet. She was so excited to finally see him!

She went shopping to buy a new dress for the banquet, and she left that weekend. Once she arrived at camp, they sent all the family and friends to the cabins so they could surprise their loved ones. My friend went with her boyfriend's parents to his cabin.

"I'm looking forward to meeting the other staffers he's told us about in his letters," said his dad. My friend didn't know he was able to write letters back. Why hadn't he written her any? Surely he had a good reason.

"Well this is a lot cleaner than I expected!" his mom expressed as they walked into his cabin.

My friend recognized the jacket lying on top of a bunk. Her eyes were drawn to a pile of letters and boxes pushed under the bunk—he'd gotten all of the letters and care packages! She smiled and went over to look at them, amazed at how the daily letters had added up: sixty-six, one for each day he was at camp. But when she began stacking them together, her heart dropped. Not one of the boxes or letters was open.

How do you think she felt after seeing a pile of unopened letters on the floor under his bed? Because camp is busy and tiring, she had already rationalized why he'd written back his parents but not her. But did he really not have time to even look at what she sent him? Did he care for her that little? If you were her, what could he say to you to make you think he still loved you?

Now just to be clear, this is a parable (a hypothetical story told for the purpose of illustrating a lesson). You see, God has written sixty-six letters to us, and they are bound together in the Bible. When we come face-to-face with Him one day in heaven, what would be an adequate reason we could give Him for not dedicating time to reading His Word?

The Lord of all creation cares about you personally and wants a relationship with you. He desires to spend time with you and for you to know Him more.

The more we know God, the more we will cherish His Word. The way to grow your desire for God's Word to increase your time in His Word. You will crave more of what you are feeding yourself. We won't always feel like reading it, but it is always worth it. I pray God continuously increases your desire for His Word, growing in you all wisdom and understanding of Him and His ways. Read His love letters to you; don't leave them unopened one more day.

HOW TO START

The Bible is a pretty big book. It's intimidating to know how or where to start. At the beginning? In the New Testament? In the Psalms? Is there a right and wrong way to do it?

The good news is it's more important to start somewhere than where you start. I would recommend starting with one of the Gospels; these are the first four books of the New Testament. Each is written by a different one of Jesus' closest followers and tells us more about the life, ministry, death, and resurrection of Jesus.

Find someone that you know is walking with God and ask them to read it with you. For almost everyone, there is someone who took the time to teach them how to read the Bible and follow God. Hopefully, they will be excited to now do that for someone else.

Choose a translation of the Bible you can understand. There are even online versions of commentaries or books with explanations of every verse in the Bible. There are reading plans on free platforms (like the YouVersion Bible App) if you are looking for specific ideas on where to start.[21] Remember, it's more important to start than to try to find the perfect way to do it.

While you don't have to do it this way, I recommend inviting a friend who knows the Lord to read the book of John with you. Ask God to help you understand. The more you open His Word, the more you will see Him revealing Himself to you.

This was the case for one of my friends that decided to focus on learning more about God after we graduated from TCU. A lot of what held her back from God was how people who claimed to live for Him had treated her. Now that she was gaining some distance, she thought it was time to see what it means to know God Himself, not just about Him through other people.

"Kath, I'm struggling to trust God. I don't agree with how some people we went to school with who call themselves Christians are living, and that's making me feel closed off from God. Can you help me?" she asked.

Rather than sharing with her what I know to be true about God, we went to the source of truth together so she could learn for herself. Over the next six months, we read the book of John together. Sometimes we read a chapter in a sitting, but other times only a verse. Between meetings, my friend would write down questions she had about Christianity or what she was reading. We went through the book at her pace, talking through her questions and searching throughout the rest of the Bible for the answers. Slowly, she began to be comfortable reading the Bible on her own. Eventually, she read the passages on her own before we met then we discussed them together.

While her heart was softening to God the more time we spent together in His Word, she was still closed off to other Christians because of the ways she'd been hurt in the past. After months of just us doing this together, she was finally open to coming to a young adult service at church with me.

"What do I wear? What exactly do people do there? What if I don't understand what they are talking about?" She asked lots of questions, and I did my best to answer them and calm her fears. I prayed that God would go before us and give her peace, helping her to clearly understand His love for her through the teaching of His Word and worship of His people.

We walked into a room of hundreds of young adults and ran into friends we went to college with—she was happy to see familiar people in an unfamiliar setting. We sang worship songs and prayed, then the pastor walked onto the stage.

"Tonight, we're going to take a break from our current series and talk about what it means to be great. Please open up your Bibles to John chapter one," he said.

My friend squeezed my hand and I smiled at her: one of her fears was not understanding what the pastor was talking about, and he chose to talk about one chapter of the book we'd been deeply studying for months. While my friend hadn't read the entire Bible or learned everything in it, God had prepared her with the knowledge she needed at that moment to hear what He had to say to her through the teaching of His Word.

Like us, God spells love T-I-M-E. It's not about doing it all or being perfect; it's simply about taking the time to invest in knowing God through studying His Word. Grab a pen and a journal, and open up the Bible. Start to write down your questions, thoughts, and prayers. Pray that the Holy Spirit would help you to understand what His Word is saying. Let's not get caught up in how we are doing it, but focus more on sitting with God and spending time with Him today.

MEMORIZING SCRIPTURE

While committing things to memory can be challenging, I've learned how crucial it is to have Bible verses in my head and on my heart at all times. This takes discipline and intentionality, but it is extremely valuable to have access at any time to the only thing that is completely true. This allows for my spiraling thoughts to be interrupted and settled.

When I was at school as a child, I was sometimes anxious that Rebecca wouldn't be alive when I got home. I would be sitting in English class repeating Philippians 4:6-7 in my head: *do not be anxious about anything, but in everything by prayer and supplication with thanksgiving let your requests be made known to God. And the peace of God, which surpasses all understanding, will guard your hearts and your minds in Christ Jesus.*[22] As I experience joys, I remember James 1:17 tells me, *"Every good gift and every perfect gift is from above, coming down from the Father of lights, with whom there is no variation or shadow due to change,"*[23] and I express gratitude to God for how He has gifted me. When I feel overwhelmed and defenseless against temptation, I remember that 1 Corinthians

10:13 says, *"No temptation has overtaken you that is not common to man. God is faithful, and He will not let you be tempted beyond your ability, but with the temptation, He will also provide the way of escape, that you may be able to endure it."* [24] If I am feeling alone or helpless, I am reminded of Psalm 46:1, which says, *"God is our refuge and strength, a very present help in trouble."* [25] When I am struggling to make a decision and filled with confusion, 1 Corinthians 14:33 comes to the surface of my heart: *"For God is not a God of confusion but of peace."* [26]

Writing God's Word on our hearts through Scripture memorization is a way we overcome sin and become more like Jesus. Psalm 119 is full of encouragement to study, cherish, and meditate on God's Word.[27] I would encourage you to take the time to read it and see the desire the writer has for God's Word. Here are some of my main takeaways:

The one who keeps God's Word and wholeheartedly seeks Him is blessed (v. 2)

The young are encouraged to keep their way pure by guarding it according to God's Word (v. 9)

We store up His Word in our heart so we can fight against sin (v. 11)

We can ask God to give us understanding as we meditate on His Word (v. 27)

Walking in faithfulness begins with setting the truth in front of you (v. 30)

As we delight in His commands, He leads us to follow them (v. 35)

Because God is good and does good, we desire to learn His ways (v. 68)

We can view our afflictions as good because they encourage us to learn more about God and His ways (v. 71)

Our hope comes from God's Word (v. 81)

His Word is guidance for our next step, showing us what will be obedient (v. 105)

God's wisdom can guide our choices, but obedience still requires faith and trust in the One who knows our past, present, and future.

In his work *A Life Without Lack,* theologian and teacher Dallas Willard beautifully describes the importance of Scripture memorization:

"Memorization is an essential element of a life without lack. It is a primary way we fill our minds with the Word of God and have our thoughts formed by God's thoughts. Memorizing Scripture is even more important than a daily quiet time, for as we fill our minds with great passages and have them readily available for our meditation, 'quiet time' takes over the entirety of our lives. Memorization enables us to keep God and His truth constantly before our minds, allowing His Word and wisdom to help us."[28]

Having Scripture memorized is my lifeline when I am feeling discouraged, anxious, confused, or joyful. Romans 8:6 says, "For to set the mind on the flesh is death, but to set the mind on the Spirit is life and peace."[29] Having truth written on our hearts and filling our minds keeps our gaze fixed on Jesus. I've experienced this truth in my own life, and have felt peace beyond explanation when I have hidden His Word in my heart.

Another encouragement to set our mind on God and benefit from fixing our focus on truth is in Isaiah:

"You keep him in perfect peace whose mind is stayed on You, because he trusts in You. Trust in the LORD forever, for the LORD GOD is an everlasting rock." (Isaiah 26:3-4)[30]

God tells us in His Word how to have this peace He promises. Perfect peace comes from keeping our focus on truth. We aren't as easily distracted and swayed by lies when we place our trust in Him.

We have peace because He is a solid foundation that will never change. If we place our hope and reliance on something that can change, we will never experience peace because we live in fear of that thing changing or a person leaving. Placing your trust in someone unchanging leads to perfect peace because you have no fear of things falling through or Him leaving. He always was and always will be. This means the God you get to know through His Word is the same God you are praying to and can spend eternity with. The truth you can learn through His Word and apply to your life through His Spirit will never change. He is a constant source of comfort and truth.

Right now, I am writing this book in a cabin on a lake in Missouri with a best friend of mine. Jill is studying for the NCLEX to become a Registered Nurse. All of college, she has dedicated hundreds of hours to studying and memorizing crucial information she will need once she is caring for patients. While memorizing that much information doesn't come naturally to most, she has done it because she is focusing on the end goal of being a Mother/Baby Nurse. To reach that goal, it is necessary for her to know this information and be able to apply it. When something is crucial for how you live your life, you learn and memorize it so that you know it well enough to apply it.

In the same way, it is necessary for us to know God's Word if we want to experience the abundance of life in Him.[31] Most of our brains have the capacity to hold verses, but we lack the desire and motivation to put in the effort. I encourage you to start with one verse. Write it on sticky notes to put around your home, make it the lock screen on your phone, write it on your hand, journal it in your prayers, share what it means with a friend, or thoughtfully meditate on it. Take the time to invest in memorizing Scripture, and the impact on your life will be greater than anything you could have imagined. I pray you understand the importance and personally see the benefits of dedicating Scripture to memory.

WALKING IN WISDOM

Wisdom is the ability to accurately apply knowledge to discern right from wrong and is rooted in the fear of the Lord.[32] Wisdom allows us to properly value the spiritual, physical, and relational aspects of our lives. God is the beginning of all wisdom, and He gives wisdom generously to those who ask Him.[33] The more you spend time in God's Word and in prayer, the more He will fill you with His wisdom and knowledge.

I often pray for discernment about what would be the wise thing to do or how to honor God in a situation. I've come to notice the difference between praying for God to affirm a decision I have already made versus praying for His best and the courage to be obedient. The wisdom we receive often goes against what we think we want in the moment. But over time, walking in this wisdom and being a part of the bigger picture of what God is doing is so much greater than any temporary pleasure.

His Word is valuable, "profitable for teaching, for reproof, for correction, and for training in righteousness, that the man of God may be complete, equipped for every good work" (2 Timothy 3:16b-17).[34] God's Word prepares us to live a life for Him, encouraging us and pointing us toward righteousness. As the ultimate source of truth, it points out where we are falling short and where He is calling us higher. It is not simply a rule book; it is a guide for how to live this life God has gifted us according to His best. Being a Christian is not only about obedience, but obedience flows from a faithful follower of Jesus. Living in a genuine relationship with God will change our heart which then affects our actions.

When making decisions, I pray for God to give me wisdom and a discerning spirit. He often gives clarity and direction on the right way to go, but other times there is no clear answer. There can be more than one obedient path, and it matters more that we are seeking Him above all else than the decision that we make.

When I was deciding where to go to college, Texas Christian University was the choice motivated by faith even though I was scared to come alone. God guided me in that decision, and four years later I see how He orchestrated my time in college to be used for my good and His glory. But when I was making the decision, I had no way of knowing how it would turn out. God's wisdom can guide our choices, but obedience still requires faith and trust in the One who knows our past, present, and future.

We can rest knowing that we can't mess up God's plan.

When Rebecca was a baby, she was having uncontrollable seizures that her medicine didn't seem to be helping. My parents took her to the hospital, desperate for a way to stop the painful convulsions. The doctor told my parents that if they didn't stop her seizures, she could likely die. There was a medication they could give her, but the dosage needed to stop the seizures could also kill her. They gave my parents the choice of either waiting it out or signing the paperwork to authorize the medication as well as a DNR.

My dad went to the hospital's prayer room and cried out to God. "Lord, show me what to do. Please help my baby girl," he cried.

God gave him peace that whatever his decision, God was going before my dad and He was the one who was going to take care of Rebecca and our family through whatever may come. Dad didn't have peace about signing it, and he returned to the room to tell my mom. When he walked in, Rebecca's seizures had miraculously stopped! Praise God that was the decision that allowed her to keep living, and we shared more time with my sister on earth because of it.

Although there will be situations like this one where making a decision seems utterly impossible, we can rest knowing that we can't mess up God's plan. He is ultimately in control of it all, and He holds us in the palm of His hand.[35] Fight against being paralyzed in the midst of making decisions. View them as opportunities to prayerfully walk in wisdom, learning how to discern God's guidance in your life. While we can't avoid all the hard decisions we will face, we can choose to surrender to the Lord's leading in them and prepare beforehand by cultivating wisdom through communing with God.

SEVEN

The Power of Prayer

Mom carried baby Rebecca down the church hallway. The walls were covered with paintings of Jesus teaching children, calming the storm, eating with friends, and healing the sick. She rounded the corner near the sanctuary and went into the prayer room. Soft candlelight drew her focus to the wooden cross draped with white fabric. Mom bent down to her knees by the cross and then laid Rebecca on the white cloth.

A Bible sat at the foot of the cross. She opened it to a passage from the book of Luke.[1] It's a story about a father named Jairus who heard about the miraculous healing power of Jesus. Jairus tracked Jesus down and begged Him to heal his dying daughter. Jesus agreed and started traveling to their hometown.

A woman who suffered from chronic bleeding saw Jesus on His way to heal the little girl. She pushed through the crowds and fought to be close to Jesus. Like Jairus, she'd heard of His power and **believed** He could heal her. She thought if she could simply touch the edge of His clothes, Jesus was powerful enough to cure her.

Sure enough, as soon as she touched His garment, she was healed! Jesus told the woman, "Daughter, your faith has made you well; go in peace."

As Jesus was speaking to this woman, someone from Jairus' house came to tell them not to bother coming anymore. The little girl Jesus was on His way to heal was dead. Jesus responded to the news by saying, "Do not fear; only **believe**, and she will be well."

When Jesus arrived, they were grieving her death. Jesus told them, "Do not weep, for she is not dead but sleeping."

They laughed at Jesus in disbelief. Ignoring their doubt, Jesus spoke to the girl and told her, "Child, arise." The Bible says that her spirit returned to her, and she was alive again!

When she finished reading the familiar story, Mom said, "Lord, I **believe** you can heal Rebecca." Mom prayed the words of the woman who touched Jesus' cloak, believing in her heart that God could heal her daughter.

As Christians, we pray to God for healing of sickness that ails us mentally, physically, emotionally, and spiritually. We pray in faith to our omnipotent God and trust in His sovereignty. It is not the strength of the one praying that coerces God into bringing about what we want; the power of prayer rests in the One we are praying to. The Bible describes God's character and documents His faithfulness over generations. Deuteronomy 32:4 says, "The Rock, His work is perfect, for all His ways are justice. A God of faithfulness and without iniquity, just and upright is He."[2] God is love and He can't sin. He is just, steady, righteous, faithful, and perfect. We can't know what prayers God will answer in what way, but we can know God hears and answers our prayers in His sovereign way and timing. We can remind ourselves of who He is and His love for us even when we can't understand what He is doing.

One morning, Mom and I were reading our Bibles beside each other in the living room. She was rereading this passage in Luke and remembering her cries to the Lord for Rebecca's healing on that Sunday morning over a decade ago.

"He has healed her. God answered my prayer," Mom said to me, "just not in the way I would have chosen. She is alive—just not in this world. And in her healing, God brought healing to many along the way."

Like the woman who was healed from her chronic bleeding by Jesus on His way to heal Jairus' daughter, God brought healing to many others through the way He healed Rebecca. The way He ultimately healed her is continuing to be used for both the good of others and the glory of God. I hope Rebecca's story can be a part of bringing healing to your hurt.

WHAT IS PRAYER?

The One who created our hearts is most equipped to heal them. Prayer is a means of communicating with God, our creator and healer. God is actually three persons in one essence: God the Father, God the Son, and God the Holy Spirit. The concept of this Holy Trinity helps us to understand how God is at work in the world and in our lives.

God the Father is the creator and sustainer of all things. Jesus is our Savior who bridges the gap between us and God. He is both fully God and fully man, meaning He understands what it is like to be human and can empathize with us while also embodying the power and perfection of God. Jesus is both the perfect sacrifice for our sins and the perfect mediator between us and God.

> "Since then we have a great high priest who has passed through the heavens, Jesus, the Son of God, let us hold fast our confession. For we do not have a high priest who is unable to sympathize with our weaknesses, but one who in every respect has been tempted as we are, yet without sin. Let us then with confidence draw near to the throne of grace, that we may receive mercy and find grace to help in time of need." (Hebrews 4:14-16)[3]

Jesus understands the pain and temptations of this life, but in His God-ness was able to withstand them and not sin. Therefore, He makes a way between us and God as the only One who fully relates to us and God. Through Jesus, we are able to experience a redeemed relationship with God permanently.

Through prayer, God calms my heart and realigns my perspective.

The same Holy Spirit that resides in God and Jesus is alive in every believer.[4] He is our comforter and helper in hardships.[5] He reminds us of truth in times of discouragement, temptation, or celebration.[6] He is our teacher, making God's Word come to life and helping us to understand it.[7] No one knows the mind of God like the spirit of God. He talks to God on our behalf in alignment with God's will when we don't have words to express ourselves.[8]

God is the almighty one we are praying to. Jesus is the one who made communication between us and God possible. To walk in the Spirit, we must surrender our lives to Jesus Christ. The Holy Spirit is alive in believers, drawing us closer to God and shaping us to become more like Jesus. When we understand the Trinity, we can be comforted by knowing we are never alone—God is always with us. His Spirit will never leave us. The more we pray, the more aware we are of His constant presence.

It is a gift to be able to speak directly to the God of the universe and know He cares for us. God knows us better than we know ourselves; He knows every detail about us from each tear we cry to the number of hairs on our heads.[9] He created us, loves us, and knows the future He has planned for us—who better to ask for wisdom and direction?

I've always been a verbal processor. Speaking or writing down everything I am thinking and feeling is what I like to call prayerful processing. Rather than venting to a friend, it is so much healthier to go to the source of truth. Prayer is how we can cast all of our anxieties on the Lord, knowing that He cares for us and wants to be the one we go to with everything.[10] Through prayer, God calms my heart and realigns my perspective.

In prayer, I draw near to God and He comforts me.[11] Although my situation often doesn't change in the midst of that prayer, my heart does. I feel more peace and security not in what is happening around me, but in who my God is. Prayer is a way we can set our minds on the Lord, which grows our trust in Him and fills us with peace.[12]

There is no secret formula for praying correctly; simply talk to God. He knows what you need before you ask Him.[13] You can be honest with Him about not knowing what to do or say—you can't scare Him away! The more you read God's Word and spend time around Christians, the more familiar God will become to you. The more you pray, the less daunting it will seem. Everyone is welcome to talk to God—even children.

For Rebecca's baby announcement, we mailed a trifold of pictures of the Gatti girls and asked people to pray for Rebecca. Both Elizabeth and I wrote a poem that was printed on the card.

My Rebecca…	**My Rebecca…**
is brave,	is a princess,
outstanding,	is loved by God,
beautiful,	precious,
healed with prayer,	God can make her better,
a miracle,	she loves me,
incredible,	the baby sister I always wanted,
can get better with God's help.	beautiful.
Love, Katherine (age 7)	*Love, Elizabeth (age 4)*

I believed God answered our prayers before when we begged Him to allow Rebecca to live. I believed she could be fully healed because with God, all things are possible.[14] Both Elizabeth and I had faith that God could heal her, but we also saw the beauty in who Rebecca was without further physical healing. She was the sister we prayed for, and the baby girl we cherished.

A mentor of mine describes prayer as entering the heart of God through the door of Jesus. Prayer includes all the ways we commune with God and spend time in His presence. It can be saying prayers, but it can also include times of silence and solitude as we sit in His presence.

The purpose of prayer is more about changing us than changing our circumstances. The more we talk to God, the more He aligns our hearts with His truth. There is no one right way to pray; it's more about having the heart to draw near to God and communicate with Him. We can pray prayers of adoration, responding to God in love as we learn more about His character. We can pray prayers of gratitude, expressing thankfulness for all God is and all He has provided.

Prayer is also used to confess our sins to God. Confession is admitting when we have acted outside of God's design for our lives. Even as Christians, we will still sin. Confession is crucial for our closeness with God because it reminds us of our need for Him. When we confess our sins, "He is faithful and just to forgive us our sins and cleanse us of all unrighteousness" (1 John 1:9).[15]

We don't have to hide from God when we make mistakes; He loves to extend forgiveness to us. When we are reminded of our sin and need for God, we are more forgiving and gracious to others. As we see the heart of God through our confession, we stop depending on our works to bring about our righteousness and remember that it is all an act of His unmerited grace.

We are invited to share everything with God who already knows our hearts. As we bring our requests to Him and are honest about our desires, the Spirit begins to reshape our desires. Bringing everything to God deepens our trust in Him and grows our reliance on Him. Peace comes from total reliance on God, and worry is a result of relying on ourselves. Times of silence and solitude where we intentionally set our minds on God are also ways we can commune with God. Words aren't needed for God to know what is on your heart, but He delights in you sharing it with Him.

IF GOD ALREADY KNOWS, WHY SHOULD I PRAY?

God knows our thoughts before we have them, and He has planned all of our days.[16] Yet He still desires to hear from His children and for us to pour out our hearts before Him. Prayer isn't needed to inform God; it's to invite Him closer.

The purpose of prayer is more about changing us than changing our circumstances.

Like anyone you are in a relationship with, communication is the key to closeness. How can you know someone if you never talk to them? Do you really have a relationship with them if you never speak? To grow in our relationship with God, we must talk to Him as well as listen.

Prayer keeps our eyes open to how God is moving and working in our own lives and the lives of people around us. Prayer is an act of obedience to God. God promises that our prayers are never in vain. Even when we don't know what to pray or have words to express what's weighing us down, the Holy Spirit intercedes for us. When Jesus gave us the example of prayer in The Lord's Prayer and in the garden before He was crucified, He prayed for God's will to be done.[17] Praying for God's will is affirming our trust that He knows what's best, and that His ways are higher than our own.

Prayer is a privilege. We have the chance to call on the name of the Lord anytime we please, and we are commanded through Scripture to pray without ceasing.[18] This means we are to be in a spirit of prayer, having prayer be our means of thinking and as natural as breathing. Having the habit of continual prayer doesn't happen overnight; it begins by going before God today and sharing all that is on your heart. The more that you experience the freedom from life's burdens and the peace from growing closer to God, the more you will pray. God doesn't like you more if you pray more, but you may like who you are the more that you pray.

What keeps us from praying? Is it because we don't have enough time or we don't know how? Jackie Hill Perry wrote this on prayerlessness:

"Prayerlessness is almost always a humility issue. We'd like to believe that we don't pray because of busyness or that we just lack discipline and need to 'do better.' At the end of the day though, we're just a proud bunch. Pride deludes us into thinking we're self-sufficient. That our jobs supply our needs. Our relationships provide comfort. Our intellect and ambition made us successful. But in fact, everything you are and everything you have is because God rains on the just and the unjust. So then, to become more prayerful, we have to be honest. Embrace the reality that we are perpetually needy even when it doesn't feel like it."[19]

Even when we don't feel like we need God, the reality is that we do need Him. Every moment, we need Him. Prayer is how we seek Him in our need. It keeps our hearts in a humble posture of seeking God and remembering that He is the one that meets all of our needs.

PRAYING FOR GOD'S WILL

My sophomore year of college, my Pops developed another type of cancer: acute myeloid leukemia. This time, it was deemed terminal. We spent Thanksgiving at M.D. Anderson in Houston with all of my mom's side of the family gathered together in the Leukemia Unit's Family Room. Pops was able to muster up enough strength to come sit with us for a little while, smiling as he watched us working together on a puzzle. Our family always enjoys just being together, especially when we're around a jigsaw puzzle. Over the years, Pops has given me a lot of his puzzles. I love doing ones he's already done because he left the edge pieces separately stored in plastic baggies. I get most of my organizational and efficiency tendencies from my Pops.

Leaving Pops at the hospital after Thanksgiving to go back to school, I was told to be prepared for this to be the last time I saw him. I prayed this wasn't true. For the next few months, I carried the weight of anticipating the grief of losing him. I felt guilty for having to be away, but cherished the days he felt strong enough to talk on the phone. He always made me laugh and showered me with kind words.

My prayer each day I was away from him was for God to work out the timing of his heavenly homecoming. I had so many things I was balancing at school, and I had no idea how to prepare for dropping it

> *God doesn't like you more if you pray more, but you may like who you are the more that you pray.*

all once the news came. Rather than worrying about how the details would play out, I prayed for God's will to be done in His perfect timing. I asked Him to heal my Pops and comfort my family.

When we pray for God's will, we are expressing our desires to God while also acknowledging that He knows better. The way God worked out the details with my Pops was more gracious than I ever could have imagined. Against all odds, Pops was able to come home for Christmas. Our family has many traditions that Pops and Nana started, and it was the greatest gift to share them with him one more time.

In February, I came home for the weekend and spent time with Nana and Pops. So many of my favorite times with my grandparents are when we sat and visited together in their wood-paneled living room of the house my Pops built when my mom was a little girl.

That afternoon, my family worked on a puzzle together. Pops didn't join; he sat at the counter watching us, looking tired but content. When it was time for me to go back to Fort Worth, I hugged him tight and he rubbed my back, telling me he loved me. In my heart, I felt this would be the last normal day I had with him. Right as he was walking out the door, I hugged him again. I held myself together, smiling as we said goodbye. But my heart was breaking.

Soon after this day, Pops went back to M.D. Anderson because he was regressing. Toward the end of his time there, the clinical trials they performed on Pops were not going to help him. He chose to endure them anyway because he knew they may help someone else.

When I had sleepovers at their house as a child, I would run into my grandparents' room and jump up into their bed and snuggle between them when I had a nightmare. They called me a crazy sleeper and would laugh the next morning at breakfast about my feet somehow ending up in their faces and my sleep talking, but they never complained or made me feel guilty for seeking that safety and comfort with them.

The last time I slept in their bed, I tearfully remembered all those times I had come in there as a child. It was a late night in March 2020, and I had just made it into town. It was the beginning of the COVID-19 shutdowns. Pops had not woken up since I'd arrived. I'd held his hand and talked to him, telling him I was home and that I loved him and missed him. This was the first time he'd been unresponsive like this. I was sitting next to Nana on the couch, and she told my Mom through her tears that she didn't think he would make it through the night. I decided to sleep at their house because I wanted to be able to talk to him if he woke up at all.

I slept on Pops' side of the bed which doesn't feel so big anymore. I prayed for God to allow me to talk to him one more time, and I thanked Him for all of the time I did have with Pops and the conversations I did get to have. Mom woke me up early to tell me that Pops had a rough night. The nurse came by and confirmed he'd entered into the active stage of dying. The shock of her statement made my heart pound in my ears. My feet were heavy as I made my way down the stairs—step by step—to the living room where Pops lay in a hospital bed.

He was moaning in pain. For a moment, it was just the two of us. I held his hand and told him how thankful I was for him. He opened his eyes, and I looked into them and told him many of the ways he's positively impacted my life and our family. Soon after, his breathing dramatically worsened and I backed away as Mom and Nana came beside him. They comforted him through their tears, and Mom read him Psalm 23 just before he breathed his last breath. She told him it was okay, that he could go on to be with Becca and Nanny (his mother). Then just like that, he was gone.

Being in the room when someone you love crosses over to heaven is an inexplicable experience. It made me reflect on life, and how in an instant our time on earth ends. Sitting next to my cousin Claire, there were no words. Her husband Kyle kindly gave us tissues while drying tears of his own.

The next week, the entire family was at Nana's house nonstop. Because of COVID-19 shutting down everything, we were able to take this time to be there together as a family. His service was scheduled just before the ban which would have made it impossible to gather. Although we were masked and trying to keep our distance, I'm grateful we were able to come together to honor him and celebrate his life.

While the heartbreak was painful, God answered my prayer for the timing to be best. Because of the pandemic, I had an extended spring break and did not have to do schoolwork. I was able to focus on loving my family and grieving alongside them. The grief was excruciating, but I felt so loved by God that He'd answered my prayers for both more time with Pops and for the timing to allow me to be with my family.

The last time I saw my Pops at the funeral home, he was wearing the same suit he wore when he escorted me on the field for homecoming court. Pops never made me doubt how proud he was of me. His constant affirmation and genuine support was the greatest gift. Not once, but twice during my freshman year at TCU, Nana and Pops made the drive to Fort Worth to see me. On their second visit, we went back to their hotel to watch baseball, and I sat on the couch while Nana played with my hair. I was going on a date that weekend, and Pops gave me some encouragement and advice I will never forget. They were concerned about taking up too much of my time or taking me away from my studies and friends, but I cared more about cherishing this time with them. I am forever grateful for the way my Nana and Pops always went out of their way to be there for me. I'm glad we get to spend forever together.

PRAYER WARRIORS

Those who are committed to faithfully praying for others are often called prayer warriors. Warrior is an accurate term, considering we are all engaged in a spiritual war whether we realize it or not. There is the devil, who is the prince of this earth, prowling around like a roaring lion looking for someone to devour.[20] He hates God and he hates Christians, and he strategically works against us. He is the father of all lies and an instigator of evil.[21] The devil can't take away our salvation or alter the eternity we have secured through a relationship with Jesus.[22] But if we live unaware that we have an enemy, he is going to distract and discourage us from living in obedience to what God has created us to do.[23] He wants to lead us astray from our devotion to Jesus.[24]

We have no reason to fear our enemy, but we must be aware of how to fight him every day. When we resist the devil, he flees from us.[25] The most effective tool we have against the spiritual forces of evil is prayer. Each day, we must intentionally fight against these unseen forces. In the Bible, this preparation is described as **The Armor of God.**[26]

"Put on the whole armor of God, that you may be able to stand against the schemes of the devil. For we do not wrestle against flesh and blood, but against the rulers, against the authorities, against the cosmic powers over this present darkness, against the spiritual forces of evil in the heavenly places. Therefore take up the whole armor of God, that you may be able to withstand in the evil day, and having done all, to stand firm." (Ephesians 6:11-13)[27]

Like soldiers readying for battle, we can put on our armor and fight with the tools God has given us for this spiritual war. These tools include the belt of truth, the breastplate of righteousness, the gospel of peace, the shield of faith, the helmet of salvation, and the sword of the Spirit. After listing these ways to stand firm, the final command is to pray at all times.[28] Prayer is crucial to our walk with God, and it is the most powerful thing we can ever do.

We have an enemy, and he is the father of lies.[29] Through God's Word, He shares with us how we can confidently withstand the enemy's attacks and fight against his lies. When we put on the whole armor of God, we are able to stand firm in His truth.

The more we study His Word, the more we know God's character and heart. As we learn more about Him, we are able to discern what is truth from Him and what are lies from the enemy. If we expect to fight the lies that so often attack us, we must remember who our enemy is and utilize the tools God has given us to fight against him.

To fight the lies, invest in knowing the truth.

To fight the lies, invest in knowing the truth. Jesus Himself is the truth.[30] Through knowing Jesus, we know truth. To discern truth from lies, you must first surrender your life to the source of all truth. Jesus told His followers, "If you abide in My word, you are truly My disciples, and you will know the truth, and the truth will set you free" (John 8:31-32).[31] Freedom is found through knowing Jesus and His truth.

Every Tuesday afternoon for eleven years, I took piano lessons. My mom would drive us to Mrs. Holbert's house and park her minivan in the circle driveway. Elizabeth and I would walk in with our Vera Bradley crossbody messenger bags that held the piano books I hadn't looked at since last week's lesson. Mrs. Holbert was kind and patient, always telling me that I was getting better. I almost never practiced, so I knew that was unlikely.

While I have minimal pianist abilities despite the hundreds of hours I spent on her wooden bench, I learned more about prayer because of my time with Mrs. Holbert. She would ask me how things were going and always check in on what I had mentioned the week before. She always asked about Rebecca and wanted to come out to the car to see her. I talked to her about big decisions or a breakup or my anxiety. She often shed a few tears and cupped her delicate hands around mine. When Mrs. Holbert told me she was praying for me, I believed her.

It sounds more like my parents paid for biblical counseling than piano lessons, and that wouldn't be an unfair assessment of how I spent my time there. Piano was never my thing, but I couldn't imagine quitting and losing my weekly time with Mrs. Holbert. It's powerful knowing someone is bringing your cares and hurts before God and praying for you. She showed me how to ask thoughtful questions, pray for others, and follow up. It's a simple yet powerful way we as Christians can be the hands and feet of Jesus.

Our prayers for each other hold significance. James, the brother of Jesus, wrote, "The prayer of a righteous person has great power as it is working" (James 5:16b).[32] As we go to God on behalf of others, we have

Prayer warriors are those who understand the power of prayer and yield it on behalf of others.

eyes to see how He is working in their situations. Prayer warriors are those who understand the power of prayer and yield it on behalf of others.

Prayer is a gift, and it's our greatest weapon against the darkness. May Christians rest knowing this ability to communicate with God can never be taken away from us, and may we never take this gift for granted.

PRAYING SCRIPTURE

Reading the Bible is essential to our relationship with God. It's His love letter to us that tells the story of creation to eternity, instructing us how to walk by faith through the in-between. This book is powerful, and we can benefit both from reading and memorizing it.

A benefit to memorizing Scripture is that it is written on your heart and easily accessible when you are talking to God. It is powerful to pray Scripture, repeating the truth to yourself as a reminder of God's promises and repeating them to God to ask Him to do what He has promised.

We can memorize the words of God and repeat them back to Him in prayer. Setting our minds on God's Word helps us to intentionally obey it.

"This Book of the Law shall not depart from your mouth, but you shall meditate on it day and night, so that you may be careful to do according to all that is written in it. For then you will make your way prosperous, and then you will have good success." (Joshua 1:8)[33]

The key to obedience and growth in our faith is where we set our minds, and the key to setting our minds on God is prayer. For us to walk in intentional obedience to God, we must be mindful of Him and His instructions. In prayer, we ask God to help us live a life worthy of the calling to which He has called us to as His children.[34]

The key to obedience
and growth in our
faith is where we
set our minds,
and the key to
setting our minds on
God is prayer.

Prayer is powerful because it draws us closer to the heart of God.

The Christian life isn't about following God's Word perfectly—the whole point of why we need Jesus is that we could never live up to the perfect standard of the law on our own merit. We study and meditate on Scripture not to modify our behavior through our own willpower, but to come to God in prayer and ask Him to help us live according to His purpose for our lives. Scripture reminds us of our need for God and outlines how we can pray and ask Him to help us.

Meditating on God's Word simply means setting your focus on Scripture. This can be done through repeatedly saying, thinking, writing, or reading a passage. At the beginning of college, I picked this passage to focus on for the next four years:

> "Trust in the Lord, and do good; dwell in the land and befriend faithfulness. Delight yourself in the Lord, and He will give you the desires of your heart. Commit your way to the Lord; trust in Him, and he will act. He will bring forth your righteousness as the light, and your justice as the noonday." (Psalm 37:3-6)[35]

Here is what my prayers often looked like as I prayed through these verses:

Lord, I trust in who You are and have faith in what You have done. Help me to have eyes to see the good You have set before me to do. Lead me into immediate obedience with a pure heart. May I not long for a past or future time, but be present here and dwell in the land where You have placed me. Open my eyes to ways I can serve others and share the hope of the Gospel. Teach me more about Your faithfulness and help me to live a life marked by faithfulness. May I love faithfulness and keep it near like a friend.

I pray my deepest desires are for You, and that You alone are what I delight in. If it's not from You, I don't want to want it. Please change my heart to desire You above all else, and align the desires of my heart with Yours.

Give me wisdom and discernment to know the difference between what is of You and what is not. Please fill my heart with desires that are from You, and give me these desires in Your perfect way and timing.

In all that I do, I want to be committed to You. My life is not my own, and I pray my aim is to please You alone and not those around me. Thank You for the work You have set before me and the people You have placed around me. I commit my ways to You and wholeheartedly place my trust in You. Help me to steward the time, opportunities, and relationships You have gifted me obediently for Your glory. Please direct my steps and lead me to walk in Your ways. You have called me to be faithful to abide in You, and You are the one that will act.

I believe You are going to bring about my righteousness as sure as the sun will rise each day. You are the executor of justice and the ultimate avenger of all evil. You will bring justice at the right time. You are my defender, and You are the one who is fighting my battles. I love You. Amen.

I wrote little prayers in the margins of my Bible around this passage throughout college. Looking back at what I prayed when certain burdens were crushing me, I am overwhelmed by the faithfulness of God to see me through each hardship. Even though I couldn't see it in the middle of the pain, He was bringing about purpose from the pain. While the prayers around these verses throughout those four years looked different from each other, the truth of these verses was constant. During college, I faced an array of trials from heartbreak to grief to the pandemic. These years also held some of the deepest joys and best memories of my life thus far. Through all the highs and the lows, I came back to these verses. When I pray God's Word back to Him, the truth goes deeper into my heart and grows my trust in Him. This keeps my prayers grounded in what is true when it is so easy to be swept away by what I feel.

Prayer is powerful because it draws us closer to the heart of God. Through spending time with God in prayer, I have experienced His Spirit changing my heart to look more like His. Even if my circumstances didn't change, my heart did. When you are hurting and praying God's Word in the midst of your pain, it will resonate with your heart deeper than ever.

PRAYER JOURNALING

In a psychology class I took in college, we began each session with five minutes of journaling. Our professor was passionate about how beneficial journaling is for our mental health. It's proven to reduce stress, sharpen memory, and cultivate emotional maturity.

This helpful habit is something we can also practice in our relationship with God. Journaling all my thoughts and emotions like a letter to God is my favorite way to pray. There is nothing magical about writing prayers down as opposed to saying them out loud or praying in your head or even singing them. It's more important that we are coming to God in prayer, not the means that our prayers are lifted up. God knows our hearts and hears the words before we even say them.

What I have personally found to be powerful about journaling my prayers is how it creates a personal track record of God's faithfulness in my life. I am so quick to forget all that God has delivered me from and the abundance of prayers He has answered. When I reflect back on the prayers I have written throughout my life, I am reminded that God hears me and He cares for me. He is answering my prayers in His perfect timing in the best way, even though I usually can't see what that will be when I am in the hardship.

As I look back on the prayers I prayed in the midst of many different storms, I have the perspective now of how God brought healing and answered my prayers. This strengthens my faith through the trials because I know God will continue to be faithful to me, just as He always has been.

One of the greatest ways to increase your faith and trust in God is to reflect on and remember all He has done. We have His Word that is full of displays of His character and heart for His people. We hear the testimonies of others and how He has redeemed them. We also have personal experiences of how He has walked us through the valleys and the mountaintops. Whether you choose to document these things through prayer journaling or not, take the time to remember the Lord and His faithfulness to you.

One night, I was sad so Mom stayed up talking with me. It was almost 3:00 a.m. when she left to go to bed and I still couldn't sleep, so

I pulled out my prayer journal. The day before while Rebecca had an intense seizure, she bit her lip so hard it ripped. It broke my heart to see her in even more pain. We planned to take her to the doctor the next day to get stitches. I wrote in my prayer journal and prayed: *God, heal Rebecca. Please, take her pain away. Give her peace and give my family the strength to endure whatever comes next. I love her so much, Father. Thank you for choosing me to be her sister.*

At this point in Rebecca's life, I knew the healing I was praying for would likely only come from her going to be with Jesus Himself. There was a shift that happened later in her life when I realized I was now praying for heaven, not for her healing here. My family wholeheartedly believed God had the power to heal her on this earth, but it didn't seem to be in His plan for her life. Because of my trust in God, I was able to pray for His will because I know that is ultimately better. I cried that night as I prayed for her healing, but was comforted knowing that no matter what we would have eternity together in heaven.

Although it was not the way I ever desired it to happen, God answered my prayer hours later and healed my precious sister. While I was sleeping that night, Rebecca went to heaven. God's ways are higher than ours, and we may never understand why He does things the way He does until we are in heaven. But even in the darkest of times, He is faithful in listening and answering the prayers of His children.

EIGHT

The Peace of Christ

My elementary school closed on a Tuesday because the roads were covered in too much ice for Louisianians to drive safely. My dad deemed this a daddy-daughter date day for Elizabeth and me, and we were off to the bookstore.

I've always loved to read. In my hometown, there was a bookstore where my dad often took me to buy as many books as I could carry. I walked through the colorful shelves, running my fingertips along the spines. We sat in red bean bag chairs and read our different books, sharing sentences we liked out loud with each other. After buying the next few Beacon Street Girls books and a Diet Coke, Dad drove us home.

K-Love played on the car radio. I watched cars slide back and forth on the bridge leading into our neighborhood. The bridge's incline was slight, but the ice and inexperienced drivers complicated the situation. My dad looked at us in the backseat and said in a goofy voice, "Challenge accepted!"

He accelerated as we approached the incline, and we hydroplaned. My Diet Coke sloshed and stained the corners of my new books. *Maybe the bookstore will give me fresh, unstained copies if I explain the situation?*

Dad's gold Yukon slipped into the bridge's barrier, holding us up like bowling balls out of the gutter. I squeezed my eyes closed and clenched my fists so tightly that my fingernails left crescents in my palms. I screamed, terrified we were going to fly right off the side to our certain demise. When I opened my eyes, we were safely in our driveway.

There was a black scrape on the side of our car, and we left a matching mark on the bridge. Aside from that scratch, we made it out unscathed. Every time I drive over the bridge into the neighborhood where my Nana still lives, I see the black marks and remember our near-death experience.

I wasn't scared to drive through the ice because I was with my dad; I was certain he would protect me. Even when we started to slip, I squeezed my eyes shut in the midst of the chaos and trusted my dad would get us through it. I didn't have to see what he was doing or where we were going to trust him because I know my dad. This is like our relationship with our heavenly Father; the more we know Him, the more we trust Him. Even when we can't see what God's doing.

I've spent countless hours with my dad, and he has proven to me how much he cares about me by how he sacrificially loves me and my family. Although I know my dad is not perfect, he taught me about my heavenly Father who has all the qualities of my dad perfected.

Sometimes, father figures aren't leading and loving in a godly way. Just like all people, fathers will inevitably fall short of perfection. There will always be a feeling of lack; sometimes that hole is larger in some relationships than others. No matter the size of the hole in your relationship with your dad, let the feeling of lack lead you toward your perfect heavenly Father.

As we faced this unknown of Rebecca's health, I was anxious about what would happen to her. I looked to my dad who has always kept me safe and made me laugh. And I saw him looking to Jesus.

PEACE IN THE UNKNOWN

When I first began to understand how drastic Rebecca's brain injury was, I struggled to understand why God would allow this to happen. *How could a loving God allow an innocent child to be harmed? What had our family done to warrant this? Why would He not heal her if He has the power to? How could He watch her suffer and do nothing to help her?*

Fear became a part of my every day. It was there when I woke up, rushing to her room to make sure she made it through the night. It was there when I left for school, hoping she would be there when I returned. It was there when I went to sleep, plaguing my thoughts and haunting my dreams. It was there in every conversation; the struggle I always knew I needed help with but did not know how to ask or where to begin.

I accepted fear as a part of me, allowing it to rob me of hope. I was not experiencing the joy I have access to in Christ because my mind was often ruled by fear and anxiety. Freedom from fear felt impossible. I thought my best option was to learn how to live with it as well as possible while hiding it from everyone else.

My thoughts frequently stayed on my sister. I talked to God about her throughout the day. Each week at church, our Sunday school teacher asked us if we had any prayer requests. *How many times am I allowed to ask them to pray for my sister?* It didn't usually feel like the right time to bring it up amongst the asks for prayers for good grades and safe travels. Besides, I wouldn't want anyone to think I wasn't okay. *Shouldn't I be okay by now?*

By the time Rebecca was five years old and I was twelve, my understanding of God's sovereignty and His will had deepened some. Through reading the Bible and being taught by older Christians, I learned about some extremely difficult situations where God allowed the bad thing to happen and still used it for His ultimate good.

The main example of this is the death of His own Son for the sake of our salvation. I knew in my head that God's best could be for her healing not to happen until she was in heaven, but my heart refused to believe it. *God can do anything. He can bring the dead back to life—how difficult could it be to heal my sister?*

I watched someone I love suffer and knew there was nothing I could do about it—this was when I realized how completely helpless I was. Whatever illusion of control I thought I had was just that: an illusion. In this circumstance, it was my lack of control and absence of predictability that stirred up anxiety.

Trust is crucial to living a life marked by peace.

As a child realizing I was not in control, I began to learn what it meant to believe God is in complete control. At first, I thought this meant asking God to promise everything would turn out the way I hoped—that life would be free of fear, loss, disappointment, or pain. I made very good cases for my suggestions, explaining why He should use His position of control to do what I would do.

I only saw what was right in front of me and made the very best recommendations I could. The only good outcome I saw during the beginning of Rebecca's life was the outcome where God answered my prayers and healed my sister miraculously. *How could any other outcome be good?*

When I was a junior in high school, Rebecca was still alive and not yet healed. I was feeling anxious about what to do with my life; I didn't want to go far away from my family without knowing what would happen to Rebecca while I was gone. I was deciding on my college and my major, and I didn't know what to do. Sitting at our tan kitchen table, I asked my dad for help making these decisions.

"I just want to make the right choice," I said.

Dad grabbed a yellow legal pad and a blue pen. He drew three circles, one inside of the other. He pointed to the outer layer and said, "These are all the things you have no control over: when you die, the weather, what happens to Rebecca, LSU football, the future."

"Now this," he moved into the second circle, "are the things you have influence over: your friend group, your church, your classmates. You can't do the right thing for the people around you, but you can pray for them and point them toward wisdom. You have the ability to be a positive influence."

"The center circle holds what you do have control over: your relationship with God, where you go to school, who your friends are, how you treat people, how you spend your time, taking care of your body, what you think about."

"You're spending 80% of your mental energy in this last circle thinking about things you can't control, and only 20% on what you can influence," my dad said. "That's why it's so difficult to make a decision because you can't control the factors you're worrying about."

"You need to shift at least 80% of your focus toward what is within your realm of influence and focus on obeying God within that. You should still be aware of what's going on in that outer circle, but just trust God with it. Spend the time you have stewarding your inner circle well and obeying God, then trust Him with the rest. As long as you are doing that, you don't need to worry about whether or not you are making the right decision about college. God will be with you and guide you, and He will use a surrendered heart no matter where you go or what you major in."

This advice from my dad has carried me through many decisions since. He's taught me that when you are obedient to God where you can be and trust Him with what is outside of your reach, you can have peace through making decisions.

Within our domain, we have the responsibility to obey God. For the majority of life that is outside of our domain, all we can do is trust God. In an attempt to control what is outside of our domain, we will be overcome with anxiety, frustration, and disappointment.

Trust is crucial to living a life marked by peace. It's a muscle we grow over the course of our lifetime as we follow Jesus. Trust is cultivated through knowing God, believing God, and letting that knowledge and belief direct our steps and affect our life. Trust is openhandedness with all that we love.

We will face an array of issues and frustrations and joys and gifts in this life, but facing all of these faithfully comes back to trusting God and setting our minds on Him. Each moment we feel anxious is an opportunity to experience the Gospel reality of our ability to draw near to God.

No matter how we landed in the anxiety we are currently facing, there is hope for peace. We are more than what we have done and what

Each moment we feel anxious is an opportunity to experience the Gospel reality of our ability to draw near to God.

has been done to us. God has gifted us His Spirit, His Word, and His people to aid us as we battle anxiety. In addition to prayer, there are situations where counseling, medication, or other resources can help. God can carry us through whatever we are enduring and provide us with the help and support we need—let's trust Him.

ANXIETY & HOPE

There is a chapter in the Bible where a mom is describing to her son what kind of godly woman he should find to marry. One of the descriptors is that "she laughs without fear of the future."[1] How often are we paralyzed by fear over things that may or may not happen in the future? How many thoughts spiral over situations that never become reality?

For as long as I can remember, I have dreamed about my future. My excitement for what my future could look like was accompanied by fears of ways that future could go wrong. When I was in fourth grade, I was sitting on the bottom of the bunk bed I shared with Elizabeth. My childhood best friend, Victoria, and I were talking about a book where a young boy died, went to heaven, and came back to life.[2]

The boy claimed he saw his dad fighting in what looked like a scene out of Revelation, the last book in the Bible. Victoria and I were scared about what this could mean. We called my mom into my room to ask her our questions.

"If his dad is our dads' age, and the boy thinks he saw a battle during the end times, does that mean Jesus is coming back while our dads are still on earth?" I asked Mom while I nervously picked at my pink and green quilt.

"He could," said Mom. "The Bible says no one knows when that time will come, but that we should be ready at any moment."[3]

"I want Jesus to come back, but not until I've lived more life," said Victoria. "I can't even drive yet!"

"I know, I really don't want him to come back until I'm a wife and a mom," I paused. "And probably a grandmother, too."

The focus of my faith is Jesus, not what Jesus can give me.

My mom smiled and said, "It's impossible to be sad when you are with Jesus in heaven. I promise you that when Jesus comes back, you won't be worried about any of those things you think you need to be happy."

The thought of our life not looking like we hoped before Jesus came back made Victoria and I anxious. We were so focused on what we planned for our own lives that Mom had to remind us that getting Jesus is the very best thing. When that day comes, we won't wish for these things we once wanted because being with Jesus will be all we desire.

When there is something we deeply desire, it can produce **anxiety** or **hope** in us. **Anxiety** comes from desperately reaching for what we want. We don't have the sovereign control to cause what we want to happen exactly when we want it; anxiety is inevitable when we take fulfilling our plans into our own hands. **Hope** results from trusting in a good God who is in control to give us the desires of our hearts in His perfect timing.

In moments of anxiety, it is helpful to redirect my mind to the things of God rather than my circumstances. When He is my focus, I don't feel alone or helpless. I will never be alone because He is with me and He promises to never leave me.[4] No matter what mistakes I make, I am not out of the reach of His redemption. I can rest knowing I am trusting in the One who is good and in control.

In seasons of waiting, we are given daily choices between **anxiety** and **hope**. Today, you have a choice between trusting God for what you desire or anxiously grasping for control. Choosing to trust God isn't easy, but it is worth it. While you can not control if and when your prayers are answered, you do not have to be anxious in the waiting.

Our attention is naturally drawn to what is missing rather than what we have. When we don't have what we desire, we can trust God knows the desires of our hearts. He knows us, loves us, and He gives good gifts in His perfect timing. As we live with unfulfilled desires, we can bring

Hope results from
trusting in a good
God who is in control
to give us the desires
of our hearts in His
perfect timing.

our honest feelings to Him in prayer. The more we talk to Him, the more we trust Him.

Prayer isn't the only thing we can do while we are waiting. We can prepare ourselves to receive what we are praying for. For example, I still very much want to be a wife and a mom one day. That is not my reality now, but I am actively preparing for that to be a part of my future. I am praying for God to maximize my singleness for His glory for however long this season may last. I am cultivating godly character and fighting sin, which will benefit my relationships with all people now and in the future. I babysit for the kindest Christian families, spending time around moms who love Jesus and disciple their children. They invite me into their homes and offer wisdom about how to be a godly wife and mom. I can trust God's timing is perfect, regardless of if I meet Jesus face-to-face before or after I get married and have children. While I can't control when or how God answers my prayers, I can faithfully steward where He has me right now.

As I pray for what I desire, I ask God to change the desires of my heart to be His desires for me. Even when my circumstances don't change, He changes my heart. Instead of being discouraged by my lack, I am encouraged by God's faithful provision. Rather than anxiously and miserably enduring the time when a desire is unmet, God has given me eyes to see how He is using this time to strengthen and stretch me.

I do not want my satisfaction in life to be based on something that is not guaranteed; there is no stability in that. If and when God chooses to change my reality is up to Him, and I will choose to praise Him no matter what. God's goodness isn't tied to Him giving me what I want when I want it. He is all-powerful and all-knowing. Regardless of my circumstances, He is worthy of all my trust.

Which is greater: your desire for what you want now, or your trust in God's goodness and timing? While my answer to this question may vary some days, the wise answer remains the same. Seeking my own plans in my own timing leaves me anxious and empty-hearted. When I choose to trust in God wholeheartedly—even when it's difficult—the peace I am filled with surpasses all understanding.[5]

It doesn't make sense that we can have joy before we have what we want, but Jesus makes this possible. The focus of my faith is Jesus, not what Jesus can give me. Then when the One who holds my heart does give me a desire of my heart, I have the perspective that they are gifts to be stewarded, not ultimate things to be praised. Only Jesus is ultimate.

FEELING MISUNDERSTOOD: AM I ALONE?

In elementary school, I went on weekend church retreats with other 2nd-5th graders. My friends' parents and my mom were always our leaders. We stayed up late laughing in our bunk beds and woke up early to our leaders playing music and singing. It is women like these leaders that taught me from a young age how to love God and live my life for Him.

I loved exploring camp during the day. Victoria and I would walk through the woods, jumping over streams and discovering gazebos where we would sit and talk. Every last night of camp, we played a game called Pitch Black Attack. It's a scavenger hunt across camp where you sneak around with everyone in your cabin while avoiding the bad guys. All the places that were so intriguing and peaceful during the day suddenly became scary in the darkness.

I have never been a fan of the dark. In high school, I paid my little sister Charlotte to grab things out of my car if the sun was down. I don't like being unable to see what's surrounding me. As you may have guessed, I was extremely anxious the first time I attempted to play Pitch Black Attack. I wanted to be anywhere other than surrounded by darkness in the middle of the woods.

"Miss Tara, I can't do this," I said to my leader. "Can you take me back?"

She walked me back to the main building, and I sat in there with camp staffers until the game was over. The next year, I decided to sit out from the beginning to avoid being scared altogether. In fourth grade, I planned to sit out again. As everyone was getting ready with their camouflage and face paint, my mom encouraged me to join them.

While there is brokenness that is unavoidable because we are not in control, we do have dominion over our actions and reactions.

"Be brave," she said. "Your cabin needs you!"

Reluctantly, I agreed. Mom braided my hair and Victoria painted my face. I may not have felt ready, but at least I looked ready. All suited up, we walked to the main building to hear the rules.

"Remember campers, no running: the trees always win!" said the camp staffer.

Ignoring this advice, everyone started running as soon as they released us. I linked arms with Victoria as we ran outside. It was cold and dark; I heard my anxious heart pounding in my ears. We followed the clues, sneaking our way from one location to the next. Luckily, no one had caught us yet. Being caught just meant camp staffers in silly costumes made you do something silly, then they would decide whether to let you continue or make you start over.

My cousin, Amy, is the same age as me and was one of the other girls in my cabin. We ended up in the back of the group. She knew I was scared, so we linked arms. Suddenly, we heard someone behind us.

"BOO! Got you!" yelled a staffer.

Amy screamed, let go of my arm, and started running—right into a tree! She fell flat on her back. I gasped and we all rushed to her.

"Amy! Are you okay?" Mom asked.

Amy groaned and put her hand on her forehead. "Well Aunt Susie, I guess the trees really do always win," she laughed at herself, wiping a little blood from the scratches on her face.

"Do you want to go back to the cabin?" I asked, secretly hoping she would say yes so I could volunteer to walk back with her.

"No way, we've got a game to win!" said Amy. She was fearless. Even when the scary and painful things I feared happened to Amy, she didn't let this keep her from moving forward.

There is no way to avoid all pain and anxiety; we must focus on moving forward when the unavoidable strikes. While I would not recommend running through a forest on a dark night, there will still be trees that pop up in your path no matter how careful you are.

Because of the brokenness of this world, there is sin and suffering. We experience the consequences of this brokenness, and that contributes to our anxiety. Sometimes this brokenness is a result of our own actions or a consequence of our disobedience to God. Other times, this brokenness simply falls on us. This was the case with Rebecca's brain injury.

While there is brokenness that is unavoidable because we are not in control, we do have dominion over our actions and reactions. Each day, we have opportunities to choose obedience or disobedience to God.

One of the most rewatched DVDs in my mom's minivan for years was *A Cinderella Story*. The quote on the diner wall in the movie says, "Never let the fear of striking out keep you from playing the game."[6] So often, we avoid situations simply for the possibility of a less-than-ideal outcome. Rather than being bold in obedience, we sell ourselves short because we don't want to be embarrassed, hurt, or abandoned. Sometimes, we'd rather forfeit than lose. I don't think we should run around taking uncalculated risks and living recklessly, but we aren't meant to strive for completely safe, careful lives.

We don't have to guard ourselves against everything; we can trust that God is our shield and protection.[7] Rather than focusing on protecting ourselves, we can focus on the One who has the power and perspective to protect us. As Christians, we can trust that even in the riskiest situations, we are trusting in a God who goes before us and beside us.[8]

While my cabin didn't win Pitch Black Attack that night, it felt like a win because I finished the game for the first time! As we were walking back to the cabin, one of the campers started bending her arm, hitting herself in the chest, and yelping. I was confused and didn't understand what she was doing.

Another girl started laughing, and the girl making the noises said, "You're so retarded—retard, retard, retard!" Then she started hitting herself again, twitching her head and making noises. Now, I understood what they were doing: pretending to have seizures.

I walked silently back to the cabin, holding back the tears. I stayed outside and sat on our front steps when everyone else went inside. I stared at the stars and cried. *God, why would they make fun of people like that? Don't they understand? Don't they know Rebecca is one of the people they are making fun of?*

I heard the door open behind me and quickly dried my tears. My mom sat down next to me.

"Hello my girl," she wrapped her arm around me. "Do you want to talk about it?"

I shrugged and rested my head on her shoulder. "I feel like no one understands," I said. "I'm always sad about Rebecca, and I don't need them to ask me about it, but I can't take it when they make fun of people like her."

"I know, sweetie. They aren't doing it to be intentionally hurtful, but that doesn't make it right," said my mom. "You're so young, most nine-year-olds don't experience things like this. I'm grateful for the big heart you have because you are Rebecca's big sister. And that is something people that aren't her sister won't be able to understand."

This talk under the stars with my mom is something I will always remember; it's when I first understood that the perspective I have because of this trial is a gift. Until this point, I felt discouraged from being misunderstood. Other elementary schoolers around me didn't know how to relate to what I was going through, so we didn't really talk about it. I felt different and alone in my emotions. Mom helped me to see that without being Rebecca's family, people couldn't fully understand what it's like. I wouldn't wish this trial on anyone else, but I wouldn't trade the faith and perspective it's grown in me.

The pain you are enduring may not look like what others are facing, but it is a means by which you can grow closer to God and eventually encourage others who are facing similar struggles. I know it's natural to feel isolated and alone in our struggles. But even if no other person can relate to what you are going through, God knows you and understands you.

He created you and He sees you; you are not out of His sight or care. While there will be pain and brokenness we experience, God sent Jesus to be our ultimate rescue from that. Despite the extremely painful things we will endure in this lifetime, there is hope for where we will spend forever when we have a relationship with Jesus. This is a truth I must return to His Word and remind myself of often.

REST & COMFORT IN HIS WORD

On a much less eventful bookstore trip than when my dad hydroplaned, I bought a Bible for Rebecca. Reading the Bible is how I learn God's character and grow in my relationship with Him, so my own Bible means so much to me. His Word brings comfort, direction, correction, and peace. Rebecca wasn't able to read on her own, but I didn't want her to miss out on the gift of God's Word. I wanted her to have a Bible of her own.

Her Bible had VeggieTales characters on the cover and cartoons in the margins. Although she was blind and couldn't see the pictures, I described them to her. When I came home from school and Rebecca was laying on her bed in her room, I snuggled up next to her and told her about my day. I would write songs and sing to her about how loved she was by God and her family. I would open up this VeggieTales Bible and read to her about the goodness of God and how He has a plan even when we can't understanding what He is doing.

A favorite Bible verse of mine is Matthew 11:28, where Jesus says, "Come to me all you who are weary and burdened and I will give you rest."[9] I remember sitting in a middle school small group when one of my leaders shared this verse with us and encouraged us to commit it to memory. She told us how this verse is Christ's promise that when we feel unsettled or overwhelmed, we can find rest and peace in Him when we come to Him.

Over the years, God's Word has revealed to me repeatedly the key to peace: come to Him. Whenever I feel swept up by the worries of this world or overcome by fears of the future, I evaluate where I am placing my focus.

> *"Come to me all you who are weary and burdened and I will give you rest."*
> *Matthew 11:28*

Do I seek affirmation from other people or find security in who I am in Christ? Am I depending on my own strength or resting in Him? Do I trust God's ways are best or am I striving to control my life? Almost always, the times when I feel paralyzed by fear are the times when I am focusing on anything but the truth of His Word.

Growing up in church, I was encouraged to memorize Bible verses. We would memorize verses together as small groups, writing them on note cards I taped to my bathroom mirror. Sometimes, we would even write the first letter of every word on our left hand for us to look at throughout the day. At the Christian school I attended for middle school where my dad taught my Bible class, we would learn songs of entire passages of the Bible—these still play in my head today! There are so many helpful tools when committing God's Word to memory.

Encouragement to memorize Scripture was definitely beneficial. I am grateful for the people who emphasized the importance of writing His Word on my heart at such a young age. But it was not until I not until I understood I was was going through spiritual battles that I realized I need Scripture. Nothing else sustains me. Nothing else is purely truth. Nothing else provides me with peace.

That is why I distinctly remember when I committed Matthew 11:28 to memory. It was the lifeline I didn't know I needed, and the truth I would cling to when all else threatened to consume me. When a nightmare pulled me awake in fear that Rebecca was gone, I would pray this verse over and over again, reminding myself of Jesus' promise of rest. My racing heart would begin to calm as He gave me that rest as I came to Him.

MIDNIGHT MEMORIES

Many nights, I was jolted awake by a nightmare where I lost Rebecca. One dream I had over and over for the first few years of her life was Rebecca dying. I would wake up and she would not, or she would be in the hospital and the monitors would go flat. My body would tense up and I would sit up in my bed, feeling the weight of grief and fear that in the room next to mine, she was not alive.

I would slide out from beneath my hot pink and neon green comforter, heart pounding in my ears as my feet pattered on the hardwood floor. Shaking and terrified, I would rush into her room. I placed my hand on her chest to ensure she was breathing. Once I felt the release of her lungs and her breath against my cheek, I released the breath I hadn't realized I was holding.

At this point, my body was completely awake, all hope of going back to sleep lost. Sometimes, Rebecca was already awake when I arrived. I began to see these midnight wake-ups as extra quality time for just me and Becca.

I would wrap her fingers around my pointer finger. She didn't like to be touched on her face or her hair, but she would let me hold her hand. It was my favorite, especially when I was holding her and she was all snuggled in. Her entire delicate hand wrapped gracefully around my finger. She couldn't control her muscles much, and I think her holding onto my finger was mostly a gripping reflex that was out of her control. But even still, I cherished holding her close.

In the middle of the night, I would read to her from the VeggieTales Bible, pray over her, and sing to her. Her room was in the front of the house, my room was closest to hers, and my parents' was in the back of the house, far enough away to where they couldn't hear me tip-toe down to see Becca. It was just us in the quiet of the night, and it was so peaceful.

Life can be really loud and hurried, but there was no rush or distractions in this time. The tears would flow because I knew this was not fair and she shouldn't have to live in such constant pain. Tears would also come because God did not have to be so kind in allowing me to be the sister holding her hand in the middle of the night.

There's messiness in the emotions of it all, being both angry that she had to experience this but feeling favored that God chose to place her in our family. I'm thankful for a God that meets me in the messiness of these emotions and gives me the grace to feel both.

My fear isn't the only thing that led to Rebecca and I spending time together while the rest of our family was sleeping. Sometimes in the middle of the night when I just wasn't able to fall asleep, I would walk down the hall to Rebecca. She was usually awake because her pain didn't allow her body to get much rest. I would sit in there with her for hours praying over her, talking to her, and just holding her hand.

It started off as me going in there when I couldn't sleep, but then I began to feel like my body would wake me up when Rebecca needed someone in there with her. I cherished that alone time with my sister, and I knew that she must feel so scared and alone during the long hours of the night.

Many nights, she shrieked in pain from non-stop seizures. She would clench her fists, her tiny hands balling together tightly as she cried through her seizures and dug her nails into her palms.

I desperately desired to give her an escape but didn't know how to help. I would hold her and try to comfort her, but it was no use. I remember praying for God to take the pain off of her and place it onto me so she could just have a moment of rest, but that never happened. Instead, I would hold her and rock her back and forth, crying so that my fallen tears mixed with hers.

One night in third grade when I went to check on Rebecca, I found my parents in the living room. Seeing my tears, they were concerned and asked me if I wanted to talk to them about it. When I told them about my dreams, they cried with me. This is the first time I remember seeing my dad cry.

This reminded me that I was not alone in the depth of pain I was feeling. My entire family was also hurting, plagued with their own fears of losing Rebecca and hurt from seeing her in pain. They prayed with me and stayed with me until I fell asleep on the couch with my head in my mom's lap as she stroked my hair.

I could not be more grateful for the example of strength and faith that she has set for me. I'm blessed to have two strong Christian parents who always modeled faith and trust in God, leading our family to do the same.

I still wake up in the middle of the night sometimes. It took a while to break the habit of going to her room. I would get halfway down the hall instinctively, only to have grief overcome me like a weighted blanket when I woke up just enough to remember she wasn't there.

Now when I can't sleep, I remember Rebecca. I talk to God about her, and I look at the picture of her sitting in a teal wooden frame on my nightstand. In the picture, our cheeks touch and her eyes look up—it's the very picture that was next to her casket on the day of her funeral. I cry and journal the moments with Rebecca brought up in my memory, and I'm thankful that God still allows me this extra time to process, heal, and grieve my sister in the quiet. These nights are one of the ways I most feel God's nearness and presence; finding the ways I feel closest to God has helped me experience His peace.

Over the past few years, God has shown me how to hold both hand in hand—my deep appreciation for being her sister and anticipation for seeing her again, and the inexplicable grief of separation I now experience. The emotions come together and coexist, needing each other to stay grounded in both hope and reality.

It's these nights when time seems to be so slow that I ponder how to the Lord a thousand years is like a day, and a day is like a thousand years.[10] Oh, how glorious it will be once these days have turned to a thousand years and all is restored in perfection in a holy, unending reunion! May I not rush past the beauty of today or the acts of obedience that are in the present because of my longing for the future.

In fact, it's the assurance of my hope for the future that enables me to be joyfully present and prayerful about all God has for me today. I do not need to worry about what's to come because He holds my future—both the one that will happen tomorrow, and the one a thousand years from now.

That frees me to be present and pray now: *Lord, what do You have for me today? Show me what faithfulness looks like in this season. May I glorify You in all that I do. Remind me that my life is not about me, and help me to be a faithful steward of all You have entrusted to me. Today I come to you again with my burdened heart. Please give me your rest as I lay down my burdens and take up my cross. May I be immediately obedient to all You call me to do, and may You allow me to be a broken vessel to carry out Your will. What an honor to be a coworker and coheir with Christ. May Your Spirit lead me, and show me what is most important. Discern my yeses and nos to honor You. Thank You for today; my life is Yours. I love You. Amen.*

NINE

The Freedom of Forgiveness

One of Elizabeth's accidental crashes was between her FJ Cruiser and my friend Emily's car. Emily parked her Jeep in the long driveway with two acres of open field around her. My family visited with Emily in our living room and reminisced about our time together in Haiti.

"Alright, I'm meeting my friends at Sonic," said Elizabeth as she grabbed her keys. "Bye Emily!"

Elizabeth turned up her music and put her car in reverse, assuming the space behind her was clear. Her reverse camera was a little off because of the extra tire on the back of her car, so she didn't like to use it. Elizabeth whipped her car backward and to the right.

We ran outside as soon as we heard the crash.

"How bad is it?" Elizabeth yelled over her blaring music. She gripped her steering wheel and rested her forehead on her hands, hesitant to see the damage she heard. The concrete was covered with shattered glass from Emily's driver's side door and Elizabeth's back window.

"Oh, no!" Emily immediately apologized, "I'm so sorry for parking there."

Forgiveness is not earned; it's freely given. If it could be earned, it would not be a gift.

"Emily, no, this is not okay. I'm so sorry," said Elizabeth.

"It's just a car—I'm just thankful no one is hurt!" Emily put her hand on Elizabeth's shoulder. "You poor thing, your back window is completely shattered. That must have been so loud and terrifying. Are you okay?"

Emily was supposed to drive back to her college town the next day and was now without a drivable vehicle. Yet her greater concern was making sure Elizabeth wasn't upset. Charlotte was holding one of our chickens while petting its feathers. She looked up at me and raised her eyebrows. "Is she serious? How is she that nice?" Charlotte asked.

Emily was quick to forgive Elizabeth's mistake, even when it came at the expense of her car. Like Emily, I want to be quick to forgive and for my reactions to show that I value people over possessions. Her car is now fixed, and we laugh about it every time we're together. Emily displayed a compassionate reaction inclined to forgive because she is someone who daily reminds herself of the way Jesus has forgiven her. Without understanding how we have been forgiven, it is impossible to truly forgive others.

Forgiveness is not earned; it's freely given. If it could be earned, it would not be a gift. The reminder to give freely is written into the word: for**give.** God is the giver of every good and perfect gift, including forgiveness.[1] Every person who has ever lived has fallen short of God's standard of perfection. We are all in need of forgiveness because of our sins.[2] Through offering the perfect sacrifice of His Son Jesus, God made a way for us to be forgiven of our sins and enter into a right relationship with Him. There's nothing we can do to earn His love; it's a gift given out of God's innate grace and mercy.[3]

When we admit our sins, God "is faithful and just to forgive us our sins and cleanse us of all unrighteousness" (1 John 1:9).[4] The impact of this forgiveness gives us purpose in our life on earth and security in our eternal life in heaven. He has forgiven us unconditionally and completely, expecting nothing in return but for us to follow Him wholeheartedly. Understanding how much we have been forgiven and the impact of this forgiveness is the necessary starting point for forgiving others.

FORGIVING WHAT FEELS UNFORGIVABLE

Forgiveness is polite and expected when the mistakes are small and the hurts are reversible. It's what we want from others when we fall short. Forgiveness is what we extend to friends who have minor, fixable slip-ups. We're told to forgive and forget, to let go and move on.

But what about the big things that you can't forget? What about when someone legitimately wrongs you and isn't sorry? What about when someone is unfaithful and dishonest about it? What about when the consequences of their actions will continuously have negative effects on you for the rest of your life?

Relational pain we experience can occur for many different reasons. Maybe someone has an unrepentant sin pattern that is causing collateral damage to those closest to them. It's possible God could be revealing their character to you in an effort to protect you from bringing that person closer and to create healthy boundaries at this time.

There was a relationship in my life that kept bringing about emotional pain and uneasiness, and I could not understand why. Walking around my college campus, I was on the phone processing everything with a mentor. I simply was not able to understand why they weren't changing or why the prayer, grace, and forgiveness didn't seem to be working. I wrongly believed if I did all the "right things," then the relationship should be better.

My mentor kindly but honestly said, "My darling, there is a difference between being kind and being a doormat. And right now, I hate to say it, but you are being a doormat."

If someone continuously reveals their character to us, it's silly to continue to be surprised each time they reaffirm with their actions what they've already proven to be true. Sometimes for people to truly

Sometimes for people to truly understand the weight of the consequences of their actions and have the space to heal and change, we need to establish boundaries.

understand the weight of the consequences of their actions and have the space to heal and change, we need to establish boundaries.

God's will for His people is for us to be holy and set apart.[5] Set apart from what? All the brokenness that causes us to be separated from God. In order to be set apart from sin, we must put up boundaries in our lives. Both in what we do and in the emotional access we allow others.

Healthy boundaries are guardrails informed by God's Word and affirmed by His people. The purpose of boundaries isn't to fix or control another person, but to guard our own wellbeing. Boundaries don't stop pain from happening; they give us guidance on how to respond when painful situations occur in our most important relationships.

When those we have given the closest access to our hearts hurt us, the wounds are deep and disillusioning. Forgiveness isn't giving the one who is hurting you a free pass to continue doing so; forgiveness is taking a necessary step toward healing instead of sitting in the hurt you didn't choose.

All hurt we feel is ultimately a result of living in a broken world filled with sin. No matter the reason for the pain, all pain can point us back to Jesus. He saw us in our brokenness and loved us enough to die for us so that we could have eternal hope in the midst of our pain. No matter how much pain we experience on this earth, nothing can separate us from the love of Christ.[6]

The concept of forgiveness sounds lovely, but it becomes trickier when we apply it to our lives. Is forgiveness really always the right thing to do? How should my family go about forgiving the carelessness of the doctor that led to the brain injury and ultimate death of Rebecca? Do we even need to forgive him?

Forgiveness is taking a necessary step toward healing instead of sitting in the hurt you didn't choose.

When doctors make questionable choices or mistakes that lead to tragedies, they are brought before a medical review board. It is the board's responsibility to evaluate the details and determine if the doctor was in the wrong. If the doctor is found negligent, the physician's medical license could be temporarily suspended or lost completely.

During this process for Rebecca's doctor, my mom said she wanted nothing more than for the results of the investigation to conclude that the physician had done everything he could to save her daughter's life. Rebecca's doctor told my parents that her brain injury was unavoidable. He suggested the birth complications were likely a result of choices my mom made while she was pregnant. For the beginning of Becca's life, my mom carried the weight of believing what happened to her daughter was somehow her fault.

But that was not the case. The board unanimously agreed the doctor was in the wrong. He missed all the signs he was trained to notice. And by the time he called for the emergency C-section, Rebecca was gone. Yet even with this conclusion, because of the medical malpractice cap in Louisiana, the hospital made more money from Rebecca's medical bills than it paid for harming my sister. The doctor was permitted to continue practicing medicine and was unapologetic toward my parents after they repeatedly reached out to reconcile. His actions had permanent consequences on our lives while it seemed like his life was unaffected.

Knowing the entire situation was avoidable but there was no way to reverse it was agonizing. The truth is valuable, but it didn't change the reality of Rebecca's brain injury and pain. These answers didn't help us know how to lengthen her life. The question that altered my family's path wasn't whether or not the doctor was in the wrong, but whether or not we would depend on the Lord's strength to forgive him of these wrongs.

Rebecca suffered her whole life because of that doctor's carelessness. Her constant pain was unchangeable. What we decided to do was unconditionally forgive the man who did this to her, even though he never asked for it or showed any remorse for his malpractice. This could never have been possible on our own strength, but is evidence of God's Spirit in us and is an overflow of God's forgiveness to us.

I remember talking to my parents about how angry I was at this doctor for doing this to our family. *How could someone be so arrogant and reckless? He doesn't deserve to be a doctor.* My parents told me to pray for him and reminded me that we were promised infinitely more time in heaven with Rebecca than we could have in this lifetime.

As Christians, we know there is a purpose for our pain and hope beyond our current sufferings because of the eternity in heaven awaiting us after this life. We know the big picture and how the story ends. But what do we do today, when the weight of what has been done to us feels unbearable?

Since forgiving Rebecca's doctor, I've had many other times when my ability to forgive has been tested. During my freshman year of college, my boyfriend and best friend wounded me deeper than I'd ever imagined possible. Over the two years of our relationship, he betrayed my trust repeatedly. In the beginning, we always found a way back to each other through grace, repentance, and forgiveness. This time, what was broken could not be mended no matter how hard we tried. We broke up, then walked our way through forgiveness over time.

The emotional pain even hurt physically, and the loss of the closeness we had and the future we planned was excruciating. I was blindsided, and my trust and heart were broken. I not only felt like I didn't really know him anymore, but in some ways, I also felt like I couldn't trust myself because I hadn't seen this coming. Because I loved him, I was motivated to forgive him. But that did not take away the pain associated with the results of his actions.

I chose to forgive my boyfriend, but there were also continuous impacts of his actions that gave me opportunities to work out forgiveness. The more I had to process the hurt and do the hard work of forgiveness, the more God proved Himself faithful to heal and mend my heart. He alone can take a broken heart and make it whole again.

As followers of God, we are told to forgive. We are not judged based on whether or not the one who wrongs us accepts or asks for that forgiveness, but only on whether or not we choose to withhold it. Withholding forgiveness potentially hurts the one who wronged you, but it is guaranteed to hurt you.

When you withhold forgiveness from fellow believers, it hurts the body of Christ and the unity of the church. Jesus gives us an outline of how we are to handle hurts, conflicts, and sins among Christians. Jesus says, "If your brother sins against you, go and tell him his fault, between you and him alone. If he listens to you, you have gained a brother" (Matthew 18:15).[7] Calmly confronting someone with what they did wrong is the opposite of what feels natural in the midst of our hurt. But God's way is best, even when it doesn't feel natural.

My ex-boyfriend and I were both Christians and walking with the Lord. However, we're still imperfect, broken humans and hurt still happened. I wanted to understand why he hurt me. I desired to explain and reverse what had been done and restore the relationship to how it was before the hurt. I wanted to pretend like I was okay, and not let him know how deeply his actions hurt me. But after studying this passage and receiving advice from godly friends, I knew this would not be a beneficial or biblical way to handle this hurt. I didn't need to talk in circles to other people about my pain. We needed to have a conversation between the two of us where I asked for forgiveness for my contribution to the conflict and addressed his sins against me.

I prayed a lot going into this conversation. I didn't want this talk to lead to more hurt or confusion, but to serve as a step toward clarity, forgiveness, and healing for both of us. While it was terrifying to do, I had complete peace going into it because it was clearly the obedient thing to do. It was the opposite of how I felt or what I wanted, but I trusted that God knew better and there had to be a reason He laid out this path for handling hurts between His people.

I stumbled my way through the conversation, getting a little feisty and emotional. The wounds were very raw. Thankfully, he was also gracious in forgiving me and understood how deeply I was hurting.

Sin hurts everyone involved and damages everything it touches.

Eventually, he admitted his faults and sought forgiveness. While the person who wronged you doesn't always ask for forgiveness and we are called to forgive them even if they don't, I was grateful for this. Although the conversation did not take away the hurt, I had peace knowing I was honoring God the best I knew how through the unavoidable hurt I was experiencing.

Talking to him also helped me to remember that he is so much more than what he did to me. It grew my compassion for him and increased my desire to help him find freedom from his shame. I encouraged him to run to God and his community to fight this sin and earnestly prayed for him to experience healing and freedom. Sin hurts everyone involved and damages everything it touches. In this situation, I was not the lone victim and the only one hurting. Yes, his sin had hurt me. But sitting across from another hurting heart, I could not deny how it was also crushing him.

The real fight isn't between people, but against the enemy.[8] Like Haymitch tells Katniss in *Catching Fire,* we must "remember who the real enemy is."[9] People are held accountable for their actions, but we must not forget who is behind all lies, pain, and sin. Just as there is a God working to redeem all of creation to Himself, there is an enemy doing everything in his power to stop it.

Until we reach heaven, there will be continuous pain, brokenness, and hurt. Jesus tells His disciples, "I have said these things to you, that in Me you may have peace. In the world you will have tribulation. But take heart; I have overcome the world" (John 16:33).[10] Jesus doesn't promise us an easy life; in fact, He warns us that the road to eternity will be marked by hardships and troubles. However, we can have peace in the midst of hardships and hurts when we have Jesus.

Through the hurt from my former boyfriend, I learned forgiveness doesn't mean you're justifying their actions or that the relationship will

Experiencing the peace accompanied by forgiveness is so much more satisfying than inflicting harm or executing justice on the one who wronged you.

be restored. Even when the right thing seems clear to me, I can not dictate the decisions of others. It takes one to forgive and two to reconcile. God offers us forgiveness through Jesus, but we must turn toward Jesus and receive it to be reconciled to God. You can have forgiveness without reconciliation, but not reconciliation without forgiveness. I am only responsible for my actions and reactions, and forgiveness is a choice I can make to keep my heart clean of bitterness. I forgave him, but our relationship never went back to how it was before. That doesn't mean forgiveness wasn't worth it; it is a freeing thing to do regardless of the outcome.

When the disciples ask Jesus how they should pray, He tells them what is now commonly known as **The Lord's Prayer**.[11] Forgiveness is mentioned more than any other topic in this prayer. Jesus says we are to pray for the Lord to help us forgive others as He has forgiven us. When we truly understand how much we have been forgiven, we are able to extend forgiveness to others. Through daily remembering the Gospel, we are drawn closer to Him and able to selflessly extend grace to others. Forgiveness is worth fighting for because of the peace and freedom found on the other side. Experiencing the peace accompanied by forgiveness is so much more satisfying than inflicting harm or executing justice on the one who wronged you.

Jesus taught to "love your enemies and pray for those who persecute you"(Matthew 5:44).[12] He shared this knowing His disciples would be tortured or even martyred for their faith. Jesus modeled this on the cross when He asked God to forgive the people who were murdering Him because they didn't comprehend what they were doing.[13] To love and forgive like Jesus, we first pray for those who have hurt us.

After my conversation with my former boyfriend, I was not able to help and encourage him the way I normally would when a friend is struggling with something because our relationship had ended. This grew my understanding of the power of prayer because it was all I could do for him, and I have seen God answer many of those prayers. Remembering the real enemy is not the one who hurt us, we can pray for God to work in them to convict them of their sins and lead them to repentance. Just as God does not hold our sins against us, we can pray to Him to help us not hold the sins of others against them.[14]

God is our Healer, and in Him healing is possible. Healing is contingent on my decision to trust God for the healing; it's not dependent on their willingness to admit their wrongs and change their behavior. Oftentimes, forgiveness doesn't transform your external situation but it does completely alter your internal heart posture.

Forgiving others can bring you peace. The hurt will likely linger, but you can be obedient to extend the same grace to others you so desperately need yourself. Unforgiveness weighs us down and can affect how we view everything after the hurt that wounded us. It's so much more freeing to live a life without grudges and bitterness; this opens your heart to receive the beauty of all God has in store for you.

The goal of the Christian life is to look more like Christ, and forgiveness is a perfect opportunity to grow in Christlike character. Christians are encouraged to "be kind to one another, tenderhearted, forgiving one another, as God in Christ forgave [us]" (Ephesians 4:32).[15] Christ sacrificed Himself for us while we were still sinners, making a way for our ultimate forgiveness that we can never repay.[16] In forgiving others, we can display the mercy of God and love of Jesus.

Before publishing this story involving my ex-boyfriend, I asked him to read it and let me know if he was okay with everything I said. While God used this situation to teach me so much, I also wanted to be respectful of this being a part of his story as well.

He was humble and gracious in being supportive, wanting the way we handled our hurt to be used by God to help others. After reading it, he said, "This was hard for me to read in some places, but your explanation of forgiveness, and the reality that you have forgiven me, made it impossible to feel the shame that felt natural in remembering the damage

I caused. You were able to articulate thoughts I had about forgiveness but was never able to formulate. I think God could use this to help a lot of people. It has helped me at least. As you point out, the way you have forgiven me is what God desires of us and is the natural implication of His forgiveness toward us, but it bears saying that forgiving me like you did is rare even in the church, and I don't take that for granted. So thank you for emulating Christ in that way, it has taught me so much. I'm sure this book will be great, you have my full permission and support."

The fact that we are able to stand on this side of forgiveness and have conversations like this is a gift from God. As Paul writes, "If possible, so far as it depends on you, live peaceably with all" (Romans 12:18).[17] Peace and unity are possible when both are living surrendered to Christ. I am so thankful that instead of deepening the wounds we caused each other, we fought to pursue reconciliation as God intended. Our relationship was lost because of this pain and we are not in each other's lives like we were before, but I feel grateful to know we are at peace with each other.

When enduring hard times, you make choices that lead you to become better or bitter. Fighting bitterness begins with forgiveness.

When you know you need to forgive and it feels impossible, you likely feel weak. In weakness, Christians have the ability to surrender to God and depend on His strength: His power is made perfect in your weakness.[18] When forgiveness feels impossible on your own strength, it's because you weren't meant to do it on your own. It is in your weakness that you can be most dependent on God. Depend on the strength of your Father who loves you in your weakness and is the source of perfect peace and unwavering resilience.

OWNING OUR MISTAKES & ASKING FOR FORGIVENESS

When I was nine years old, I accidentally ran over my cousin with a golf cart. We were at my Uncle Robbie's house for a big Fourth of July party. An older girl was driving the golf cart full of my friends. The driver pulled up next to my cousin, Hal, and started flirting with him.

"Get off or you're gonna get soaked!!" yelled Hal, "3-2-1!"

It is in your weakness that you can be most dependent on God.

While the other girls jumped off and shrieked in fear of the water, I was not phased by my cousin's threat. Immune to his cuteness most girls fawned over, I rolled my eyes at my cousin. The solution seemed obvious to me: drive away. Since I was the only one left on the golf cart, I just scooted over and pressed down on the pedal as hard as I could.

After getting a hundred yards away from the water hose, I turned around to smirk at Hal and taunt my victory in keeping the golf cart from him. But when I turned around, no one was there.

My friend Victoria's younger sister, Olivia, ran up to me and screamed, "You killed Hayden! You ran him right over!"

I realized the bump allowing me to catch a little air on the golf cart was no hill, but Hal's younger brother, Hayden. I was mortified and terrified I just killed my cousin and friend. I later learned that Hayden crawled in front of the golf cart to grab a wiffle ball when he heard Hal's threat, thinking the girls would easily surrender the golf cart.

Hayden ran into the house screaming, holding his throbbing head. As the adults learned what happened, my mom said, "Well I know it wasn't my child who did it. They know they aren't allowed to drive that thing."

Uncle Robbie examined Hayden's head injury. "Good, it's going out, not in."

Hayden was rushed to the hospital. He luckily had no lasting injuries and was able to come home that night.

I felt so guilty. Not only had I disobeyed my parents, I had also almost seriously injured my cousin. As my dad drove me to Hayden's house the next day, I prayed my cousin would forgive me. When Hayden opened the door, he excitedly took the plate of brownies I made him—they were his favorite.

"Hayden, I'm so sorry. I feel— " I said.

"Oh don't worry about it, it's all good! Thanks for the brownies! Will you ride on the golf cart with me?" Hayden asked.

He was quick to graciously forgive me, and this is something we can thankfully laugh about together today. We jokingly say it's Hal's fault for spraying the water hose, even though I know good and well the blame is on the girl behind the wheel.

When we do something to hurt someone else, even when it's unintentional, it's important to humble ourselves and ask for forgiveness. It often helps when you have a little gift in hand when you are doing so. Whether they extend forgiveness to us or not, this is a step toward unity and peace with others.

When we are wronged, we often want nothing more than for the one who hurt us to acknowledge what they did and ask for our forgiveness. Then when we are the one who does the wrong, we can justify not apologizing because we know the pain we caused can't be reversed. We tell ourselves there is no point in apologizing because it won't change anything. While it might not change anything for us, it could change everything for the one we wronged. In an effort to treat others as we wish to be treated, let's be quick to own our mistakes and humbly seek forgiveness from those we have wronged.

When we sin against God and others, confession and repentance are how we receive forgiveness and healing. James, the brother of Jesus, writes, "Therefore, confess your sins to one another and pray for one another, that you may be healed. The prayer of a righteous person has great power as it is working" (James 5:16).[19] Rather than hiding our mistakes and sin, Scripture calls us to bring it into the light. This removes the power the enemy has when we keep it in the dark, making us susceptible to his lies and deception. After confessing our sins, we have the ability to pray for each other and experience healing in community as God designed.

RECEIVING FORGIVENESS & GRACE

Sometimes it is easier for me to extend grace to others than to believe I can receive it. Because I have grown up around Christianity and had a relationship with God since I was a little girl, it's easy for me to think I shouldn't make mistakes anymore. When I mess up, I imagine God is upset and He is disappointed in me because I should know better by now. This faulty way of thinking affected my relationship with God and view of myself.

My senior year of college, a mentor and friend, Amy, reminded me the goal of the Christian life isn't to avoid mistakes and be perfect. When our focus is on our perfection, we are forgetting the Gospel and our continual need for it. Being a Christian isn't about perfecting our behavior; the focus is on closeness with God which leads to Christlike character. Our aim is to turn quickly away from our sin and toward Jesus, knowing sin is unavoidable until we are made perfect in His presence.

"What makes someone who is faithfully following Jesus stand apart from someone who is living in sin is that the one who is faithfully following Jesus is quick to return humbly to the path God lays before us, desiring to walk in His ways and repenting the many times they fail," said Amy. "David was a man after God's own heart who still made mistakes, but he always returned to God."

David is a man in the Bible who was a murderer, adulterer, and liar. He committed great wrongs that had immense consequences, one of them being the death of his child. After he was confronted for the sins he committed, David wrote Psalm 51. This is a passage I pray through often as a way to confess my sins to God, repent, and ask for His forgiveness and healing. I encourage you to read the entire chapter, but here are a few verses:

"Have mercy on me, O God, according to Your steadfast love; according to Your abundant mercy blot out my transgressions... For I know my transgressions, and my sin is ever before me. Against You, You only, have I sinned and done what is evil in Your sight... Purge me with hyssop, and I shall be clean; wash me, and I shall be whiter than snow... Create in me a clean heart, O God, and renew a right spirit within me. Cast me not away from Your presence, and take not Your Holy Spirit from me. Restore to me the joy of Your salvation, and uphold me with a willing spirit... The sacrifices of God are a broken spirit; a broken and contrite heart, O God, You will not despise." (Psalm 51:1,3-4,7,10-12,17)[20]

I want to be someone after God's heart, not after my own perfection.

While David wronged other people, he knew his sins were ultimately against God. He came to God brokenhearted by his sin and sought forgiveness, asking God to purify him from the inside out. As Amy explained to me, maturity is shown not through perfection but through quickly returning to the only One who can clean up our mistakes. Our mistakes do not surprise God; He sent Jesus to die for all of our mistakes because He knew we couldn't stop making mistakes on our own. Like you and me, David wasn't perfect, but God described him as a man after His heart.[21] I want to be someone after God's heart, not after my own perfection.

But what is God's heart? To truly be freed from the weight of the mistakes we make, we must first understand God's heart toward His children. Jesus addressed the people of Israel who were burdened by the legalistic demands of the religious leaders. They were weighed down by all they are supposed to do and not do. Similar to how I often feel, they just wanted to do everything right but were scared of making a mistake and disqualifying themselves.

Jesus expressed His heart to them; rather than affirming their need to flawlessly follow all the rules, Jesus told them "Come to Me, all you who are weary and burdened, and I will give you rest. Take My yoke upon you and learn from Me, for I am gentle and humble in heart, and you will find rest for your souls" (Matthew 11:28-29).[22] He desires to give His people rest, and He is gentle and humble when we come to Him. Jesus doesn't overburden us with rules and scare us with standards; He wants us to come to know Him more and more, then let the Holy Spirit change our hearts and affect our actions. Our behavior shifts as a result of knowing how loved we are; our right behavior doesn't earn us His love. Right behavior and repentance flow out of a heart surrendered to Jesus.

Fighting bitterness begins with forgiveness.

Right behavior and repentance flow out of a heart surrendered to Jesus.

When describing Jesus' heart as depicted in these verses, Dane Ortlund in *Gentle and Lowly* said:

"The posture most natural to Him is not a pointed finger but open arms…You don't need to unburden and collect yourself and then come to Jesus. Your very burden is what qualifies you to come…This high and holy Christ does not cringe at reaching out and touching dirty sinners and numbed sufferers. Such embrace is precisely what He loves to do. He cannot bear to hold back."[23]

He desires to bring us rest that can only come from Him, and draws near to us as we draw near to Him.[24]

On the last day Rebecca was alive on this earth, I was sitting in the living room with my mom. We'd just gotten back from church, and Mom was holding Rebecca in a position where she was sitting straight up facing me. She'd been fussy and uncomfortable all day, and she had finally settled down. I wanted to hold her but didn't want to disturb her now that she finally seemed comfortable. So I didn't hold her, and Mom and I kept talking about a hurtful situation that was going on between me and a friend.

That was the last time we were together before she passed away. For months, I felt an overwhelming amount of guilt for not being present with her and holding her on that last day. I regretted spending that time talking about a meaningless situation with my mom rather than being attentive to Rebecca. While I know we will have forever together, heaven still feels like forever away. This one missed opportunity ate away at me, and I was distraught.

Looking back on this last day with Rebecca knowing what I know

now, I would do things differently. When I opened up to another mentor about how I was feeling and that I wasn't able to shake the guilt, she kindly said, "Oh sweetie, Rebecca knows how much you love her. Don't discount years of love and hours of time together because of this one moment. You had no way to know what was coming. If anything, you gave your mom more time with her."

What a different perspective this was than the one weighing me down. While I can't change what happened that last day, I can choose to remember and cherish the quality time I did get to share with my sister. When I reflect on her life, I pray God shows me His perspective of how He was always working things together for our good and His glory. Shifting our perspective can't change the past, but it can redeem our remembering of it and save us from additional and unnecessary pain.

I often place higher standards on myself than God ever asks of me. I want perfection, but He only asks me for surrender and obedience. Then when I make a mistake, I feel completely defeated. Living a life weighed down by regret takes the focus off of Christ and places it on ourselves. This is exactly where the enemy wants us: doubting the freedom we have in Christ and distracting us from sharing the hope that is within us.

As Christians, we don't have to live under the bondage of shame and regret from our past mistakes, no matter how big or small. Why do we so quickly forget that He offers us complete freedom? When I hyperfocus on my mistakes or things I wish I could change, I often miss the big picture of what God is doing or how He has blessed me. Fully embracing the Gospel looks like daily reminding yourself of who you are in Christ and who His Word proves Him to be. Rather than trying to live up to the standard of perfection I place on myself, God is teaching me to humbly accept His grace and run to Him in the midst of unavoidable imperfections.

FORGIVING GOD

God is sovereign, meaning He is all-powerful and in complete control; nothing is too hard for Him.[25] He loves us perfectly, and His perfect love casts out fear.[26] He is a giver of good and perfect gifts, and His mercy and goodness endure forever.[27] God is good, He does good, and He teaches us to do good.[28]

How do we reconcile these truths with realities that feel anything but good? At the beginning of Rebecca's life, I did not understand why a good God who loves us would hurt Rebecca. *Why are You withholding healing when You have the power to take her pain away?* When we face completely unfair and inexplicable situations, we have to decide what we truly believe. In this case, I had to decide if I believed God is both completely sovereign and perfectly good in all things.

My family loved God and truly did our best to honor Him with our lives—so why did this have to happen to us? *What did we do to deserve this? What can we do better to make You undo it?* My prayers sounded a lot like bargaining with God when Rebecca was a baby. *If you heal her fully, I promise my family will continue in our faith and honor You in all we did for the rest of our days. I promise to do whatever You want with my life, just so long as Rebecca doesn't die.*

The more I learned about God and His sovereignty, my prayers shifted. Rather than praying toward the outcome I desired, I began to pray to know and understand God more, and for His will to be done. I realized that no matter the outcome, God would use it for good. Some outcomes would feel good and some wouldn't, but God's definition of good is beyond what I can fathom and isn't based on how I feel.

A common question Christians are asked is, "Why does God allow bad things to happen to good people?" Rebecca experiencing a traumatic birth and living with a debilitating brain injury can be described as anything but good. Through her life, God brought about more good in my family than any blessing He's bestowed on us. His grace is just as evident in allowing my family to endure this trial as it is when He gives us what our hearts desire. God's ways and thoughts are so much higher than mine, and His omniscience gives Him a perspective beyond what I could ever comprehend.[29] I truly believe that even in the pain and suffering Rebecca and our family endured, God is using it for good.

When sharing this with a friend in college, he asked me, "Do you really believe God would let a kid suffer and die just for the faith of your family?"

I paused, then responded, "Well, it's what He did for all of us through letting His own Son die on our behalf. It won't ever fully make sense to us, but He takes even the greatest tragedies of death and uses them for His divine and good purposes."

God is full of mercy, compassion, and love. We deserve nothing, yet God gives us His best. He does not delight in sin, and He has offered us the ultimate freedom from the consequences of sin. While on earth, the only escape we have from the brokenness around us is the refuge we find in the hope of the cross.

Even though I have no way to guarantee what I desire to happen in the short term, like Rebecca's healing, I find peace knowing what will happen in the longer stretch of eternity. Staying angry with God for allowing her to suffer on earth would have stopped me from grasping the gift that eternity is and enjoying the life Rebecca did have.

Through facing the reality of Rebecca's brain injury, I chose not to build up a wall between me and God but to fully rely on Him every step of the way. While the effects of sin and death have robbed me of the relationship I desired with my sister on this side of heaven, in Jesus I have an eternity sealed and promised that no one and nothing can take away. This truth allows me not only to release my anger toward God but to praise Him for how He's worked through my sister.

I pray that the closer you become to God through investing in your relationship with Him, the deeper you understand His love for and forgiveness of you. He sees you in your pain, and you are not forgotten. Remember who the real enemy is, and hold tight to the friend you have in Jesus. Today, take one more step toward our gracious Father who cares for you.

TEN

Faithfulness

The power of a promise is determined by the character of the promise maker. Remaining faithful to your promises takes integrity, devotion, and selflessness. If the promise is not accompanied by action, it's empty and can not be trusted. For someone to be worthy of trust, they must be faithful.

At a wedding, two people stand in front of their loved ones and promise to always be faithful to each other, no matter what. The ring placed on their left hand is a daily reminder and declaration of this promise. Marriage is vowing faithfulness, devotion, and sacrificial love to your spouse. When a marriage covenant is broken, the one who broke it is referred to as unfaithful because they did not keep their vow of faithfulness. Unfortunately, unfaithfulness in marriage often leads to divorce.

Parents of children with special needs are significantly more likely to divorce. The highest divorce rate occurs for couples in their early thirties. For spouses who experience the death of their child, the divorce rate is also extremely high. My parents were thirty-one and thirty-two when Rebecca was born. They spent the next decade being parents to a daughter with special needs until she passed away.

How did my parents not only stay married but strengthen their marriage through the death of their daughter? They chose to remain faithful to each other. Faithfulness is a choice rooted in trust and played out in loyalty. In the midst of grief, anxiety, depression, and uncertainty, they invested in their relationships with God and relationship with each other. This does not mean their marriage is without trials, but they go to the Lord in the midst of these trials.

The author of Hebrews describes faith as "the assurance of things hoped for, the conviction of things not seen" (Hebrews 11:1).[1] God is the most faithful and reliable one to enter into a covenant with. Placing our trust in God creates the opportunity to be full of faith in Him. We inevitably fall short of living a perfectly faithful and holy life, but this does not surprise God or disqualify us from being His children.

Lack of faithfulness in our relationships with others leads to disloyalty, abandonment, and brokenness. We have all been damaged by the unfaithfulness of other people, even people who are Christians. But when we fall short in our relationship with God, God doesn't pull away from us. Our times of imperfection and unfaithfulness do not disqualify us from the grace of God. His faithfulness to us is not dependent on our faithfulness to Him. Even when the people of God live outside of His design, this does not change the faithful character of God.[2]

We choose how to spend our time and where to set our minds. The priorities we make and the schedules we keep can help or hurt our pursuit of faithful living. While we don't need to strive for God's approval because we can't earn it on our own, God does value intentional effort and investment in our relationship with Him. There are practices called **spiritual disciplines** that are transformative for those seeking to live a life worthy of the manner to which we have been called.[3] Walking faithfully with Jesus includes our personal time with God, growing in community with others, and sharing hope with those who don't know God.

ABIDE

"I just feel like I'm not growing and I don't know why," she said. As a sophomore in college, my sweet friend Reese was experiencing the same defeat common among a lot of us. She felt stuck, and doubts filled her mind: *Why do I not feel like I am growing in my faith right now? Am I doing something wrong?*

Faithfulness is a choice rooted in trust and played out in loyalty.

Sitting in my car, Reese reflected on moments in her walk with God where she saw Him working so evidently. These times had strengthened her faith and grown her confidence in Him. These highlights are stark contrasts with her recent mundane moments. Without seeing the same immediate results she'd seen in the past, it was difficult to feel like she was on the right track and be motivated to keep going.

Christianity isn't a roller coaster that only goes up; it dips and turns, drops and rises. Faith is an unknown ride, but you take it with Jesus sitting next to you. It's not constant productivity and fruitfulness. I reminded Reese that just because we don't see immediate growth doesn't mean we're doing something wrong. As we see in God's creation, blooming is only part of the process. There are seasons of sowing, growth, and harvest.

Anytime my family is somewhere with trees, my dad is scanning the ground for acorns. He gathers the tree seeds into his pockets, places them in empty plastic water bottles, and labels where they're from. At home, he plants the acorns in separate containers of loose soil and lines them up along the back of his shop. Given water, sunlight, and time, they start to grow. A taproot shoots downward into the soil. As the roots deepen, another shoot begins to grow upward toward the sunlight. Eventually, the acorn becomes a sapling that can be planted at our family's tree farm. Years later, it becomes a little tree that produces acorns of its own.

Growth takes time, and a lot of it happens under the surface where we can't see progress. In the book of Psalms, King David compares a righteous person to a tree:

> "He is like a tree
> planted by streams of water
> that yields its fruit in its season,
> and its leaf does not wither.
> In all that he does, he prospers." (Psalm 1:3)[4]

This tree isn't healthy because it's constantly yielding fruit, but because it's yielding fruit in its season. If there are seasons for producing fruit, that means it's not constant and there are seasons without fruitfulness. In the off-season, the tree remains planted by the water and is

Like a healthy tree stays planted near its source of sustenance, a righteous person abides in the Living Water.

constantly refreshed. These fruitless times are no less important; they are crucial for the future production of fruit.

Water is crucial for life, both for trees and for humans. For the majority of history and still in some countries today, people traveled to the nearest well to get water. Then when the water ran out, they went again. Because without this water, they couldn't survive. The Bible documents a time when a woman coming to a well to get water ran into Jesus. He told the woman, "Everyone who drinks of this water will be thirsty again, but whoever drinks of the water that I will give him will never be thirsty again. The water that I will give him will become in him a spring of water welling up to eternal life" (John 4:13b-14).[5]

Jesus made a way for us to have eternal life and a restored relationship with our Creator. While everything else (including water) is only a temporary refreshment, Jesus satisfies completely and forever. Like a healthy tree stays planted near its source of sustenance, a righteous person abides in the Living Water.

Abiding is the essential starting point and sustainer of the Christian life. This is how the Holy Spirit changes our hearts and consequently changes how we live our lives. Abiding means to remain and dwell. In John 15:1-11, Jesus describes what it means to abide in Him and why it is essential. The original Greek word used here for abide has the same root as "abode," sharing the connotation of making a home.

Remaining in Jesus means standing firm in who He is and who He calls us to be. When we drift, we are quick to return. We become familiar with how it feels to be in close relationship with God, and His heart draws us to return and remain. We study His Word and allow it to impact our decisions. Christ's heart becomes our home, and He is the solid foundation we build our life upon.

This life of faithfulness is built through small, daily decisions we are diligent and consistent in over time. Don't be discouraged by how far you feel from where you want to be. Instead, focus on taking one step closer to Jesus today. He is the one that does the work of spiritual formation in us, and all we do is abide and submit to His leading.

As Christians, we have the ability to take part in the eternal work of God. We are living for a kingdom not of this world that will never pass away. In the midst of temporary pursuits, we have the option to invest in the eternal through partnering with Him. If we want to live out God's purposes for our lives and to walk in "the good works He has prepared beforehand for us," we must abide in Him (Ephesians 2:10).[6]

Jesus says, "As the branch cannot bear fruit by itself, unless it abides in the vine, neither can you, unless you abide in Me. I am the vine; you are the branches. Whoever abides in Me and I in him, he it is that bears much fruit, for apart from Me you can do nothing" (John 15:4-5).[7] Just as silly as it would be for a dead branch on the ground to think it could grow flowers on its own, we can't expect to produce anything of lasting value apart from Jesus. We must remain connected to Jesus to be sustained spiritually and live obediently.

As we spend time investing in our relationship and abiding in Him, the Holy Spirit will produce fruit (or evidence) of this relationship in our lives that is visible to those around us. This fruit produced in public from investing in your relationship with God in private is one of the ways God gives us a full and abundant life in Him. These fruits include "love, joy, peace, patience, kindness, goodness, faithfulness, gentleness, and self-control" (Galatians 5:22-23).[8] When you are living in the joy and peace of the Lord, you will have deeper satisfaction in this life, even if your circumstances are painful. This character will be most evident in the midst of disappointment and trials because it's contrary to our natural reactions to hardship.

Abiding in Jesus involves the production of fruit as well as the pruning of what's hindering our fruitfulness. God prunes and cuts away at the things in our lives that are not bringing about our good or His glory.[9] This isn't to rob us of fun or keep us from doing what we want; it puts us in a healthier place and allows us to produce beneficial spiritual fruit.

As I've said many times before, this comes out of a relationship with God and a trust that deepens the more we know Him and His Word.

The emphasis of this pruning is on cultivating our relationship with God, not on perfectly following rules. When the focus is incorrectly placed on rule-following, everything is distorted and discouraging. I've seen many people muster up their own strength and attempt to modify their own behavior. Then when they fail, they feel defeated and want to give up on Christianity. Change of this magnitude feels impossible, so why try?

When you study the Bible, you see that God doesn't ask people who are not Christians to live like Christians. The way He's laid out instructions in Scripture is for people who have chosen to surrender their lives to Christ. If you do not yet have a relationship with Jesus, the Gospel is the focus. Rather than trying to clean yourself up, simply focus on understanding what Jesus did on the cross and accepting what that means for you today.

Once someone becomes a Christian, there is a way God has called us to live. Part of surrendering your life to Christ is submitting the way you live your life. In a letter to the church of Ephesus, Paul wrote:

> "I therefore, a prisoner for the Lord, urge you to walk in a manner worthy of the calling to which you have been called, with all humility and gentleness, with patience, bearing with one another in love, eager to maintain the unity of the Spirit in the bond of peace." (Ephesians 4:1-3)[10]

The calling of Christ on believers' lives means we should live distinctly. Not so we can walk around with our heads high with a holier-than-thou attitude, but to live in humble awareness of our need for Jesus and appreciation of the Gospel. This call to humility, gentleness, patience, love, unity, and peace is not done by trying to force change in ourselves. These are holy dispositions that come from an inward surrender to Jesus.

Behavior change is a result of resting in Jesus and having His Spirit cultivate faithfulness in you. Outward change occurs after inward change, not the other way around. All else is striving to attain perfection we were never expected to achieve.

Christianity is about consistently refixing our gaze on God. When we focus on perfecting our behavior, we are setting an impossible standard for ourselves. If we are focused on all the things that we "aren't supposed to do," we will drift and crash. We will inevitably fall short, which will leave us feeling defeated and like we will never be able to be good enough to follow God. But God never asked us to live this way. In fact, He sent Jesus to be perfect for us because He knew we could never achieve it on our own.

Rather than reaching for this impossibility, rest in the Savior who was perfect on our behalf. We are saved by grace through faith in Jesus, not a result of anything good we can do or take credit for.[11] When we believe our worth increases with the good we do and decreases with every mistake, we are forgetting the grace of God that is foundational to our relationship with Him. We will never be good enough, and that is precisely what qualifies us to have a relationship with God. We are not chosen because of the good things we do; He chooses us simply out of His love and mercy.

I encourage you to abide in Jesus and pray for Him to change your heart to look more like His. God cares so much more about what your heart desires and where your mind is set than how you look or what you are doing.[12] God values our obedience, not our effectiveness. Don't focus so much on what other people think of you; invest your time in cultivating godly character through spending time in God's Word and growing in your devotion to Him. This investment will be difficult; the things that are most worthwhile are often the most challenging. In order to have the strength to pursue God, we must depend on the strength we gain from His Spirit. He is both the means and the end.

Through reading His Word, we can learn what God's ways are and get to know His heart. And the more we know His heart, the more it changes ours. Jesus says, "By this all people will know that you are my disciples, if you have love for one another" (John 13:35).[13] As you abide in Christ and live in the reality of how loved you are by Him, this love will overflow into your interactions with others.

ACCOUNTABILITY

My junior year of college, I lived in an apartment behind the business school. After Tuesday morning classes, I was walking home with one of my best friends, Lauren. I wore a suit and heels because I'd given a presentation to my Marketing class.

"What do you want to do for lunch?" she asked. We discussed our afternoon plans as we walked around the construction on the sidewalk.

Suddenly, I tripped over nothing. My foot slipped out of my shoe, my ankle rolled, and the top of my foot bent against the concrete with a dreaded *crack*.

"Katherine!" Lauren grabbed my arm and helped me stand up. "Are you okay?!"

Lauren and I both laughed; I'm always tripping over nothing and almost hurting myself. I stopped laughing when the pain set in, then the tears came.

"Actually, I don't think I am okay," I said. We hobbled back to my apartment, and my foot was already swelling and turning all kinds of unnatural colors.

Lauren filled a bag with ice and stacked pillows for me to elevate my foot. I called my Uncle Robbie for advice, and he said, "If you wake up in the middle of the night in excruciating pain, then you know it's broken."

What a lovely thing to look forward to.

My foot went numb under the ice, and soon I was bored with sitting on the couch and doing schoolwork on my laptop. I'd planned to make lasagna that night for Lauren and our friend, Jackson, so I decided to give cooking a try. I hopped around and gathered everything I needed onto one section of the counter, sitting on one barstool and propping my foot up on another.

It took much longer than usual, but I finished the lasagna. When Jackson and Lauren showed up that night, Jackson immediately asked about my wrapped foot. We told him what happened, then he asked, "Are we laughing about this yet, or are we still processing it?"

I laughed and said, "We can laugh about it, but there may be some more tears when I get an X-ray tomorrow if it's broken."

Accountability within biblical community is a safe place to be fully known and pointed toward truth.

Lauren, Jackson, and I ate our lasagna and laughed about me tripping over nothing. I am grateful to be their friend and for the way they help me to laugh when I mess up or hurt myself. We were in a business honors program together called Neeley Fellows, and all of us had struggled with anxiety about school and perfectionism in our academic performance. As we took these classes together, we helped each other study and do well. But more than that, we held each other accountable to finding our peace in Christ regardless of our performance. Together, we fought for our ultimate aim to be pleasing God, not performing well in school.

Their fellowship and encouragement helped me to honor God in school and in other areas of my life. God has graciously provided people to hold me accountable in different ways and areas, and the support of a godly community helps me to live obediently and faithfully.

Sometimes accountability comes from the Christians we are doing life with, and we naturally call each other to a higher standard through speaking into each other's situations we are witnessing firsthand. Other times, accountability looks like a group scheduling a weekly time to meet. It can be extremely structured or more spontaneous, but it must be prioritized to be effective.

No matter how accountability shows up in your life, it must be intentional. It is not natural to want to show other people your weaknesses and ask them to call you higher. However, the more we reveal the things we desire to keep in the dark, the less power they hold over us. Accountability within biblical community is a safe place to be fully known and pointed toward truth. As we are honest about our struggles and sin, we are reminded that none of us are perfect. Our goal is not perfection, but holiness; accountability is one of the ways we pursue this.

Thankfully, I did not break my foot that day coming home from the business school. The doctor was unsure how I managed to completely roll my foot around and cause only a severe contusion. This kept me limping around for a while.

At the time I hurt my foot, I was training with my friend Nicoletta who started a workout program for college girls. She also happened to be discipling me, which means she was mentoring me in my faith. I'd just gotten into the rhythm of running when I hurt my foot, and I was so discouraged. I was not looking forward to losing all my hard-earned progress. The first day I decided to run again after my injury, my friend Ash joined Nicoletta's class.

"Kat, run with Ash and show her the loop!" said Nicoletta.

"Okay! I'm just warning you, I'm not the best runner and I have a hurt foot, so this may be a little slower than you'd like," I said to Ash.

"Oh my goodness, no worries. You're doing great!" Ash encouraged me the whole way, and we kept perfect pace with each other. I ran even farther with her that day than I'd been able to before I hurt my foot!

When you have someone staying in step with you and encouraging you, you are able to persevere and go farther than you would be able to on your own. Through accountability and encouraging each other in community, we are able to help each other do hard things for the glory of God.

Now in my postgrad season of life, accountability looks like early Tuesday mornings before work with my three roommates. We sit on our living room couches and each share about our time with God, temptations, trials, and triumphs. We pray over each other and ask how we can intentionally help one another. Even in the busyness of starting our first jobs out of college and creating new rhythms, we prioritize time to come together with people who know and love us and the Lord. It is an answered prayer to live with other young women who share my faith and season of life. I'm so grateful for the way these ladies care about me and my walk with the Lord, pushing me out of my comfort zone and into deeper communion with God. We invite each other into the messiness of our emotions and thoughts, asking for correction and wisdom. They won't let me hold onto the comforts in life that I am turning to instead of

Through accountability
and encouraging each
other in community,
we are able to help each
other do hard things
for the glory of God.

God, and they lovingly point me back to truth when I'm going through life so fast I've seemed to have forgotten what matters most.

I pray you find your people that challenge you to fight sin and pursue faithfulness. When you share your love for God and foundation in Christ, there is a different depth and accountability to that friendship. It's vulnerable to invite people into your life. There's a good chance you will hurt each other because Christians are still broken people. Fight for community anyway; it's worth it.

DISCIPLESHIP

I love Google Calendar! It took me until my sophomore year of college to transition away from my physical planner, but now there is no going back. I learned how to insert my own color codes and separate my priorities into different colored calendars. To ensure how I am stewarding my time reflects my priorities, I use it to document almost everything and then occasionally evaluate how I'm spending my time.

Google Calendar comes up in conversations with my friends because it truly does help me to better organize my life and reach my goals. Because of this, I have helped countless friends create a calendar that can do the same for them. I'm an evangelist for Google Calendar, and I teach others how to utilize it, too.

When we care about something, it naturally comes up in our conversations. When we invest our time in something, it is more top of mind. If something is a core part of how we structure our lives, it is a known trait about us.

More than being known for my affinity for Google Calendar, I want to be known for my relationship with Jesus. When we are abiding with God and privately investing in our relationship with Him, the overflow will be clear to those around us. In the same way that we can teach others how to share in other things Christians value, we are called to teach others how to have a relationship with Jesus.

Jesus' last command to His disciples before returning to heaven is referred to as the Great Commission. Jesus said, "Go therefore and make disciples of all nations, baptizing them in the name of the Father and of the Son and of the Holy Spirit, teaching them to observe all that I have commanded you. And behold, I am with you always, to the end of the age" (Matthew 28:19-20).[14] Pastor and author Jonathan "JP" Pokluda defines discipleship as "intentionally spending time with people around you to help them know Jesus."[15] Making disciples is simply sharing the Gospel and teaching others how to follow Christ.

A disciple of Jesus lives their life marked by imperfect but whole-hearted faithfulness to God and teaches others to do the same. A disciple is both someone who teaches and learns. This is one of the gifts of being a part of a body of believers in the church: being discipled and discipling others. We have direct access to God through Jesus, but He has also given us the gift of His people. Lean into the community around you to help you learn more about what it looks like to mature in your faith.

During college, I had the privilege of being discipled and discipling others. While I expected to learn from those wiser than me who were intentionally pouring into me, I learned even more from those who I was teaching and encouraging.

Seeing someone understand the Gospel for the first time is the most magnificent gift—their life and eternity are forever changed! Walking alongside them as they ask you questions about what it actually looks like to follow Jesus teaches you to go back to His Word and seek His wisdom in prayer. Now it's not just your relationship with God you are impacting; someone else is trusting you to speak into theirs. This pushes you to go even deeper because of the weight and responsibility you feel pouring into others.

Most of all, discipleship reveals your flaws and struggles. While it can be tempting to hide those from people who view you as a mentor, don't. Let them into the areas where you are still fighting sin and learning to trust God. They will learn more from how you handle your struggles and mistakes than from hearing about your perfections.

One of the discipleship relationships I was blessed with during college was with a girl named Abby. I was her small group leader at a retreat designed to help freshmen find a church home. We started hanging out and becoming friends, then we began reading the Bible together.

A disciple of Jesus lives their life marked by imperfect but wholehearted faithfulness to God and teaches others to do the same.

We are just people who know Jesus helping other people know Him.

I love how she texted me questions about God and genuinely desired to know Him more.

It's evident God placed Abby in my life for a reason, because almost every struggle I endured during college, she faced just a few months after me. As I was honest with her about where I was struggling and how I was fighting to trust God in my weaknesses, she was encouraged to do the same. Abby became one of my closest friends and is a testament to the joy of discipleship and the benefit of transparent accountability.

Watching Abby fall more in love with Jesus and blossom into a wise woman of God is one of the greatest honors of my life. Abby chose to take one step closer to God at a time and was always honest with me about where she was at and how she was struggling. God has continuously used our friendship to point us both closer to Him, and I am so grateful. Watching her discipling and mentoring others now makes me excited to see how the Great Commission truly works and the kingdom of God expanding.

Every believer is a coworker with Christ and other Christians in the goal of spiritual multiplication. We are just people who know Jesus helping other people know Him, and I can not think of a greater purpose for our lives here on earth.

Share your life with others and invite them into your daily tasks. There seemed to be more nights than not in college when a younger girl was sleeping on my couch to escape the dorm life as they were learning how to walk with God. This means they were there when I woke up a little cranky or heard me snap at my mom on the phone. They saw if I didn't read the Bible in the morning because I was on social media. They hopefully also saw how even though I am not perfect, my heart is to seek the Lord in all that I do.

It is tempting for me to want to put on a perfect front for others as they are beginning to look into what a relationship with God could mean for them. As they are considering surrendering their lives to Him, I want to make the Christian life as appealing as it can be and show them truly what God's character looks like the best I can. But if their faith is dependent on my ability to act just like God, then that would make me their savior. And Lord knows I would make a lousy savior! Only Jesus holds that ability, weight, and honor.

When we show others how we come to Him in our weaknesses, trials, mistakes, and doubts, they see the reality of someone living as a Christian. When they see all of your life, it can help remove the stigma of hypocrisy amongst Christians. Even if we do our best to only show our best, they are bound to see our mistakes. If we proclaim our own goodness and never own these mistakes, that makes us a hypocrite. Use your life as a means to display the grace of God, both in His forgiving us of all our sins and welcoming us back into His arms when we run the other way.

Who in your life can you help know Jesus more? What walls can you bring down to show them the genuineness of your love for them and your relationship with God? You don't have to know all the answers to disciple someone; you're just bringing them alongside you as you follow the One who holds all the answers. A common saying amongst Christians is that God doesn't call the qualified; He qualifies the called. Because He has called all Christians to be disciples and make disciples, pray for Him to help you be obedient to this calling He's placed on your life. All you need to disciple someone is the Holy Spirit and a willingness to be obedient.

SURRENDER & OBEDIENCE

As your trust in God increases, you seek to live in obedience and look more like Him every day. When you are abiding and resting in Jesus and teaching others to do the same, you learn to surrender daily to His leading. You grow in understanding that your life is not your own, but you are to steward it well.

Living in daily surrender looks like fixing your mind on truth each day, then holding your hands open to whatever God may have for you.

Everyone has two main purposes in life: to love and serve God, and to take as many people with you to heaven as possible.

We have our desires and our plans, but we are constantly asking the Lord to lead us to His best. As Jesus prayed in the garden before He went to the cross, "not My will, but Yours, be done" (Luke 22:42).[16] God will do anything He wants done with a heart posture of "here I am."

Christians are funnels: open to receive whatever the Lord gives us, then serve as a conduit to extend those gifts to others. God uses us not because of our qualifications or good works. He chooses to use broken vessels to carry out His work, displaying His omnipotence in our weakness.

Growing up with the Gatti girls, I was sad that Rebecca couldn't take part in the things we were doing. She didn't have to go to piano lessons or get to go to the lake. She had to be pumped full of medication every few hours and stay in quieter places that would help her to stay calm.

I had to surrender my expectations and desires for Rebecca's life and trust God to fulfill His perfect plans for her life. I talked to my parents about feeling disappointed about Rebecca missing out on the sister things we did together, and they reminded me that everyone has two main purposes in life: to love and serve God, and to take as many people with you to heaven as possible. Even after only a short time of living, Rebecca was already fulfilling that purpose.

While it was easy to see where Rebecca's life lacked, she experienced many things in abundance that those who are able-bodied can sometimes miss. Those who hear her story hear of the faithfulness of God and are given a new perspective on the hope of eternity. Viewing our lives through the lens of what God says is valuable and leads us to a holy view of our circumstances. Otherwise, it is easy to be weighed down by what is right in front of us if we are not lifting our eyes above it and fixing them on God's higher ways.

The goal of our relationship with God is not to feel steady, but to know we are steady regardless of how we feel.

Living a faithful life will impact how you interact with others, view relationships, and make decisions. The Holy Spirit changes you to look more like God from the inside out—this is a process called **sanctification**. The more you know God, the sooner you will surrender all of yourself to Him because you know He is trustworthy. Until you take the time to grow in your faith and knowledge of Him, trust will not feel possible. Getting to a place where you can genuinely trust God is not about having all of your questions answered; it's about knowing His character well enough that He is the one you want to come to with your questions.

I soon learned I don't need to know all the answers or explanations to know that God is good. He holds me and He draws near to me as I draw near to Him.[17] I have experienced such closeness with the Lord through being Rebecca's sister because it had led me to draw close to Him. Now no matter how heavy or carefree my day may feel, I have learned the importance of dependence on God. He is the safest place to put my trust.

While circumstances leading us to deeper faith can be a good catalyst for spiritual growth, I don't want to wait for a crisis to seek the Lord. When we choose to seek God through His Word and prayer each day, we are building a firm foundation of faith. Each day, we can be nourished by the Living Water. The more my life is about God and the less it is about me, the more peace and security I have in living out my purpose.

No matter the state we are in today, we can pick up the first stone and begin to build a solid foundation for our lives through our relationship with God. Then when the storms of life come, which we know they will, we have built a strong and unshakeable foundation in Christ.

No one wakes up with complete assurance, security, confidence, faith, and trust. This is built through consistently seeking God through His Word, His church, prayer, community, and other avenues for spiritual growth. An unshakeable house is built one brick at a time. The goal of our relationship with God is not to feel steady, but to know we are steady regardless of how we feel. He is a firm and secure anchor for our hope.[18]

What is one step you could take closer to God today? It can even be a cry of desperation, saying, "God, I don't have the strength; please come to me." And He promises us in His Word that when we come to Him when we are weary and burdened, He will give us rest.[19] You don't have to do anything to make yourself worthy of coming to God. Jesus sees us in our brokenness, and He comes closer. He wants to clean us up of the sin that separates us, but first He wants to hold us in His arms and care for our broken hearts as a loving father comforts his children.

ELEVEN

Proclaim His Glory

When we were in elementary school, Dad took Elizabeth and me to a local arcade. He purchased a seemingly endless amount of tokens and we played skee ball until our arms were sore. After we used all our tokens, Dad waved us over to meet him by the prize booth.

"Okay girls, how many do we have?" He looked at our receipts holding our grand totals and added them up in his head. "928 tickets—that's your new record!"

"Really? Does that mean we can get something from the top shelf?" Elizabeth asked.

"I had another idea. We got to have a fun afternoon sharing time together. What if you were to give them away to another kid? We don't need more things, and you could make someone's day." Dad shared his idea with us, and we were silent. "What do you girls think?"

We looked at each other with raised eyebrows. "Um, do we have to?" I asked.

"You don't have to. Just remember the tokens that gave you the ability to earn the tickets were a gift, and you had the joy of having fun with your sister. Think about the joy you could share with someone else. It's better to do things that make other people happy than what makes you happy. In fact, it usually makes you happier to give something away than to get something," Dad explained.

The first time we did this, it honestly made us a little upset. *We worked hard to earn these tickets—why should we give them away?* Dad never forced us to give away our tickets; it was always a nudge in the right direction. He encouraged us to give selflessly to others the way we had received someone else's generosity. Dad always likes to turn everyday moments into life lessons.

When we were obedient to his suggestion and gave our tickets away, I was always filled with so much joy. The shocked look on strangers' faces from our generosity was heartwarming, and it gave us opportunities to learn how to share the love of Christ with others. Admittedly, it was often a little awkward and uncomfortable. But over time, I began to look forward to giving at the end just as much as the playing.

This simple action taught me the joy resulting from selfless giving, and that value is not found in material things like prizes from tickets but in the time spent with people I love. When Charlotte came around, Elizabeth and I took her to the arcade to repeat the lesson. She wasn't a fan of it either at first, but seeing her grasp the meaning and begin to give joyfully was sweet.

Looking back, I am so grateful for what Dad taught us through this. The only reason we had the tickets was because our dad brought us there in the first place and provided the tokens. Everything the tickets earned was a result of his generosity, and all the fun we had was because of him. When he encouraged us to give away what we had been freely given, it didn't seem fair to us. We were selfish and wanted to keep what we falsely believed was ours.

This life I now live is a gift from God, and every good thing in it is a result of His mercy and grace.[1] Rather than holding on tightly to the good things God has blessed me with, I want to hold it all with an open hand in surrender. When I remember that it was never really mine to begin with, I am a better steward of the good gifts God has entrusted to me.

HOPE IN SALVATION

As Christians, our lives are not our own because God has purchased them with the blood of Jesus. God created you and loves you. He desires a relationship with you. God is light, and in Him there is no darkness. In our sin and darkness, we can't be in an eternal relationship with the God of light.

Everyone who has ever lived has sinned, falling short of the perfection and glory of God. Rather than leaving us in the darkness alone to face the consequences of the actions we earned, He sent Jesus—His perfect Son of light—to take on the righteous punishment for our darkness. We can't change the reality that we are sinners born into a dark world; we can't escape the darkness on our own.

Through acknowledging our sin and darkness, we cry out to God about our need for light and salvation. Accepting His gift of light means rather than God looking to us to pay the punishment for our own sins, He looks to the cross as the complete payment. Without submitting to His Lordship and surrendering our lives to Him, we aren't able to receive the payment for our sins. God gives us His Son, and He asks us to give Him our lives. He also gives us peace, purpose, and perspective that we could never have apart from Him.

In the book of Romans, Paul dives deep into different aspects of the Gospel truth and how that impacts our lives. Here is one of the ways he explains the Gospel:

"For while we were still weak, at the right time Christ died for the ungodly. For one will scarcely die for a righteous person—though perhaps for a good person one would dare even to die— but God shows His love for us in that while we were still sinners, Christ died for us. Since, therefore, we have now been justified by His blood, much more shall we be saved by Him from the wrath of God. For if while we were enemies we were reconciled to God by the death of His Son, much more, now that we are reconciled, shall we be saved by His life. More than that, we also rejoice in God through our Lord Jesus Christ, through whom we have now received reconciliation." (Romans 5:6-11)[2]

Jesus died for us while we were weak, knowing we were sinners. This reemphasizes the fact that we are not saved by anything that we can do on our own merit, but simply as an act of grace and mercy from a perfect God.

Paul speaks to the fact that most people would be hesitant to die for a good person, but Jesus died for us at our worst. His love is that deep and genuine. Jesus is capable of perfect love because He knows us fully, yet loves us completely. He doesn't love a future version of you or the person you present to others; Jesus loves you in the messiest moments that no one else sees.

Through the blood of Jesus, we are **justified**. This means the debt of our sin has been paid in full. We are no longer in debt for the wrongs we have committed, but have been covered by the only one able to live perfectly and pay it fully. But Jesus didn't only die for our sins and accept that punishment. Three days after dying on the cross, He rose again! He took on the payment of the sins of the world, then conquered death itself. Now through His life, we are **reconciled** to God. This means because He lives, we are able to have an eternal relationship with our Father in heaven. There's nothing left to be made right once we are in Christ's righteousness.

Without Jesus, we are the ones who have to pay our sin debts. If we don't have a relationship with Jesus and trust in Him before our time on this earth comes to an end, we will spend an eternity paying the debt our sin earned us. This heartbreaking reality is why the Gospel is so important.

Through Jesus, the enemy has no claim on you, even as you continue to sin. Our aim is to live a life worthy of the Gospel grace we have received, but we will still mess up and sin despite our best efforts not to. God isn't after our good works; He desires our hearts.

God isn't after our good works; He desires our hearts.

There's nothing left to be made right once we are in Christ's righteousness.

God sent Jesus to die out of His love for the world.[3] Jesus not only pays our debt but also leads us into a relationship with God. We don't need to earn favor with God; Jesus opens the door for our constant access to Him. The author of Hebrews describes Jesus as our perfect high priest.[4] This means He bridges the previously insurmountable gap between us and God. As Christians, we can focus our time and efforts on praising God for who He is, not being discouraged by who we are not.

"Therefore, since we have been justified by faith, we have peace with God through our Lord Jesus Christ. Through Him we have also obtained access by faith into this grace in which we stand, and we rejoice in hope of the glory of God. Not only that, but we rejoice in our sufferings, knowing that suffering produces endurance, and endurance produces character, and character produces hope, and hope does not put us to shame, because God's love has been poured into our hearts through the Holy Spirit who has been given to us." (Romans 5:1-5)[5]

Because of Jesus, we are at peace with God since Jesus has paid our outstanding debt. We now stand in His **grace**, which is the unmerited and abundant favor of God. We are saved by grace alone, through faith alone, in Christ alone.

Because of the Gospel, we can have hope in our sufferings. The verses above (especially Romans 5:3-5) are the verses that brought my family encouragement through Rebecca's life and death. They are the verses I wrote on the tombstone we designed together as sisters. Because of everything you just read about the Gospel and our right standing with God, we can genuinely rejoice in the midst of the most difficult sufferings. It produces in us endurance, character, and hope.

In times of desperation, we cling more desperately to what brings us comfort and security. Apart from Jesus, all of these comforts will fail. Whether they are friends, family, or finances—none of them can sustain you the way that your Creator can. Our hope in Jesus doesn't lead us to shame or disappointment because Christ Himself is the source of unending hope.

As Christians, we are indwelt with the Holy Spirit. This means that God's presence is always with us, comforting and guiding us. He grows us in wisdom and produces in us fruits of the Spirit. It is one of the ways God fulfills His promise of never leaving us alone. This Spirit is a constant reminder of God's faithfulness, presence, and hope. Without my relationship with God through Jesus' sacrifice and the comfort of His Spirit, I would never have been able to endure the trials I have and still have hope. But because of the Gospel, my hope remains secure even when everything crumbles. Rebecca's life taught me the importance of sharing this hope with others and the urgency to do so; none of us are promised tomorrow.

There are two categories of people in this world: those who have no hope and those who are ambassadors of hope. We all desire lasting, secure hope. Trying to find rest or purpose in anything else besides Jesus will leave you confused, disappointed, and broken. Once you hold onto the hope you can have in the Gospel, your perspective and purpose change: you are now an ambassador of eternal hope and entrusted to share it with the hopeless. Us ambassadors are no better than those without hope; we all began in the same position of hopelessness. We're simply pointing others in the direction of Who has graciously saved us.

I want to encourage you to take a moment to reflect on your own beliefs about God, eternity, and the Gospel—which category do you see yourself in, those without hope or those who are ambassadors of hope? Have you placed your trust wholeheartedly in Jesus for the forgiveness of your sins? Are you living the assurance this hope provides? If you have not placed your hope in Jesus, there's no better time than right now. He's right here waiting for you, and He loves you. The Bible says, "everyone who calls on the name of the Lord will be saved" (Romans 10:13).[6] Come to Him in surrender—is there really a reason to wait?

Our hope in Jesus doesn't lead us to shame or disappointment because Christ Himself is the source of unending hope.

If you are a Christian, I hope you're reminded of the Gospel and encouraged to love other people enough to share it with them. If this is something you don't believe in, please know I share with you because I love you. I am confident this is the only way to eternal life, and I love you enough to tell you. While I would love for everyone reading this to place their trust in Jesus, I know it may take time. It's okay to have questions and doubts; don't be afraid to bring those to God in prayer or to other people walking alongside this faith journey with you. As I've said before, surrender typically takes time and getting to know God first. Trust is a process; rather than expecting change to happen overnight, take this journey one step at a time.

SHARING HOPE

One of the first people I remember sharing the Gospel with is Taylor Swift. I listened to a lot of her music and I noticed a common theme in her songs: she was always brokenhearted or angry or lonely or disappointed.

When I was ten, I told my dad, "I wish Taylor Swift was finding her hope in Jesus, not in boys. Then maybe she wouldn't be so upset. She could find a boy who would treat her the way God wants her to be treated."

"Katherine, you are so right," said Dad. "Why don't you write her a letter telling her about God and I will send it to her?"

In my best cursive, I wrote her a letter on fancy paper with pink, green, blue, and yellow stripes. I explained how the hole in her heart could only be filled by Jesus and the perfect love she wanted was only found in God. Folding the paper into thirds, I sealed it into an envelope and wrote "To: Taylor Swift, From: Katherine Gatti" on the front.

Obviously, I don't think this letter ever made it to Taylor Swift. Although I still pray her heart ultimately finds satisfaction in God above all else. The same thing that's true for Taylor is true for all of us: we have a hole in our heart that only God can fill. And for those of us who have this hope, it's our responsibility to share it with those who don't yet have it.

Two of my favorite people in the world are Riley and Haley. Both of them grew up in California before moving to Fort Worth for college in the fall of 2020. I met them my junior year when they were freshmen. I was Riley's small group leader during sorority recruitment and Haley was in my sorority.

During their freshman year, they both asked questions about faith and sought to understand what it means to truly trust God. We studied the Bible together and had meaningful conversations. They were also really silly and brought so much fun into my life. Whether I was driving them around or they were sleeping on my couch, I saw them almost every day and had a front-row seat to God changing their hearts.

Sometimes when they stayed over, I'd come downstairs and they'd still be sleeping on the couches. I would sit at the end of one couch next to Haley's curled-up feet, praying over them and spending time with God in the morning before they were awake.

They'd wake up and see me there, and Haley would gasp, "Woah I did not expect to see you there." I'd laugh and apologize for scaring her, then keep reading my Bible.

Often Haley would ask, "Will you read out loud to me?" Then she would lay her head down next to me, closing her eyes while I read to her.

I couldn't help but remember the times I'd read the Bible out loud to Rebecca. Haley and Riley hold special places in my heart like they are my sisters, and teaching them about God is one of the greatest honors and joys of my life. I'm grateful God chose to bless me with their kind hearts and faithful friendships.

After spending the year growing in their knowledge of God and the life He offers, spring break was a turning point for both of them.

They chose to spend their weeks in different ways, but God was sovereign and brought about good through both choices.

They'd both committed to spending the week with their sorority sisters in South Padre, a trip common for freshmen and notorious for being a week of nonstop partying. Our college ministry was going to Broken Bow for a more lowkey getaway in light of the lingering pandemic. In my prayer journal, I wrote: *God, please make a way for them to come if it's Your best. But either way, please use this week and wherever they are to draw both Haley and Riley closer to Yourself. Lead them to wholehearted surrender and trust in You.*

Riley went to South Padre with her sorority friends for her spring break while Haley and I were in Broken Bow. Riley spent the week surrounded by people doing everything opposite of how God calls us to live. She describes this time as complete darkness and feeling hopeless.

The first night Riley was back on campus, we got dinner together like we did every Monday night. Riley grabbed us both Chick-fil-A salads on her meal plan, then ran across campus in the rain to meet me.

"I understand more now than ever why God calls us to live a certain way. Because giving yourself away to these things is draining and painful." Riley didn't share many details from the trip, but it was evident she'd seen and learned a lot during her time there about what truly matters to her.

We ate our salads and talked about how life with Jesus is truly what is satisfying. God doesn't give us rules to restrict us unnecessarily to rob us of fun; He is protecting us from unnecessary pain and leading us to His best.

Sitting there in her South Padre sweatshirt eating Chick-fil-A, still wet from the pouring rain, Riley said, "I'm ready. To really trust God." I prayed, Riley prayed, and we both cried. She was exuding pure joy and freedom. I was overjoyed because Riley's eternity was changed in this moment, and her salvation seals her for eternity through Jesus! Through placing her trust completely in Jesus for the forgiveness of her sins and eternal life, Riley now has access to the peace of Christ as she lives the rest of her life.

That same day Riley decided to go all-in with Jesus, Haley and I were processing what she was feeling and thinking coming back from spring break. Haley went with our college ministry to Broken Bow, and she was fiercely wrestling with God. Something especially difficult for her to grasp was that people who did not believe in Jesus were not able to go to heaven. This is a sobering reality, that apart from faith in Jesus there is eternal punishment for our sins and separation from God. That is why God loved us enough to send His Son as the perfect sacrifice and the only way to atone for our sins completely. This is why it is crucial for us to understand and share this truth. Not out of judgment for those who don't believe what Christians do, but out of love for them knowing where they will spend eternity apart from this relationship with God through His Son.

Haley sent me this text late that night: "I know I will give my life to Christ eventually and see myself pursuing Him later. This makes me question why I'm holding back when I'm confident that's how I want to live my life. My heart has changed, but my brain is holding me back from just letting go of the things I am holding onto. I know I want to give everything to God but I just can't seem to make myself take that final step."

The next day, I had my phone turned off while I took an online exam. After finishing the exam, I turned on my phone to three missed FaceTime calls from Haley and a text that said: "I just gave my life to God!! I confessed I'm finally done fighting this battle and just want Him to take control. I'm completely at peace and feel so much relief."

Calling her as fast as I could, I screamed with pure excitement—Haley wholeheartedly surrendered her life to Jesus! She came to my house, and we walked around my neighborhood and talked about what was going through her mind.

"I just finally decided to stop fighting God and trying to figure it all out. He's been chasing me, and I realized I don't have to be perfect before I can be a Christian. Then there was no more reason to wait! I feel like the largest weight has been lifted off my chest—I just want everyone to experience this feeling." Haley became a new creation and her heart changed. Rather than fighting to change herself from the outside through sheer willpower, Haley found peace and purpose through first giving Jesus her heart.

He asks us for our devotion and lives, then does the work of changing us to look more like Him. When done in this way, it's so much more life-giving than pressuring yourself to do everything perfectly on your own strength. Haley has continuously grown in who she is in Christ, and now shares that with confidence and conviction with those around her out of love. She's a bright light and gives all the credit to Jesus.

During spring break, Riley immersed herself in darkness and craved the light; Haley was around the light and realized she wanted that light for herself. They both had just enough understanding of the truth to be uneasy about where they were. This was the point when it finally clicked for them: they wanted to truly surrender wholeheartedly to the Lord. It was so freeing for them to grasp that it wasn't about their behavior or performance, but about their belief and their heart.

A month later, they were baptized at our church. This was a public declaration of their inward trust in Jesus. When each of them came out of the water to me, I hugged them and wrapped them in a towel. This is one of the greatest joys we can experience on this side of heaven: seeing people go from death to life, giving them present and eternal hope. My heart could not have felt more full! The way He pursued both Riley and Haley allowed His love to be revealed to each of them in a personal way. God's timing and ways are perfect, and His love for each of His people is evident.

LEAD THE WAY

My junior year of college, I led a Bible study for freshman girls. One week in the fall only two girls came: Haley and Riley. We met at my house in my room and talked about the importance of building our house on the rock.

"Christ alone is a solid foundation, and everything else you give your life to in college and in life will crumble," I explained.

Individually, they had both talked to me about feeling lonely and desiring genuine friends who were also seeking to grow in their faith. I really wanted them to be friends, and I wasn't being subtle about it.

God's timing and ways are perfect.

"It's crucial to surround yourself with people who are also wanting to follow God because it's so much easier to do it together."

They exaggerate when telling this story now. "Riley, remember when Katherine locked us in a room together and tried to force us to be friends?" Haley screams and grins at me, knowing this is not what happened but laughing when she sees my eyes get big.

"Haley stop it, you know that is not what happened!" I try to defend myself and share my side of the memory.

But first, Riley continues with her perspective. "But it didn't work! Maybe if we listened to her then we would've become best friends sooner."

They love to mess with me by telling that story in a dramatic way, but even them making fun of me together makes me happy because I have such gratitude for the way their friendship and faith have grown. Not only have I benefited from having them in my life, but I have seen God use their friendship with each other to grow their relationships with God. They love each other so well and are loyal to each other. It is a testament to the kind of friendships possible when they are founded on mutual trust in Jesus.

At my graduation, they surprised me with a gigantic cutout of my face they waved throughout the ceremony. They sat right where everyone could see them when they walked off the stage—it was such a sweet and funny gift. They love to play the music as loud as it goes in the car and embarrass me by yelling out the car window at strangers. When they came to Louisiana for our big crawfish boil our family hosts every Good Friday, they were not a fan of the little mudbugs. They are great friends and are always willing to be helpful and serve others. They always show up, and they love and serve me more than I deserve.

One of the biggest ways they have ever served me happened on a Saturday morning. My friend Jill and I had gone to a Surfaces concert in Dallas the previous night, and I had a flight to Nashville the next day at 6:00 a.m. to visit my sister. Haley and Riley offered to pick me up at 4:30 a.m. to take me to the airport.

I called Haley on my drive home from Dallas. "Can y'all just stay the night with me before so I can make sure you're up in time?" I asked.

I didn't want them to oversleep and leave me without a ride to the airport.

"I'll wake up, I promise. I'm already in bed," Haley said. "Can you just call me at four o'clock to make sure I am awake?"

I was nervous she was going to oversleep, but I agreed. I started packing around 1:00 a.m., then decided I could throw the rest in my suitcase in the morning and went to sleep.

The next thing I know, I'm jolted awake by a banging my back door. I looked at my phone: 4:45 a.m. I jumped out of bed and ran to open the door.

"Finally!" Riley screamed.

"Katherine you literally gave me a heart attack," Haley leaned her head down, letting out a sigh as she put her hands on her knees.

"I'm so sorry guys, I just need to finish packing real quick then we can go." I ran back to my room and threw everything in my carry-on. Hoping I had what I needed, I zipped up my purple suitcase and ran down the back stairs to Haley's car.

"Do you think this is enough gas to get to the airport?" Haley's gas gauge was hovering just above E.

"Let's just take my car," I said. Riley opened Haley's trunk to move my suitcase. But when I turned on my car, my low fuel light also came on.

"Well Haley, I hope yours is enough, let's go!" We got back in Haley's car and I handed them Celsius energy drinks. They told me everything they'd done to try to wake me up for thirty minutes before resorting to banging on the door.

"We threw rocks at your window, screamed your name, called your roommates, and rang your doorbell," Riley said.

"We even called your mom! But she didn't answer. I'm not sure what she would've done to help but we were desperate," Haley laughed.

At 5:35 a.m., we pulled up to the Dallas Love Field Airport. I grabbed my suitcase, hugged them goodbye and said thank you, then jogged through the doors. This airport usually isn't busy, especially at this time of day. I prayed I'd make my flight, knowing that as soon as I told my dad he would remind me that this is why we always get to the airport three hours early no matter what.

In all my years of flying out of this airport, I have never seen such a crowd. There were people packed all the way between the lines to check your bag and the doors with no room to move. The end of the security line was wrapped all the way past where I could see.

Standing in the back of the security line, I knew I needed a different plan. With ten minutes before my flight started to board, there was no way I was making it through the line in time. I contemplated being that annoying person and explaining my situation to people in line to get to the front. Even if that worked, the stanchions set up put hundreds of people zigzagged between me and the front of the line.

I called Haley and Riley to explain the situation and asked them to keep waiting for me just in case I didn't make it on the plane and needed a ride back home. After hanging up the phone, the young lady next to me asked, "Is it always this crazy?"

"Oh no, it's never like this. I've never seen it this bad." I just shook my head and tried to think of something to do. Past the crowded line, I noticed a shorter line. There were two attendants standing at the entrance, stationed like guards. I told my new friend that I was going to see what that line was for.

"It's worth a shot! I know if I stay here I am definitely going to miss my flight." I invited her to come with me. She hesitated, then decided it was worth the risk. We jogged over to the empty line with the two guards.

"Excuse me, who is this line for?" I asked, hoping they would make an exception.

"Are you a member?" He pointed to the sign behind me. It's an advertisement for a membership that uses retinal scans and a background check to expedite your process through airport security.

"I'm not, can I join here?" At this point, I knew this was likely my only chance of making it on the flight.

"No ma'am, you need to go back there and sign up at the kiosk." He pointed to a blob of people frantically registering for this membership. I thanked him and we rushed back.

While we waited in line at the kiosks, my new friend from Chicago told me more about herself. She just moved to Dallas but was going home to visit her family. I told her I was going to see my sister. Finally, it's our turn at the kiosks. We entered our information and then hurried to the short line.

In this line, we talked about change and fear of change, and I talked to her about my faith and the peace that comes from that. We separated into two different security lines, and I made it through before her. I realized we never exchanged our names. Unable to finish our conversation, we waved goodbye across the room and I went up the escalator toward my terminal.

Over the intercom, a flight attendant said, "If you are one of the twenty-five people heading to Nashville that got held up in security, we are still waiting for you! You've got three minutes, you can do it!"

With the flight attendant cheering me on, I sprinted to the gate and rolled onto the plane just before the doors closed. My flight attendants clapped for me and helped me find an open seat. Less than two hours later, I arrived in Nashville as my mom and sister were waking up. They couldn't believe I made it with all that happened. Just as I predicted, Mom told me what Dad always says, "See, this is why you always go three hours early! You never know what could happen."

When I asked my new friend from Chicago if she wanted to try to find a faster way with me, she didn't have time to figure out if I was right or not. She just had to trust me. Because of the knowledge the airport worker at the empty line gave us, we knew the way to make it through the crowds. As we passed others in the long line, we shared the good news and told them there was a faster way! Some people would rather stay where they were because they didn't want to risk leaving and going to the back of the line. Others chose to trust us and come too, then they were able to make it past all the lines and onto their flights in time.

As Christians, we know the Way and we have the answer. Unless others know it too, they won't make it. Are we sharing it like we genuinely believe it is the only way to eternal life?

In the busyness of life, we get caught up in all that is happening around us. We are pushed and pulled in a thousand different directions so hardly anything feels intentional. Rather than having eyes to see what

There is purpose in the mundane and reasons for the reroutes.

the Lord is doing around us, our eyes are fixated on screens and our feet are rushing from one thing to the next without even truly noticing the people around us.

What would happen if we slowed down and noticed? Who are the people around you that you are rushing past? What could God have placed you there to do besides the tasks on your neverending to-do list?

When we remember one of the reasons we are on this earth is to point other people to God and make disciples, we see these setbacks differently. In all situations, whether it is as predictable as the person who sits next to you at work or as random as the friend you make in the airport, look for what God could be doing or showing you.

I don't want to rush through this life and miss all the good God has placed right in front of me because I am too busy to notice. There is purpose in the mundane and reasons for the reroutes. While we won't see the full picture until we are with God in heaven, we can trust that He is working through all things for the good of His people and the glory of Himself. Looking at all of life through this lens, it's impossible not to see endless opportunities to partner with God in proclaiming His glory.

Riley and Haley tried everything possible to wake me up because they knew if they didn't I would miss my flight. This is one of the kindest ways they have served me, and I would not have even made it to the airport if it wasn't for them. Do we go to this extent to share the Gospel with people that they did for me not to miss my flight? While missing a flight is sad and disappointing, missing out on eternity in heaven is so much more devastating. I want to love others enough to go to the greatest lengths to share the truth with them, patiently walking with them one step closer to God at a time.

No matter who we are or where God has placed us, all Christians are coworkers with Christ in His ministry of reconciliation. This ministry of reconciliation is God bringing the world back to Himself. Paul encourages Christians with this call and reminder of who they are in Christ:

> "Therefore, if anyone is in Christ, he is a new creation. The old has passed away; behold, the new has come. All this is from God, who through Christ reconciled us to Himself and gave us the ministry of reconciliation; that is, in Christ God was reconciling the world to Himself, not counting their trespasses against them, and entrusting to us the message of reconciliation. Therefore, we are ambassadors for Christ, God making His appeal through us. We implore you on behalf of Christ, be reconciled to God. For our sake He made Him to be sin who knew no sin, so that in Him we might become the righteousness of God." (2 Corinthians 5:17-21)[7]

Jesus became sin for us so that we could be reconciled to God through a relationship with Him. God allows us to be His messengers of the Gospel, and we are all working together to accomplish this mission of sharing it with the world. And not just sharing it so that people hear, but imploring with our hearts so they understand and believe. When this is the focus of our lives, we are filled with purpose that can not be shaken.

TWELVE

Eternal Hope

It was the last night of summer camp. All the middle schoolers gathered into the auditorium for a worship night. I closed my eyes to help myself not be distracted by the people around me. As I sang songs of praise to the Lord, my heart was comforted by a thought. I pictured myself in heaven greeting the Lord face-to-face. Everything was light all around me. Jesus stood up from sitting beside His Father's throne and ran down the stairs to me.

With the biggest smile on His face, Jesus said, "Follow Me. I want to show you something." He wrapped His hand around mine, and my thumb dipped into the hole where the nails hung my Savior on a cross. Locking hands, we walked together until we approached a garden full of the most marvelous flowers.

Jesus walked steady and unhurried; His peace seemed to flow out of His being and into my Spirit. We approached someone in the garden with her back turned toward us. My heart caught in my throat at the sight of her. She's wearing the whitest dress with her golden hair braided and draped over her back.

Jesus called out her name and confirmed what I knew to be true: "Rebecca, your sister is here!" Her braid whipped through the air as she turned to greet me, her smile spanning across her entire face. I saw her dimples, her sparkling blue eyes.

I can trust God will bring about good ultimately no matter what happens immediately.

We embraced, and my heart swelled. This was pure joy, being with Jesus and my sister in the heavens. What an undeserved gift.

The three of us walked through the garden. My sister and I got to do what girls like to do: we talked, laughed, and shared time with each other. All the simple things we never got to do here. It was a gift to be in her company, telling her all the ways she has impacted so many for the better. I thanked Jesus for God's planning of it all and His sacrifice on the cross to allow us eternity not only with Him but with each other. Now those years on earth that were marked by excruciating pain couldn't feel farther away.

With hope in my heart for what's to come, I opened my eyes at the worship night and wiped my tears. I was smiling, understanding that I can trust God will bring about good ultimately no matter what happens immediately. I wasn't sure if He would choose to miraculously heal Rebecca or not, but I knew the end of the story had already been written. And I can't wait for this ending!

Because of Jesus, forever is not a complete mystery. Rebecca and I will both spend infinitely more time after this life than we do in it, and God has made a way for us to do that together. Of course Jesus Himself is the object of my faith, and He alone is worthy of my complete devotion and praise. But how kind of Him to also allow such a sweet assurance of knowing those we love that are in a relationship with Him will have eternity to live in fellowship with one another. In the middle of hardships, this hope is sure.

GRIEF

If I had it my way, my life would be free of hard times and full of happy moments. People wouldn't leave and words wouldn't hurt, change wouldn't happen and hearts wouldn't break. However, if my life really looked like that, I truly believe I would not know the Lord the way I do after He carried me through times of difficulty and grief.

I used to see the hard times as something I wanted to rush through, keeping my head down to make sure no one noticed anything in my life was less than the perfection I wanted to portray. When I have instead faced hard times with vulnerability and complete dependence on the Lord, I have felt peace, joy, confidence, and hope like never before, regardless of the outcome. While my circumstances aren't often inherently joyful, God has taught me how to experience His joy in all circumstances.

Rather than seeing Rebecca as a burden, she is the greatest blessing God has given me. Through experiencing the grief of watching her suffer and then the grief of losing her, I learned how to depend on the Lord for strength and to lean on the people He placed around me for support.

I would not trade any of the heartbreaks I have gone through, especially being Rebecca's sister, because they have revealed the Lord's character to me and taught me more about Him than any joyful period of my life. These hurts have taken the promises of Scripture, which I know to be true, and shown me the reality of them in my own life. God does not just care about His children; He cares about me and loves me. We read in the Bible that He is the God of all comfort, but it was on the days when my body ached from the pain of losing someone I love that I personally experienced God comforting me. His Word says He is sovereign, and it was when He used even the darkest times to shine His light that I knew it to be true in my own life. I know God is love, but it wasn't until someone I deeply trusted was unfaithful that I truly understood His faithfulness and self-sacrificial love for me.

Through being Rebecca's sister, I learned that I don't need to know all the answers or explanations to know that God is good. When we choose to seek God through His Word and prayer, we are building upon a firm foundation of faith. The more my life is about God and the less it is about me, the more peace and security I have.

Faith is deciding ahead of time no matter what brokenness we face in this world, Jesus is worthy of all trust and devotion. Not because we blindly believe that, but because of who He has proven Himself to be.

I don't need to know all the answers or explanations to know that God is good.

Everything happens for a reason. I know it; I believe it. But knowing God is in control and believing the pain is really part of His perfect plan is not easy to accept.

Tragedies provide crossroads. They're often things we never asked for or expected. We can pray for God to bring healing or change, but we can't guarantee that is what He will do. When our prayers seem to go unanswered, it's natural to question if God is real, and if He is real does He even care about what you are going through? In times of crisis, our character takes shape. When we choose to trust God while we are grieving without understanding why the tragedies are happening, we cultivate godly character and dependence on the Lord. His Spirit in His people who are submitted to Him produces endurance, perseverance, strength, and hope.

God is near to us when we are brokenhearted; He's no stranger to grief or loss. God gave His only Son whom He loves to die in our place so that God could save us, who He also loves. He watched His Son suffer and die on the cross for the sins of the world; the light was coming, but the darkness still affected His Son.

Remember the God you can pray to is Father, Son, and Spirit: our Father who is in control of all He created; the Son who took on flesh and died in our place; the Spirit whose power raised Christ from the grave and now lives in all believers. He created you, He understands you, and He loves you. In your grief that is overwhelming and uncertain, turn to Him.

HEAVENLY HEALING

Rebecca's doctors never gave a solid prediction for how long she would live because her brain injury was not the result of a disease or disorder, but of a series of mistakes. They roughly guessed she would live to be around five years old. When April 2017 rolled around, Rebecca had been fighting the odds for an entire decade. At this point, my family allowed ourselves to become hopeful for a longer future for Rebecca. We'd become so used to our lives with her that we never expected to have a life without her. My parents even drew up new house plans after

Rebecca's tenth birthday. We thought of every possible accommodation for her—but the house was never built.

On a July summer night, my mom and I stayed up until 3:00 a.m. talking. My best friend broke my heart, and I didn't know what to do. Mom let me talk through it all one more time, and encouraged me to trust God and get some rest.

"As long as you are focusing on Him and letting the Lord guide your steps, you'll make the wise decision. You can't control His will for your life; just trust Him." Mom hugged me goodnight, turning off the light and closing the door behind her as she left.

My mind was still racing as I sat in my room alone, so I flipped the light back on and opened my prayer journal. I wrote about the relational hurt weighing me down and the wisdom Mom shared that I wanted to remember. I asked God to give me discernment in the midst of so much confusion. I also prayed for my sister: *God, my heart is hurting for Rebecca. She bit her lip during a seizure again, and it's ripped now worse than ever. God, heal her. Give her comfort. Give her rest. Give my family and me the strength to handle whatever may come, and reveal to us all that we can do to help Rebecca live a more comfortable life. I love her with all my heart. Thank you for choosing our family to be blessed by her. May your goodness and glory be shown through her. Amen.*

Feeling the peace that always washes over me after talking to God, I closed my prayer journal, turned off the light, and went to sleep.

The next morning, my mom woke me up.

"Any plans for today?" Mom asked.

It was only 8:00 a.m., so I told her I would sleep a little longer. Mom told me she'd come back later, then left my room. I closed my eyes, but they popped back open to the sound of my mom screeching, "Ryan! Rebecca's gone!"

Confused by her outburst, I rushed into Rebecca's room. *Did someone take her? What does she mean, gone?*

Then the reality hit me: Rebecca died.

I walked in and saw my mom sitting on Rebecca's bed. She was holding my sister's body, rocking back and forth as she cried out in complete despair. Sitting down next to them, my shaking hand held onto Rebecca's. Our sobs poured out of our bodies and bounced around the room. I stayed there for as long as I could bear to hear my mom's cries, but they were soon too much for me. Her scream from when she first found her filled my thoughts and nightmares for years to come.

I stumbled slowly to the living room. My dad embraced me, sobbing. He called Rebecca's sitter, Miss Cathy, who cared for Rebecca for over nine years.

"She didn't wake up, Miss Cathy. She's gone, I'm so sorry," Dad said.

I stood frozen in the living room, unsure of what to do and unsure if I would be able to do anything if I tried. I saw my sister, Elizabeth, walking in from outside. Our eyes met through the French door, and her gaze dropped to where Mom was still holding Rebecca. Her hand raised over her quivering lips and I saw her heart breaking; we were all breaking. She came inside, and we embraced.

I called my grandparents, and my Pops answered the phone. I couldn't bring myself to say that my sister was dead, so I instead used the words that were still haunting my mind, the words ringing through my brain accompanied by my mom's piercing cry.

"Rebecca's gone. She passed away in her sleep."

"Oh honey," Pops said, "I'm so sorry." Our cries are the only thing heard over the phone for a moment. He said, "Well sweetheart, your Nana is about to go into a blood pressure test, so I am going to wait to tell her because I think this would affect the results."

I was not able to bring myself to actually laugh, but for a moment his comment lifted my spirits. But only for a moment. Even on this tragic day, Pops was still thinking of how to protect my Nana's heart. He loved her so well.

Charlotte also woke up to Mom's scream. She was seven years old at the time—the same age I was when Rebecca was born ten years earlier. Charlotte ran out to see what happened. When I heard her cries, I knew she was broken, too.

Charlotte and Elizabeth followed me into my room. We fell to our knees and literally cried out to God.

Elizabeth held onto my hand and laid her head on my shoulder. Charlotte wrapped her little arms around me and buried her face into my arm. With a sister on each side and one in my heart, I prayed out loud, "God, thank you so much for choosing us to be Rebecca's sisters. Thank you for bringing her home to You peacefully in her sleep. Thank you for all the days we spent together, and for the forever we will have with her in heaven because of Jesus. Thank you for healing her. God, help us to get through this. We need you, and we love you. Amen."

Sitting on the floor in my bedroom, we hugged and cried together. At that moment, as my sisters and I collapsed into each other's arms, I remembered my prayer from the night before: *God, heal her.* Although it broke my heart to be apart from her, the only consolation for my soul was knowing that she was healed and no longer in any pain.

We went back into Rebecca's room and huddled together in the place where Rebecca slept. I held her body, stroking her hair and holding her hand. I studied her face, wanting to cherish this last moment and memorize each detail. I couldn't believe this would be the last time I held her.

As the news traveled, my entire extended family trickled in and filled our home. People took turns holding her. Some told sweet stories about times they've shared with Rebecca. When the time came for the paramedics to take her body away, everyone was silent. Rather than bringing the stretcher inside and wheeling her out, my Uncle Robbie scooped up his niece and carried her outside so we didn't have to see a stranger take her away. The next time we'd see her was at the funeral home.

The whole day was a blurry daze of tears and hugs. I felt numb. People came in and out, and we used so many tissues. The extra soft ones with aloe. I was surrounded by family and my best friends. We were also visited by people we didn't know as well or hadn't spoken to in awhile; death has a way of bringing people back together.

There was no unique cause of her death other than the wear on her body from a decade of seizures; her little body just gave out while she was sleeping. July 31, 2017, was the longest day of my life. Seeing the love people had for Rebecca and feeling the care they had for us as her family helped me to endure it. Even still, nothing could have prepared me for this day, or the days to follow.

OUR LAST GOODBYE

The next day, the funeral arrangements began. My dad wrote the first draft of her obituary, then had me sit down at the computer at the funeral home and make edits. He had to discuss with the groundskeeper how many plots he wanted to purchase. They only had one child-sized casket; it was white with gold trim. We chose the flowers to go on top of her closed casket: white and pink, roses and lilies. We received countless arrangements holding beautiful flowers. Our house was packed to the brim with them. Everything beautiful still reminds me of Rebecca, especially flowers and butterflies.

Two days after she passed away, I started my senior year of high school and Elizabeth started her freshman year. I'd been looking forward to this day when Elizabeth and I finally got to go to school together again. We talked about not going, but decided it was probably for the best to do something normal and get out of the funeral planning bubble.

I backed into my parking spot in the middle of senior row. Elizabeth and I sat in silence after I parked. We watched as everyone ran around, smiling and taking their first-day-of-school pictures. In the midst of so much joy for a new beginning, I felt so out of place as I was grieving an ending. My cousin, Amy, was also starting her senior year. She walked over to my car, and we hugged and cried as the bell rang. I linked arms with my sister and cousin, and we walked into school together.

It was one of the hardest days of my life, filled with so many people with puzzled looks. A kindhearted professor gave me a tearful hug as soon as I walked into his classroom. Friends squeezed my hand and told me they were so sorry. Mostly, people looked at me with heavy eyes without knowing the words to say. I was relieved when school was over.

When I got home, every black dress the Gatti girls owned was draped over our living room couches. Elizabeth and I found dresses to wear, but Mom and Charlotte weren't as lucky. My friend Savannah offered to go to the mall to pick out dresses for them. She's a great friend, then and now, always finding ways to take care of me and my family.

When Rebecca was in the hospital during one of my parents' wedding anniversaries, my dad bought my mom a ruby ring. He said the strength she'd displayed throughout her life, especially through being Rebecca's mom, proved her to be a Proverbs 31 woman. He read the chapter over her, and praised her for her godly character:

"An excellent wife who can find? She is far more precious than rubies…Strength and dignity are her clothing, and she laughs at the time to come. She opens her mouth with wisdom, and the teaching of kindness is on her tongue. She looks well to the ways of her household and does not eat the bread of idleness. Her children rise up and call her blessed; her husband also, and he praises her: 'Many women have done excellently, but you surpass them all.' Charm is deceitful, and beauty is vain, but a woman who fears the Lord is to be praised." (Proverbs 31:10,25-30)[1]

The night before Rebecca's funeral, my dad gave Elizabeth, Charlotte, and I ruby necklaces. Through his tears, he told us through being Rebecca's sisters and walking faithfully with God, God has shaped us into strong Proverbs 31 women.

"I can't imagine better sisters for Rebecca and I could not have asked for better daughters. I love y'all so much, and I'm so proud to be your dad." He clasped the necklaces around each of our necks, and we cried together.

The next day was the funeral—the last day we'd see her face until heaven. Traditionally, there is a viewing with the close family before the larger funeral service. Rebecca's funeral was closed-casket, so the viewing was the last time we'd see her. My parents, sisters, and I gathered around her casket. In all Rebecca's life, she'd never looked so calm. She was beautiful in a pure white dress and braided hair. Mom came in early that morning to make it look just right. They even stitched up her lip.

We stood there in silence, leaning on each other. Us girls cried silently, but the room echoed with my dad's sobs. Charlotte gripped his coat sleeve, and her eyes peeked around his arm barely enough for her to see our sister. I'm not sure how much time passed before Dad said, "Let's all pray and thank God for what He has done for us through Rebecca."

I wanted to reject the idea, thinking there is nothing that would make me feel worse than doing that right now. I couldn't take anything else; I was already beyond broken. Being in that room together with her body but knowing she wasn't there made me nauseous. But I knew this was the time for us to grieve and praise God together as a family, even if the pain seemed unbearable.

Dad went first. Then Mom. My parents looked at me to go next, but I shook my head. I wasn't ready. Elizabeth went next. Charlotte couldn't bring herself to speak, burying her head into Mom's black dress.

Now, it's my turn. I let out a shaky breath and prayed silently. *God, help me. Give me the strength to do this. I need You. How can I say goodbye to her?* I reached down and grabbed her hand, placing her fingers around my pointer finger like she always did.

"Rebecca, I love you. Thank you for helping me understand what it means to love God and to live for eternity." I paused and wiped my tears. "You're my best friend. You're strong, brave, and kind. I'll never be able to thank God enough for making me your big sister. You made our family strong and grew our faith. We love you, and we will be with you again soon."

I let go of her hand, then softly stroked the dutch braid my mom stranded together across the crown of her head. It circled the top of her like a halo. I noticed again the similarities in our features and felt grateful that I get to carry a part of her with me in this way. I realized that for the first time, her muscles were completely relaxed. She looked peaceful.

Looking at my sister's face for the last time, I said, "Goodbye, my sweet Becca. I love you." Holding Elizabeth and Charlotte's hands, we walked out of the room. The funeral was next.

The impact her life made was evident by the number of people at her funeral. We combined her visitation and the funeral, so our family stood in front and greeted everyone as they entered. Our church was full. People wrapped around the sanctuary and lined up in the foyer. I looked each of them in the eye and saw the grief they were feeling.

> *I have never felt so close to my family as in these moments when we shared the pain of her loss.*

Some knew us well, and those were the friends I leaned into and let the tears come as we embraced. Others I was meeting for the first time, but they were moved to tears at what they were witnessing.

Our family sat in the front row during the service. The casket was right in front of me, the reality of the tragedy staring me in the face. I have never felt so close to my family as in these moments when we shared the pain of her loss. We all felt the presence of the Holy Spirit comforting us. Apart from His strength, I would not have made it through this day.

Next to the casket was a white frame holding a picture of my beautiful Becca. It's cropped in on her face, but her head is resting on my cheek. You could see my left dimple against her forehead, and my arms wrapped around her holding her close. Her hands were wrapped around my fingers.

My mind wandered back to when it was taken. The picture was from our final set of complete family pictures from our Christmas card the previous year. Behind my Nana and Pops' house is a hill rolling down into a little swamp with lots of trees. Our family always took pictures there.

I remember while Elizabeth and Charlotte alternated taking their individual pictures, I held and bounced Rebecca as I walked around with her. This was one of the only ways we knew how to calm and comfort her. She let out a soft cry, extending her legs slightly.

"Oh, I know, sweet girl. We'll be done very soon and you can take these boots off." Rebecca almost never wore shoes because she never walked. We put little boots on her feet if we were taking pictures or if it was freezing outside. Since we only take family pictures once a year and Louisiana is rarely that cold, Becca wasn't used to shoes and didn't like them. She didn't like most things touching her, so this included shoes.

Almost every outfit of Rebecca's included a loose top, usually with long sleeves, paired with leggings. These tops were easy to flip up to access her feeding tube. The leggings were comfortable for her and made it easier for us to change her diapers. When she died at ten years old, she was 4ft 3in tall and weighed 32 pounds. She got older and taller, but not wider. Her body was long and thin. This made the leggings that fit her waist end in the middle of the shin. We'd cover her feet with socks that came up just below where the leggings stopped.

This day, she was wearing a maroon long-sleeved top with white stripes. The maroon leggings matched her shirt. She wore white socks under her boots. Her foot kicked up slightly and she cried again.

"Alright, let's just be done with these for today, okay?" I slipped off her shoes and placed them on the bricks surrounding the flower bed. I walked us back to where our sisters were taking pictures. The four of us got together to pose for what we didn't know would be one of the last times all together.

"Mom, will you take one of me and Bec?" I straightened her up and rested her head against my cheek. This was the best way for us to show her face in pictures since she wasn't able to hold her head up on her own. Still slightly bouncing her, we pose for the picture. I smiled, and Rebecca leaned into me.

Every time I look at this picture, I want nothing more than to be able to hold her in my arms again. To communicate with her even though she was never able to speak a word. To be able to comfort and care for her despite the many barriers that stood in the way of us knowing and understanding each other. To listen to her and help her voice to be heard. She's my little sister, and I don't know how I am supposed to go on without her here with me.

Throughout the service, I was distracted by my memories of Rebecca. From the family and friends who traveled from all over to be there, I heard the message was beautiful. Our pastor shared the Gospel and spoke of the eternal hope we have in Jesus. My friend Victoria's mom sang.

The four pallbearers lifted her away—what a painstakingly accurate picture of what it looks like for your brothers in Christ to literally bear your burdens. Our family followed them out of the sanctuary. Charlotte remained tucked behind my dad and clung to his arm.

The sunlight bouncing off the white concrete made my eyes squint when I walked outside. We were directed to enter the hearse before they put the casket in the back. We rode as a family to the cemetery in silence. It was a humid, Louisiana August afternoon. I handed my black sweater to my friend when we arrived. The condensation quickly collected on the outside of my water bottle.

There were more prayers and kind words from people I hadn't seen in years. There wasn't time to speak with each of them, but their presence meant more than any words we could have shared. Nothing could remove the pain of Rebecca's absence, but being in the presence of so many who loved her and our family was comforting.

My sisters and I walked with Mom to the casket. She picked off a pink rose for each of us from the beautiful arrangement on top. Charlotte put hers in Dad's front coat pocket. Later, Mom would place these dried flowers into shadow boxes for us along with a pair of Rebecca's socks Miss Cathy knit for her. I'm thankful for this little piece of her to keep with me.

Rebecca was my best friend. She knew all my secrets. She was the first person I told when I liked someone and the person I vented to when I was hurt by a friend. Just holding her, stroking her hair and holding her hands with her face pressed against my chest, was my favorite place to be.

Because of the way I love my sister, I have a better grasp of how the Father loves us as His children. Our family may have to face this storm of deep pain and loss, but I know that each of us could not be more grateful for the miracle of Rebecca in our lives.

HOPE FOR TODAY

Loving Rebecca made death a glaring reality; this makes me even more eager for heaven. Rather than seeing her brain injury as proof that God doesn't care, it is the very thing that proves to me that God loves me beyond all understanding. He blessed me with the most perfect

Walking by faith is not about earning God's love, but responding to the love that's been freely given.

*We can not control what happens to us,
but we can choose how we live through it,
respond to it, and who we trust through it.*

sister who is such a breathtaking representation of His amazing grace. Rebecca has changed my heart, making me not only love God more but others, too. She is a reminder of the brevity of life and how no one is guaranteed anything near perfection on this side of heaven.

God alone changed my eternity, but Rebecca gave me a reason to believe and an opportunity for the Lord to strengthen my faith. It's often in these unexpected hardships that we grow the most. It's in the seasons of tragedies and questions that we learn what it means to lean on His understanding rather than making decisions based on what we can see. Whether it's something large or small, what opportunities have you been given to grow your faith? What is one step you can take today toward trusting God?

We can not control what happens to us, but we can choose how we live through it, respond to it, and who we trust through it. Our lives on this earth are filled with many opportunities to trust God. Each day, every step, every decision, every moment. Walking by faith is not about earning God's love, but responding to the love that's been freely given. Trusting God is an act of faith, not performance. Abiding in Him and depending on His strength each day is the key to enduring whatever may come this side of eternity.

I hope this book has shown you that even when your worst fears come true while your sincerest prayers go unanswered, God is still good and you can still trust Him. This doesn't mean you won't feel fear, grief, or disappointment; it does mean there is a possibility for peace, comfort, and contentment that's not contingent on your circumstances.

After Rebecca died, I didn't think I would ever feel genuine joy again. Over time, God has brought healing to my heart and light back into my soul. I still miss her every day, and I can't wait to be reunited with her in heaven. I can't see the full scope of what the Lord is doing, and there are still times when I question why He didn't write Rebecca a different story. Even still, I find rest knowing that God doesn't need me to completely understand Him to wholeheartedly trust Him. God is kind, and He brings beauty in His perfect timing. I hope you find peace and rest by trusting God right where you are.

Afterword

We were in an orphanage in El Salvador on a mission trip when Katherine was in middle school. She held a sick baby, and I saw God give that sweet baby comfort through Katherine. For years, she planned mission trips to Haiti and the children flocked to her, playing with her hair and listening to every word of the Gospel. Just like her mother and sisters, Katherine intentionally brings light to darkness. She's been through the darkness and is an ambassador of God's light. I love being her dad.

I remember being at the hospital with the love of my life waiting on our third child. I knew before the doctors admitted it that something was wrong. I watched as they scrambled short-handed to find anyone to help with the C-section. Precious hours were lost. When I saw Rebecca for the first time in the NICU, she looked just like Katherine. She was in intense, unconsolable pain; my grief and anxiety were overwhelming. All hope felt lost.

The deceptive question of "Why?" kept interrupting my thoughts. My analytical brain went on unintentional, repetitive spirals of possible explanations and outcomes. I could not turn it off. I feared my other daughters would walk away from their young faith and never look back. No one would blame them if the light within them grew dim. I couldn't have known this grief I wanted to guard them against would be the very thing that helped them cling to God.

While I was on my knees in the hospital in prayer, the Holy Spirit reminded me of Proverbs 3:5: "Trust in the Lord with all your heart, and do not lean on your own understanding." On that day, I made a decision to trust God and forgive the mistakes made even though I didn't understand. God gave our family the power to get better and not bitter. Please know that anything we did as a family was accomplished because God equipped us through His Word and wisdom to face grief with faith.

Katherine spent many hours researching what really happened to Rebecca. She read Rebecca's medical records, looked at videos, and talked to witnesses. Even though it has been sixteen years since Rebecca's birth, the smells and sounds of the traumatic memories easily flooded my mind and heart during these conversations. I wept uncontrollably retelling the stories. Opening up those deep wounds was very painful for all of us. But if one person is encouraged by this book as they walk through a difficult time, it's all worth it.

I always enjoy hearing of healing miracles. Many books have been written to commemorate answered prayers. *Wholehearted Trust* addresses growing your faith in a fallen world when things don't work out according to prayers or plans. I hope this book showed you how to respond to a crisis without losing your faith. I encourage you to come back to these words or share them with a friend who is facing deep grief; God is with you in the overwhelming sadness and unanswered prayers.

— RYAN GATTI, KATHERINE'S DAD

Stories from Rebecca's Family

While *Wholehearted Trust* reflected on Rebecca's life, I wanted to share with you a glimpse into my family's perspectives in real time. At different points after Rebecca was born in 2007, we all turned to writing to process our grief, document her story, and share lessons we learned. Collected here are just a few of the many pieces the five of us have written.

The writings from my parents are excerpts from their Gatti Girls Blog, which was started to keep friends and family updated on Rebecca's health (see **gattigirls.blogspot.com** for more). The ones by my sisters and I are essays we wrote for school. They are ordered chronologically and marked with the author's name and age. Read through our hopes, prayers, and disappointments as we fought to trust God through it all. I pray they serve as an encouragement to you through whatever storm you are enduring.

"BLESSINGS" BY SUSAN GATTI (AGE 31)
JUNE 16, 2007

So often God bestows blessings on us all so freely that we take them for granted. For example, we take for granted that our children will be delivered into this world healthy and rather uneventfully. We take for granted that we will be able to hold our child after their birth. We take for granted that we will be able to introduce siblings to the new baby shortly after their birth. The examples are endless, as are the lessons that this experience and my children are likely to teach me. I will no longer take my childrens' health for granted. I will do my best to appreciate every smile, every touch, every word from my children—and so much more, in the good moments as well as the bad.

My Rebecca is one of many examples of God's miracles of healing. Only God can restore her health completely, and I fully believe in His power to do just that. He knitted her together in my womb and is the only One who can restore her. Her life was saved for a purpose. It has already demanded the faith of her family that God is in control.

When my baby was taken from my being, she was without life. While I heard the physician's words, "Oh My Lord," and I did not hear the sound of my baby, only one thought brought me solace: GOD IS IN CONTROL. God chose to heal her, to allow her sisters the opportunity to hold her hand, and to bless her family with her homecoming. The blessings that have been bestowed upon our family are a result of God's grace. There are many unanswered questions left, and we remain in a place of faith. I am more appreciative than words can express that I have an almighty and merciful God in which to place my faith in rather than the things of this flawed world. I pray that each of you can recognize and appreciate all the blessings, big and small, that God has provided to you. Mostly, I pray that each of us can take solace in the fact that God is in control.

"LESSONS FROM A 7-YEAR-OLD" BY SUSAN GATTI (AGE 31) JUNE 21, 2007

As my Katherine was taking care of her mother and her baby sister, she shared her insight with me. She told me that we do not deserve such a wonderful gift. Katherine said that we make so many mistakes and sin so much that it is amazing God would give us a beautiful baby girl. We can all gain some perspective from the God-given wisdom of a child.

"OUR MIRACLE" BY SUSAN GATTI (AGE 31)
JULY 18, 2007

I write this to assure each of you and to announce that Rebecca is a miracle of God. People say she never should have opened her eyes following her birth. They said she would likely need a feeding tube. But I say to you, God is faithful. His Word is living and His grace is true. We prayed for her to breathe independently—she did. We prayed for her kidneys to function independently—they did. We prayed for her to be able to regulate her temperature—she did. We prayed for her to be able to eat—she did. We prayed for her to not only be able to eat, but to nurse—she did.

All of these acts and so many more are evidence of God's love and faithfulness, and He is not finished with her yet. God has healed my child—He has made her whole. Surely her life has already been more successful and meaningful than my own. For we were made to worship our Father and to introduce the lost to Him. Rebecca started working in His fields to increase His harvest from her first breath. May each of you who reads this know the Father who forgives our sins and cures all diseases and the Son who was wounded and sacrificed that we may be healed.

"PLACING FAITH" BY SUSAN GATTI (AGE 31)
JULY 26, 2007

I now recognize that many of you are using this site to keep up with Rebecca's health. She has been through a great deal since my last post. In summary, she was placed on a medication that is not appropriate for infants. Since she metabolized the medication so quickly, her episodes worsened again. Following an additional hospitalization, God led us to Dallas Children's Medical Center where we were treated with compassionate and knowledgeable physicians and staff. Following the immediate treatment of her seizures, another EEG confirmed that she was in fact having seizures. Nothing was stated that suggested Dystonia, which means we do not know whether this is present or not. They had already started her on the appropriate medication when the seizure was recorded. She appeared to be on an appropriate dosage, but she has had additional episodes. The recent seizures have been much less severe. We are following up with our pediatrician today to check her medication levels.

What has sustained us all during this process is that our faith has been in the Lord to direct us, not the physicians. No offense intended to medical professionals. The Lord guided us from physicians without much hope to physicians that have clearly seen and believe in God's workmanship and healing.

Please continue to pray for Rebecca. The most pressing need for her right now is for her seizures to be controlled and for her to be able to latch on and take a bottle with ease. Overall, she is doing much better. In the past, she has either been crying or sleeping. She has clearly been in a great deal of pain over the last several weeks. With the new medication it is as though we have our baby back most of the time. She sits contently and explores her environment as a baby should. Her sisters are at long last able to hold her and kiss her again. Thank you for your thoughts and prayers.

"A SECRET TRUTH" BY SUSAN GATTI (AGE 31)
JULY 28, 2007

I am now more terrified because not only has Ryan informed others about this site, but it also appears that people are reading it. Thank you for your compliments. Please know that I may not always respond appropriately to them. My verbal abilities have always been questionable. What I want to convey is that it is not by my vision that I am able to see things clearly or by my strength that I am standing. It is God and God alone. Do not be convinced that I am always in a clear mind or strong either. For each day I ask God for the strength and wisdom to make it through the day (as well as anything else He knows I may need).

What I am about to share may have you convinced that I need to be institutionalized or convinced that God revealed a secret truth to me. I am hoping it is the latter. The other day I was watching the typical lives of those around me continuing as usual. I was alone with Rebecca at that moment. God revealed a secret to me that was too amazing to keep to myself and too mysterious for words to describe. I believe that He intended it to be too difficult to convey with words so that He alone has the power to reveal the truth in His perfect timing to each of us. I will do my best to describe it for you. It had something to do with the nothingness with which we consume ourselves and the temporary nature of this life. It had to do with the beauty of His grace and His eternity. For this life is not intended to be about us but about our Creator. What we do has eternal meaning only to the extent that it brings glory to God. I pray that each of you who reads this may also experience this secret truth that was revealed to me.

"SCHOOL BEGINS" BY SUSAN GATTI (AGE 31)
AUGUST 15, 2007

Welcome to the day Katherine started school. Much to our amazement, our oldest baby started 2nd grade! Rebecca looked around for sources of entertainment. Katherine had left for school, and Elizabeth was sleeping off a respiratory infection. Rebecca was not happy with the result—only a mom to entertain. Fortunately Katherine arrived home after not too long and saved her. To add insult to injury, I had to go back to work this week, and Elizabeth begins preschool after Labor Day. Preschool can begin for Elizabeth because she accomplished her summer goal—swimming independently across the pool!

I apologize for the lack of posts—not typically a good sign. Let me get the health updates out of the way. When we returned from Dallas, Rebecca continued to have seizures. To complicate things her seizures have also presented similar to an infantile reaction to severe gastric reflux. We confirmed the presence of reflux and adjusted her medications and things improved. Now it was Elizabeth's turn. She suffered from a very high fever and vomiting as a result of an upper respiratory infection for several days. Rebecca was next to share in the illness. We are still trying to return her to health and stop the vomiting. Nutrition is far too critical for her at this point for her to lose any nutrients. My prayer warriors need to pray that the vomiting has been a result of the infections and not a more lasting GI complication. We have an appointment to make sure it is not the latter. Katherine has now started coughing, and dad is taking Tylenol Sinus. I believe God has bestowed immune systems of steel to mothers.

Yes, you did read that I returned to work and survived. I was pleasantly surprised that I have some memory left! As I struggle with leaving my children, I was given the knowledge that **as long as we glorify God in our actions these actions are worthwhile.** I was highly remorseful because it occurred to me that my past work actions have not glorified God. I have not consistently prayed over each child and family I have worked with in the past. I had neglected to use my work to serve the Lord in the most simple of ways. This error has been corrected. My limited knowledge from graduate school and working experience has been helpful professionally and personally. However, I am only an endlessly flawed sinner. My direction needs to come from the Lord if I am to make wise decisions. I have told several friends that my psychology books have been on the shelf collecting dust, and my Bible and spiritual books are on my nightstand. I now recognize that this needs to happen in both my home and my work if my professional career is to be worthwhile. I pray that each of you is able to find a way to make your actions worthwhile, and I would appreciate the same prayer for me in return!

"GOD'S UNDERSTANDING" BY SUSAN GATTI (AGE 31) AUGUST 16, 2007

Those of you who know me best can appreciate a colleague declaring the SGSTS (Susan Gatti Scattered Thought Syndrome) in my honor. The scattered thoughts raced through my head as I am not even attempting to sleep yet. I am thinking of all the comments people have made to me, all well intended. Some comments are worthy of a blog and some not so worthy. I would just like each of you to have a reference point for your thoughts that orient you to my own. Perhaps this perspective can help you as you talk with those who have been through a difficult time.

I am NOT skilled to understand what has happened to my family.

I have often cried and repeatedly stated that I do not understand. Each time I come to the same conclusion: **I do not have to understand because God does.** Some comments from others and thoughts from my own head have questioned the timing of Rebecca's birth. Some statements have even questioned her revival in fear of a difficult life. Many remarks have noted nothing was wrong prior to that night. Please remember that it is not our place to question God's plan for our lives or the lives of those we love. His understanding is perfect. I believe that when I am seated next to my Heavenly Father He will have some "videos" prepared for me. One will demonstrate what my life and the life of my family would have been like if Rebecca's birth had occurred without complication—the other if Rebecca had not survived. Perhaps only then will I completely understand why she has had to endure the pain and suffering she has. Until that time, I trust that God knows best and remains in control. He will sustain my family and carry out His plan according to His good and perfect will.

"MIRACLES" BY SUSAN GATTI (AGE 31)
AUGUST 31, 2007

I cannot count the number of times that others or myself have made the following statement: "How could people directly see Jesus perform miracles and then doubt and lack faith?" Given recent experiences, I have been forced to ask whether we are any different. My evidence lies in the beautiful blue of my sweet Becca. Not only did non-blue-eyed parents contribute to her genetics, but she is now four months old. It is by God's grace alone that she has been spared. So many miracles have occurred on her behalf in such a short time period, yet some assume the worst outcome possible for her as a foregone conclusion. This assumption leaves no room for the possibility of continued miracles in spite of evidence to the contrary. Rebecca is doing very well. She started to take a bottle so well that we decided to begin nursing again. This has been a blessing for us both. This, in combination with her recovery from the upper respiratory infection, has resulted in her being much more content.

She has also begun to talk to her sister Katherine and myself. Rebecca even manages a partial smile as we smile at her. She also enjoys pushing up off her loved ones and supporting her weight on her elbows. She had her follow-up visit to neurology in Dallas where we learned that her head circumference had not changed in two months, which suggests that her brain is not growing at an acceptable rate. So, prayer warriors out there can continue to pray for the healing and appropriate development and recovery of her brain. We have already seen some growth in her circumference since the visit. Thank you all for your ongoing prayers and support.

"THOUGHT FOR THE DAY" BY SUSAN GATTI (AGE 31)
SEPTEMBER 11, 2007

A thought for myself that perhaps someone else will benefit from as well: I hope to live in appreciation of what I have been blessed with rather than spend my time focusing on what I do not have.

"PRAYER REQUEST" BY SUSAN GATTI (AGE 31)
SEPTEMBER 23, 2007

To all of you prayer warriors out there, please keep Rebecca and her sisters in your prayers. Over the last two weeks Rebecca has had "tremors" for lack of a better word. They became troublesome by increasing in frequency and severity last Thursday. They make her very upset, tense, and uncomfortable. We have tried to adjust her medication to control them unsuccessfully. So, we are back to Dallas tomorrow whether they want us or not. We need to make sure that these are not seizures that she is continuing to experience. Please pray for her healing, for the physician's wisdom, and for her sisters as they go without their mom, dad, and baby sister once again.

"REBECCA UPDATE" BY RYAN GATTI (AGE 33)
SEPTEMBER 26, 2007

After a few weeks of calm, Rebecca started having seizures last Wednesday. This concerned us because she is on strong medicine and should not be seizing or having spasms. We decided to go back to Dallas to have her medicine changed. The seizures became worse in frequency and duration, so the doctors decided to run an EEG.

Rebecca's EEG was not good. In fact, the doctor told us that the test results could not be worse. She is having what seem to be constant seizures and spasms. The neurological team has changed her medicine and she is now on several different kinds of seizure medicines. We will have an MRI tomorrow and another EEG before the end of the week. A feeding tube has been placed in her nose so she can continue to get nourishment. The medicine has sedated her and she cannot suckle a bottle.

Susan has remained very strong through all of this; she is a true woman of God, and God has kept us close to Him during the last few weeks. We can feel all the prayers for our peace of mind and wisdom in making decisions.

Please continue to pray that Rebecca will not suffer and the wonderful doctors at Dallas Children's Medical Center will continue to meet her physical and our spiritual needs. Also, I ask that you specifically pray for Susan's mom and dad, Al and Marcia Lockhart, as they have really been a blessing in caring for, loving, and nurturing Rebecca.

When we left Monday morning, we thought this would be a quick trip to Dallas for a medicine change. We were not prepared for the news that we received. Please pray for Katherine and Elizabeth as they go through this tough time with their sisters' illness. Pray that this experience will draw them closer to God.

Once again, thanks to all of you for your prayers and kind words.

"DALLAS NEWS" BY SUSAN GATTI (AGE 31)
OCTOBER 4, 2007

I apologize for not having posted sooner. Things get hectic when you are unexpectedly gone for a week and illness strikes upon your return. The Gatti girls are temporarily camped out at their grandparents' house, not due to their illness, but to their daddy's illness. Ryan has been struck with an awful bug that the rest of us are trying to avoid while giving him some much needed rest.

We returned home on Sunday from Dallas. I will do my best to inform you from the technical to the layman's lingo. Official terminology on the discharge papers is as follows: severe hypoxic-ischemic encephalopathy with secondary infantile spasms, hypsarrhythmia with intractable seizures, and severe developmental delay. Translation—before and after her birth Rebecca suffered from a lack of oxygen to her brain for an extended period of time. This resulted in a significant injury to her brain, which has resulted in a loss of structure to her brain overall and in critical areas, as well as a lack of appropriate brain growth. Her brain also has not developed much, if any, myelin sheath, which typically occurs by six months of age. This is what allows the electronic impulses to travel and allow the brain to communicate effectively with the rest of the body. Rebecca is now over five months old. This has resulted in a disorganized pattern of electronic impulses in her brain and the development of infantile spasms. This makes it difficult to differentiate what are seizures and what are involuntary muscle movements.

In the neurologist's words: "The EEG could not look any worse." The pattern is typically associated with profound delays, which is what they predict for Rebecca. In their words, she may never sit up or crawl or do many basic things. Her seizure activity is likely to continue, and the medical professionals hope only to be able to make the level of activity manageable for Rebecca. The delays are already evident. At one point, she was looking at us and tracking, but even these basic skills are no longer present. She is currently functioning as a baby of less than one month of age. However, the neurologists were surprised at the amount of brain matter left given her history, and she has done things that are unexpected. She has gained weight and tolerated feedings well.

To dismiss rumors: she is no longer in imminent danger of dying. At one point in the hospital her seizures were severe and not stopping in spite of medication. During this time she received a great deal of medication that placed her at-risk to stop breathing as they loaded her and rescued her with several medications. This risk has passed.

The good news is Rebecca remains in God's hands. Only He knows what He has planned for her life. Someone who loves Rebecca very much reminded the doctors (who were telling us that everything happens for a reason) that everyone has two main purposes in life: to love/serve God and to take as many people with you to heaven as possible. Rebecca is already fulfilling her purpose. If she or her sisters have touched your life in a special way, please leave a comment that I can share with them to help them gain a more complete understanding of the true purpose of living. Thank you for your continued prayer and support.

"ALL I WANT FOR CHRISTMAS" BY SUSAN GATTI (AGE 31) DECEMBER 14, 2007

I never have been one to receive gifts well. My responses are always so awkward that the person giving the gift has surely regretted it. Perhaps this is because I do not typically want tangible gifts. The same is true now more than ever. There is nothing I want that someone can purchase or make. This year, I can honestly say there is only one thing that I want for Christmas. This is a gift that only my Heavenly Father can grant: I want my Rebecca to be healed.

I recognize that this is a loaded request. I want her to stop hurting and suffering. I want to see her smile. Perhaps I have not updated the website because I want to share the positive with you. However, there has been no change for Rebecca, which actually makes it worse. She is almost eight months old and has lost her ability to track objects with her eyes and her ability to look at others. We have yet to see any purposeful movement from her. Her brain is not growing, and her seizures and spasms are not stopping. A recent increase in medication is hoped to improve her condition, but it has not as of yet. I expect we will be adding yet another medication for her in January to help ease her suffering and to hopefully stop her seizures.

Her doctors give us the expectation for her to function somewhere within the severe to profound range of retardation. Translation, she may never do many simple things such as sit up. For example, right now her "mental age" is that of less than a one month old baby, so she is not expected to do anything that a one month old can do. This is why she appears so young to most who see her.

I paint a bleak picture intentionally. She was dead for a minimum of fifteen minutes, much likely for a lot longer in utero. The doctors expect very little from her. It is a miracle that she is able to eat, and she has been able to eat baby food as well as take a bottle. Everything she does is a direct result of God's grace. Anything she is ever able to do will continue to be a direct result of God's grace. Please continue to pray for this mother's deepest wish. For God is not confined by the parameters of this physical world and all things are possible through Him. May you each feel the full weight of your blessings this Christmas season.

"THANK YOU" BY RYAN GATTI (AGE 33)
MARCH 1, 2008

I just wanted to thank each of you for your prayers and I thank God each day for everyone who calls or emails to uplift us. It is amazing how I can hold Rebecca while she is seizing and not cry, but a kind word, note, card, or email reminds us of God's working through the members of the body of the church and our tears begin. God is good and His presence is evidenced in the persons who pray for us and request that He keeps us close. It is evidenced in the hope that we have in our eternal life and our gift of salvation.

Many of you have said that we are strong, but we are not—any strength you see in us is Christ. God provides us with the strength to get up and make it through the day. He is carrying us through this and He gives me enough troubled grace each day to make it through. I will be honest that some days, when I take my eyes off Him, I sink into darkness much like Peter sank in the sea. Pray that Susan, Katherine, Elizabeth, and I keep our focus on Christ. We crave heaven now more than ever. Please pray that no weapon formed by the enemy will be successful against our family. I may not have the words to thank you for your prayers today, but I thank God for your kind thoughts and prayers for our family. Also, when you are going through something like this, you don't always know what to pray for, so please pray for us.

Rebecca is now ten months old. She is having no purposeful movement as a result of her brain injury and we were told a few weeks ago at the neurology appointment that her beautiful blue eyes are blind. Although she responds to light she has cortical blindness. Her seizures and spasms are still constant, but the medicine numbs her response. We have changed her medicine numerous times, but she is now on topamax, clonazepam, depakote, amoxicillin, and prevacid. Because the seizures and spasms are still present, even on these meds, our neurologist has suggested that we try hormone therapy. This will not heal her, because her injury is permanent and severe; however, it may ease her constant pain. During this treatment she can develop ulcers and her immune system will be greatly compromised. So please pray for her comfort and health and that we will have the strength to make it through this next round of searching for her comfort.

Susan and I are not really sure why this is happening. It is deeply painful to hold a child that is seizing because you know that it is painful, but you cannot help. When I read or talked to her while she was in Susan's womb, she always responded to my voice. She would roll around in mama's tummy when her sisters would read to her. Now, she cannot respond and we don't know if she can even perceive that we are here. There's nothing you can do to stop the neurons from short circuiting around the dead cells in her brain, the unwanted contractions of muscles and the failure of other muscles to rest or respond.

It is also painful, because Rebecca does not smile, laugh, giggle, coo, reach for you, or do anything else that her sisters did when they were young. She most likely will never do these things. But I know one day I will walk with her in heaven and I will not be amazed that she is healed, because we will be in the presence of Christ and He will have our full attention. God is good and His love is everlasting. I worry now less about where my girls will go to college; I worry more about where they will spend eternity. Where will you be in 500 years? Take a minute and reflect, what are you doing today that will count 500 years from now.

In the last ten months, I have studied endless information about pediatric neurology, obstetrics, gynecology, infant brain injuries, nursing, fetal heart monitors, placentas, and seizure disorders. I thank all my friends who are nurses and doctors who have helped us understand what happened to Rebecca during birth. She was perfect in the womb. If you're about to have a baby, I urge you to read about the birthing process and study it. Do not be afraid to ask questions. Dads, you must thoroughly interview the person who will take care of your wife.

There really is no protocol for resuscitation of a baby. One doctor told us that he would not have resuscitated Rebecca after five minutes without a heartbeat; Rebecca did not have a heartbeat until fifteen minutes after delivery yet resuscitation continued. I have not found a neurologist yet that would tell me that Rebecca would have a good outcome with a 0 Apgar score at 10+ minutes.

I did not know until a few weeks after Rebecca was born that Susan was so close to death—she lost so much blood that she could have passed away. I thank God each day that Susan is still here; by all accounts she should have died. I shudder to think what our family would be like without Susan. It is a blessing and a miracle from God that she is alive.

Susan feeds Rebecca and this takes quite some time because Rebecca's seizures disrupt feedings; however, she is still able to take a bottle. Rebecca has no control over her muscles. So she is either limp or experiences random contractions of different muscle groups. Daily life is horrible in a situation like this. Luckily, God gives us enough anesthetic to numb the pain, but not so much that we cannot experience suffering and draw closer to Him. He is faithful to His promise to transform us if we are willing to seek Him; however, conforming to the sadness in this world is a daily struggle.

Rebecca's head circumference has not changed in several months. This is a major concern because it means her brain was so damaged that it has stopped growing. This is common in babies who go without oxygen for longer periods of time. Also, she has certain muscle groups that stay contracted constantly, so the complementary muscle groups do not flex and therefore don't grow.

I did not comprehend the severity of this until we were at Children's Medical Center in Dallas last year. Our doctor asked if we were having trouble changing her diaper because of her muscle contractions in her legs. I told her that we could massage her legs and she would eventually relax so that we could change her diaper and wipe her. Then she said we should always take the time during a diaper change to perform a few basic physical therapy steps with legs and hips. I gave a puzzled look and she said, "This will make it easier when you are changing her diapers when she is six or seven, sometimes the contractions make it to where you cannot open the hips to change the diaper and that can be problematic."

I am glad God was with me that day. It was His strength that kept me from falling to the ground and weeping. After all we had been through, I thought nothing could surprise me, but this did. This statement seemed so matter-of-fact to the doctor. It had not been revealed to me that she would never stop using diapers. I knew she was going to miss out on a lot of things, but I didn't realize that she would not advance at all. In responding to the overwhelming crisis, I had really not looked that far down the road. Susan, because of her occupation, had known for a long time what the long term outcome would be. This was a long, quiet ride home.

Good news: God is still in control.

Susan had to resign from her job as Associate Professor at LSU Health Science Center. I asked her to pray about it and it was hard, but she decided to resign and give up her position so she could continue to be with Rebecca full-time. So, we were going to eventually lose our health insurance. My concern was health insurance for Rebecca, as I could not find anyone to insure our family. A few days after she resigned, I received a call that a judgeship was opening at the workers' compensation court. I applied and was hired! The insurance is with the same company that Susan had at LSU! Lesson: Turn it over to God, take a step in faith, and He will provide.

I was working two jobs and Susan was taking care of Rebecca around the clock. This was wearing her out mentally and physically and we had no time to share with each other or Katherine and Elizabeth. I wanted to help her get through this, so several months ago I started calling around. I called several nurse staffing places and could not find anyone to return a call to even offer a few hours of help during the day giving medicine or letting Susan rest while I was at work. Back in July, God placed a man in our hospital room one day who came to comfort us and told us a story of his grandson and a special nanny who was taking care of him. Months later, I randomly bought a paper (I always read it online). I began reading and noticed a child had passed away. It was the man's grandson. I prayed about it and asked Susan to call him to inquire about the nanny. God put it on my heart to have her call, even though it was awkward. He immediately called back and said that he had been hoping for her to find a good job with a good family because she has been such a blessing to his family. He remembered visiting with us and referred her to us. So she came by and introduced herself. She has over thirty years of experience working with terminal and special needs children. She lives within a mile of our house. She loves Rebecca and has only been with us a week, but she is an angel from heaven. Lesson: God is not bound by time; He sees your whole life at the same time and He will put people in your path to bless you when it is most beneficial to you. Also, obeying God usually makes you feel awkward, or different from the world, so if it seems awkward, then God is more than likely a part of it.

We talk to God more now about things that really matter. For some reason, I cannot go to God anymore with certain prayer requests. I can only ask for Him to guide me and carry me.

"THE VALLEY" BY RYAN GATTI (AGE 33)
APRIL 5, 2008

Once again, thank you all for your prayers and kind words. Please continue to pray for us over these next few weeks as Rebecca goes through hormone therapy. Please pray that we will welcome God's will. God bless you all.

Rebecca is still having seizures with the hormone therapy. The medicine is aggravating her stomach and she sometimes throws up her bottles. Please pray for her comfort and that the medicine will stop her seizures.

Her birthday is coming up in a few weeks, please pray that we make it through that time. There are so many hard memories from her first year, it is overwhelming. Please pray for Susan and the girls to get through this.

I cleaned out the garage. Haven't had time to do it over the last year in getting ready for the baby and dealing with the aftermath of her birth. I was going through things to take to the Biedenharn House when I stumbled across a plastic storage box. It was full of baby toys. Then, I remembered getting them down from the attic at the beginning of April 2007 to put in Rebecca's room. Susan had saved baby toys that were Katherine and Elizabeth's favorites. Last May, I was going to wipe the toys down and put them in Rebecca's room, but we never got around to it.

One toy was a piano that Elizabeth would pound on. Another was a cube with specially shaped holes in the sides that you place the correctly shaped block in the correct hole. There were also a few hardback baby books like *Good Night Moon* and *Polar Bear, Polar Bear*. These were books Katherine read to Elizabeth to teach her to read. It was hard for Susan and me to put these back in the attic. I guess, in the back of my mind, I have left them out all this time in case she got better.

"THE BIRTHDAY" BY SUSAN GATTI (AGE 32)
APRIL 25, 2008

Friday April 25, 2008, was Rebecca's first birthday. I thank all of you for your continued prayers. Rebecca's condition has not improved, but we are hopeful for a miracle if it is within God's plan for her.

"THE INFAMOUS QUESTION" BY SUSAN GATTI (AGE 32)
MAY 6, 2008

No matter where I go, there is one question I am naturally guaranteed to be asked: "How is the baby?" There is no way for the numerous persons asking to know just how difficult of a question it is to answer. I will try to provide a more complete answer for those few who keep updated through this blog. In providing this answer, I feel compelled to make you aware that the answer is unlikely to change—possibly ever.

Rebecca's daily life is something that I am not sure anyone can comprehend. She continues to have almost constant seizures. This is difficult to understand for those who do not know much about seizure activity other than the dramatic scenes provided in the movies. However, reality is much different. She experiences a wide variety of seizure types, which result from her incomprehensible brain injury. Seizures are merely a "misfiring" of the brain and its neural pathways.

Rebecca's brain is severely impaired as a result of the extended time period that it went without oxygen (that she was dead). You have to understand that she was completely dead for at least fifteen minutes after her birth and for an undetermined amount of time prior to her birth. There is little comparison for us because persons do not usually become revived after this time. This lack of oxygen and reintroduction of oxygen resulted in detrimental injuries. Even though the brain is supposed to increase in size dramatically over the first year of a child's life, Rebecca likely has less brain matter now than she did prior to her birth. Furthermore, as of the last MRI the brain did not develop the "white matter" necessary for her brain to communicate with her body. As a result, her seizure activity stems from multiple locations in the brain and is very difficult to control.

She has infantile spasms (a condition that makes anyone aware of it shudder). This is just a special kind of seizure that is associated with very negative outcomes for a child's development and for the ability to control the seizures. Each of these is evidenced in Rebecca. Her seizures vary from her eyes deviating to her head jerking to her legs/arms bicycling. They happen so frequently and so differently that it is impossible to track how many occur in even a day or an hour. Some appear to be a welcomed escape for her while others seem to scare her into a horrific state of fear. A recent trip to the neurologist made me aware that not only does the medical world not expect her to ever be seizure-free, but it appears that the physician does not necessarily expect them to be any more controlled than their current state. Eventually, it is expected that the infantile spasms will transform to a syndrome that is characteristic of multiple and varied seizures that are potentially far worse in presentation than she currently experiences. Furthermore, the longer the infantile spasms occur without response to treatment, the worse the prognosis is for seizure activity and developmental outcomes. Rebecca has had these spasms without improvement since she was five months old.

A recent trip to the eye doctor also revealed that Rebecca is "not processing visual stimuli," as we had expected. Translation, she is not seeing anything. The doctor informed us that this is due to either the constant seizure activity masking processing abilities or to a lack of ability to process visual information in the brain as a result of its injury. Rebecca also has problems with congestion that is interfering with her ability to eat. She has a blackened tooth and tongue as a result of all the medication she takes. Rebecca has not yet smiled or indicated any enjoyment of life. She has no purposeful movement, and her muscle tone increases (tightens). We have an appointment tomorrow to determine how she is processing auditory information. We do know that she startles to loud sounds, but does not process the information to the point that she can orient toward sound.

I believe that this is a fairly full account of "how Rebecca is doing." Having said all this, it is impossible to convey the emotions of a mother's heart. I love her dearly. I am glad I can hold her, am saddened by her pain, and am aggravated when she does not allow my kisses (which is most of the time). She is able to communicate her emotions very clearly in spite of an absence of words or smiles. If you doubt this, come by when she is getting her medicine. You don't even need to come in, you will hear her communicating from the street.

It does seem to be the worst kind of punishment to have to wait for heaven to completely meet her, but I believe we will recognize each other. As many of you know, my husband says our time here is "the dot" and our time in heaven "the line." I will have spent far more time with her in heaven than we can imagine here in the dot. God has assured me that she will be in heaven waiting, and I believe that part of her already is. As for my other girls, they have the opportunity to choose their eternal destiny. I can only pray that they will join their baby sister in heaven. I trust that in the presence of God's glory, we will be hard-pressed to mourn the experiences we missed with Rebecca during this mere dot.

After writing this, I am likely to get the other infamous question: "How are you doing?" I fear I have no good answer other than I am not doing anything. It is through the grace of God alone that I am able to breathe, to stand, and to act. Sometimes I feel as if I am the silver being purified, but as long as God the Father is the silversmith I am in good hands. One thing is certain, God is still in control.

P.S. This is a formal announcement that Ryan appears to have hijacked my blog as a result of my neglect and a formal apology for the picture he posted (which will be removed) of me on the eve of the greatest sickness I have had in fifteen years.

"CABLE TV" BY RYAN GATTI (AGE 34)
FEBRUARY 26, 2009

About ten months before Rebecca was born, our pastor Dr. Fred Lowery gave a sermon on how people in church are not significantly different from people that don't go to church. Same or higher rates of divorce, addictions, and TV viewing. He challenged us to think of what God could do in our life if we acted like we were supposed to and maybe even gave up TV. Dr. Fred also said we should spend quantity time with our kids and that is the only way that we can get quality time. He also said kids spell love T-I-M-E.

I wasn't ready to give up my vices, so I thought I would give up TV and spend more time with my kids. I was going to show God how good I was by giving up FOX News, HGTV, Seinfeld, NFL, and Tiger Football. I had no idea what He had in store for me. At that point in my life, that was a sacrifice. The girls got restless without TV, so I bought all nine seasons of *Little House on the Prairie* for them to watch. And for the next ten months, that's all we watched. Sounds corny, but me and my kids could tell you anything about *Little House*.

We also heard a sermon that talked about how infinite eternity was. I read a book about how the time between birth and death, geometrically, is like a dot, and that the time after our death is like a line. The dot represents our time between birth and death and the line represents our eternal life. The majority of our life happens after we take our last breath here on earth. After I read the book, Katherine asked me where her great grandmother was, who had passed away. I told her that Nanny was in heaven and that we would spend more time with her in heaven than we could ever spend with her here on earth because most of our life happens after we take our last breath on this earth. That comforted her. I almost did not tell her this, because I thought it would be too much for her to wrap her mind around.

Months passed.

The night Rebecca was born the whole family was in the waiting room. Katherine was interviewing everyone with the video camera and Elizabeth was coloring with Hollye-Faye. Labor was taking longer than expected and the doctor seemed to be acting unconcerned. Susan went into shock and she was given oxygen. A fear came over me that I had not felt. As the nurses rushed around, I walked over to Susan and asked her, "Are you ready for the worst case scenario?" She pulled the oxygen mask away from her face and said, "Yes." I asked, "Who are we relying on?" She pulled down the mask and said, "God." Her voice was strained and quiet. Even though there was chaos in the room, peace was in both of us.

I then called my brother Robbie from my cell phone and asked him to get everyone together in the waiting room and pray. Eventually, the doctor decided to do a C-section. We later found out that he had misplaced the internal monitor and therefore what was supposed to be Rebecca's heartbeat on the monitor was Susan's. As they whisked Susan next door for a C-section, they told me to go to the lobby and wait. I kneeled down in the hallway and prayed. God gave me peace and told me not to rely on my own understanding. He reminded me of Peter walking on water to meet Christ. As long as Peter kept his eyes on Christ, he did not sink, but once he focused on the storm, he sank. So I knew that I had to stay focused in my mind's eye on Christ. Believe me, this worked. He told me not to rely on my own understanding because I am a nerd and I have to figure things out. He reminded me of Peter because Peter got a scolding from Christ ("ye of little faith") and because I was new in my faith.

The next few hours were crazy. The baby was transported to NICU in south Shreveport and Susan stayed at Willis Knighton Bossier. Susan's mom and dad stayed with her and I stayed with Rebecca. Curt and Jeff took me to WK South at 2:00 in the morning.

At 6:00 a.m. they clean the NICU so everyone has to leave. I went back to Bossier to wake up our girls and tell them what had happened. They are smart, just like their mom. They are intuitive and loving.

It was a long drive from WK South to North Bossier, so I had time to think about how I would tell the girls that their sister had died, was revived but was in severe pain, and their mom was going to be in the hospital away from Rebecca for a few days. I thought about each of their personalities and how I could tell them without upsetting them. This could be the most important conversation I ever had with them in their life and I just prayed that God would give me the words to comfort them and keep them from losing faith in Him. I planned a ten minute explanation that I thought would cover both of them and leave them with hope and understanding.

I called ahead and told Elizabeth Guice, who took them home from the hospital and stayed with them, to start waking them up. I got home and told them I needed to talk to them about something serious. They were still excited from the night before. So I told them again that we needed to sit at the kitchen table, because I wanted to be serious.

At that time, Katherine was seven and Elizabeth was four. They both sat near me and I said, "You know girls, sometimes babies come easy and sometimes they come and it's difficult..."

Before I could finish my sentence Elizabeth said, "You mean like on *Little House* when baby Charles died?" Then Katherine put her arm around ME and said, "You know Dad, we're gonna spend more time in heaven with Mom and Rebecca than we could ever spend with them here on earth."

Elizabeth then said, "We can make it through this." Then I told them basically where the situation was at that time. That Rebecca could die and that Mom was better. The conversation was over, Elizabeth said a prayer for Mom and Rebecca and I had time to run by Willis Knighton Bossier to see Susan before the NICU reopened at 8:00 a.m.—GOD IS GOOD.

You know, if I had never given up cable, I would never have known how God uses our decisions to help prepare us and our loved ones for adversity in the future. By giving up cable time, God filled it with *Little House*. By watching *Little House* instead of Disney and Nickelodeon, my four-year-old learned a biblical truth. More importantly, Elizabeth had a point of reference on how to get by after the death of a loved one.

I almost did not share the "line and the dot" with Katherine because I thought she was too young. But God says we should teach our children these truths. I am glad I did, because I had forgotten this concept and when Katherine said this it comforted me. God's truth returned to me from her mouth.

Since then, my kids have struggled with Rebecca's pain. They have had to learn how to "break" her seizures and feed her through her stomach tube. Most kids would be sad that their sister was blind and could not smile and could only experience hunger and pain. But my girls talk to Rebecca like she's fully healed, because they know that even if they all lived to be 120, they are going to spend more time with her in heaven than they could ever spend with her on this earth.

Just my thoughts for the day and why I gave up cable for 40 days of purpose/lent. God bless you!

"GLASS HALF FULL" BY SUSAN GATTI (AGE 33)
FEBRUARY 24, 2009

Typically I come from the glass half-empty perspective and Ryan from the glass half-full perspective. However, when I read his last post I believe he was taking my view for a change, so now I will try to take his.

Yes, Rebecca did receive her "Kids Rock" chair, which is a nice word for her pediatric wheelchair last week. Must add that I was shocked that it far exceeded the expense of my first car! While it does not fit her as well as it should, we are working on it. It was nice to be able to let her mother, father, and sisters take her for a walk. She seemed to calm just being outside in the beautiful weather with a slight breeze. It was nice to see her seem to relax. The transition should be interesting, but is going better than expected.

For those of you who do not know Rebecca well—she is spoiled rotten. This started at an early age (one month) when brain injuries make for irrationally irritable babies. Kristin Mosura discovered the "jog" that seemed to help—but this involved literally bouncing around the room in a fashion that my calf-muscles were not prepared for. Since that time, she has essentially been held almost every waking moment and often for sleeping moments. This occurred because the standard rules have not applied to her. When she gets too upset, it promotes even more seizure activity. No mother in her right mind can allow that to happen.

She is now approaching nineteen pounds and consistently holding her is not as easy as it once was. Needless to say, we are all hoping for a smooth transition that will allow for her seated position to improve. This is important for all of her muscular difficulties. She also received Botox injections in her arms and legs which should help to relax those muscles again. This is her second round, and we are hoping that it will go as well as the first.

Life is always an adventure though. Rebecca seemed different Saturday morning, and she was running a fever by that afternoon. Her fever got as high as 103 and was not improving significantly with medicine or baths! A three hour doctor visit on Sunday revealed a flu-like virus was the culprit. She is still highly irritable, but her fever appears to have dissipated. So far, so good for the rest of the family staying well. We'll just keep our fingers crossed. She is gaining weight in spite of it all, which is an accomplishment for her.

Rebecca is also gaining some head control. She is able to hold her head up for about thirty seconds at a time. I have also convinced myself that she says "oma" to me. Let's just ignore the simple fact that it is the only word approximation that she has and let me believe it is for me. She also knows her routine and when it is disrupted for all of her delays. Simply put, she may be the most stubborn of us all! A difficult title to receive in this family. She is by far the bravest of us all—always giving love in her own way no matter how bad her day has been. Thanks to everyone for their prayers and support.

"MY SISTER, REBECCA" BY KATHERINE GATTI (AGE 9)
OCTOBER 25, 2009

Before I tell my story, I want to say that this story shouldn't make you cry, it should make you happy.

People look at SpecialEd kids differently. Why, because they're in a wheelchair? Do people treat you differently because of your skin color? Did you choose your skin color? No. Do people get to choose if they have a brain injury? No. So why do people treat them differently? But all people have feelings just like we do, and they should be treated equally. So, here is my story.

My family was in the hospital waiting for my new little sister. I was so excited, interviewing everybody with a video camera! It was getting late so my mom's friend took care of us at home that night. The best surprise was right around the corner the next morning! Our dad was waiting for us, and we were anxious to find out if mom had the baby yet. We found out her name was Rebecca Leigh Gatti. We kept throwing questions at him like, "Who would get to hold her first?"

Then came the bomb. My dad said, "Girls, your little sister has something wrong with her brain. They had to cut open mommy's stomach to get the baby out. Mommy and Rebecca will have to stay in the hospital for a while. Rebecca is going to be sick when she comes home. But don't worry. Everything will be fine." Neither my sister nor I really understood, we thought, "Hey, she has a cold, no big deal. She'll get over it."

Then my dad asked if we wanted to go to see Mom and Rebecca, and we sure did. You know when a kid asks every couple of minutes, "Are we there yet? How much longer?" That was exactly what my sister and I were doing.

We got to meet Rebecca at the hospital. It was love at first sight. What I realized as I spent more time with her was how beautiful and wonderful she is. She can't really control her muscles that tighten up and has more seizures than you can count. Rebecca is blind and will not be able to walk. She had surgery to place a feeding tube in her stomach so she doesn't have to take medicine through her mouth anymore.

Everyone says Rebecca likes me the most. She lets me do things to her that she won't let anyone else do. She could be screaming bloody murder in my dad's arms and be showing off her dimples the second she's in mine. I dance around with her in my arms and we touch noses.

I love Rebecca with all my heart, and I don't know what I'd do without her. You should appreciate that you have a working brain and the ability to use it. So why don't you? I hope you treat people better and judge them by their characteristics instead of what they look and sound like. You can make a difference.

"REBECCA'S 3RD BIRTHDAY" BY SUSAN GATTI (AGE 34)
APRIL 13, 2010

It's hard to fathom that Rebecca has been fighting for three years. She has constant seizures and the pain is overwhelming. I spent a few extra hours with her this morning trying to modify her chair so that she would be comfortable. I cannot wait for God to remove these seizures from her. He understands the pain of watching your child suffer, because He saw His Son beaten and crucified. I am in constant awe that God has given us the grace and strength to endure and prosper during this time. He has held us together and kept us at peace.

I long for the day that I will see her run the bases in that softball field in heaven, cheer as she swims a lap, teach her to fish, listen to her play the piano, or help her draw. Can't wait to see her smile for the first time—hear her laugh, her giggle, her voice. Can't wait to walk with her and hold her hand and just visit. But for God's promise of heaven and eternal life, I would have no hope.

But is it really that bad that the very first thing she will see with her eyes will be our Savior? That her first words will be spoken in heaven and will be "Holy is the Lamb!"? That Jesus will tell her to see and walk and she will? That God will erase the pain of this world from her memory bank?

Sometimes I wonder if she won't know I love her until then. I talk to her like the eternal being that she is—one that I will recognize in eternity. Job, after losing all he had including his children, said, "Naked I came from my mother's womb and naked I will depart, The LORD has given and The LORD has taken away, may the name of The LORD be praised." We should praise God in these storms, because our turning to praise is the evidence of movement toward the ultimate end result of our salvation—becoming like Christ.

This is what it feels like to be loved by God—the comfort provided when this world strikes at the heart of what you love most. When heaven has to be real or the suffering of this world makes no sense. That God's provisions of love and grace will satisfy the hungry heart that longs for still waters. When an examination of the facts of your life provides enough circumstantial evidence to reveal beyond all doubt that God's intent is to hold onto you in the storm. He is in the boat and ready to calm the storm by revealing His authority over it.

God provides wisdom to those who seek it and fear Him. He provides comfort to His flock. He provides redemption to the surrendered and comfort to those in need. The comfort He provides is in the form of a deeper understanding of the rescue that will occur when He returns or calls each of us home.

Please take a minute on April 25, 2010, Rebecca's third birthday, and pray for our family. We need your prayers.

"COURAGE" BY ELIZABETH GATTI (AGE 8)
JANUARY 25, 2011

I had to have courage when my sister was born. You might think she's just an ordinary baby, but she's not. When she was born the doctor messed up and she died for fifteen minutes. Good thing another doctor came in and brought her to life, but she wasn't the same. She can't see, talk, or move. She's three-years-old now. I had to have courage so she wouldn't be so scared. I got courage by praying to God to help me go through the rough time.

Just a few weeks ago, Rebecca had to have casts on her feet. If she didn't her hips would pop out of socket. For three weeks she had to have them on. Now she has AFOs, they are still on her feet but they are better than casts. She has seizures and she arches with her feet and sometimes her arm twists all the way around. She can't control her body at all, not even a little, teensy bit. But she can hear every word you say. She's perfect because she cannot sin. She is so sweet, loving, adorable, precious, ONE OF A KIND! She is everything good you can imagine and more! I love her so much! If she weren't with us, I would lose a big, huge, enormous part of me. But she'll always be my Rebecca!

"APRIL 25, 2007–JULY 31, 2017" BY RYAN GATTI (AGE 43) AUGUST 1, 2017

Monday morning, Rebecca passed away in her sleep. Susan went in to start Rebecca's day and Rebecca was already in heaven. We were quickly surrounded by all her grandparents, aunts, uncles, cousins and loved ones. We wept, prayed, and held her body one last time.

It was an honor to call ourselves her family. She, without speaking a word, transformed our hearts and minds and gave us the courage to speak out. She, without walking a step, gave us courage to walk on mission trips. She, although blind, taught us to dream about the beauty of heaven. We wanted her here with us, but God called her home. She inspired us as a family. Your prayers, texts, calls, posts, cards, gifts, and presence have been soothing like a healing ointment to a wound.

As I looked back over this blog last night, I was reminded that God has carried us through this journey by commissioning our friends and those around us to be His hands and feet. We are honored to receive your prayers. You have been a blessing to us.

Rebecca Leigh Gatti's Obituary

A celebration of life for Rebecca Leigh Gatti will be 4 p.m., Thursday, August 3, 2017 at Cypress Baptist Church. Officiating will be Brother John Fream and Dr. Fred Lowery. Visitation will be from 3 p.m. to 4 p.m. at the church. Interment will follow in Rose-Neath Cemetery, Bossier City.

Rebecca Leigh Gatti passed away in her sleep on Monday, July 31, 2017. Rebecca bravely battled a birth-related brain injury for over ten years. During her brief time here on earth, she impacted and inspired many. She is survived by her parents Senator Ryan Gatti and Dr. Susan Lockhart Gatti. She is survived by her loving sisters Katherine, Elizabeth, and Charlotte. Her sisters loved her every day of her life and blessed her with true compassion. She is survived by all of her grandparents Allen "Al" and Marcia Lockhart, Robert and Jean Gatti, and honorary grandparents Mel and Glenda Allen. She is also survived by her aunts and uncles Robbie and Jennifer Turner Gatti, Allen and Casey Allen Lockhart, Randy Gatti, Robert "Bobby" Lockhart, and Regan Gatti. She is survived by her cousins Allison Lockhart, Claire Lockhart, Brandon Lockhart, Amy Lockhart, William Lockhart, Hal Gatti, Hayden Gatti, Hunter Gatti, Maigen Gatti, Moregan Gatti, and John Robert "J.R." Gatti. She is also survived by numerous great aunts and great uncles.

Cathy Jacks was Rebecca's best friend and caregiver for 10 years. She spent countless hours caring for Rebecca and humming her favorite songs to her. She made a point to spoil Rebecca every day.

Honoring Rebecca as pallbearers will be Kyle Kirsch, Jeff Patterson, Josh Pettigrew, and Mark Rodie. Serving as honorary pallbearers will be the ladies who attended to Rebecca during church services and the professionals who provided her with specialized care in her home.

Special thanks to her physicians Dr. Scott Ritch, Dr. Pena-Miches Aristoteles, and Dr. Sunny Hussain for the love and compassion they shared with her.

In lieu of flowers, the family suggests that donations may be made to the Cypress Baptist Church Night to Shine Event or the Cypress Baptist Missions Fund at P. O. Box 340, Benton, LA 71006.

Romans 5:3-5 "Not only that, but we rejoice in our sufferings, knowing that suffering produces endurance, and endurance produces character, and character produces hope, and hope does not put us to shame, because God's love has been poured into our hearts through the Holy Spirit who has been given to us."

"THE MORNING THAT CHANGED EVERYTHING" BY CHARLOTTE GATTI (AGE 11) NOVEMBER 20, 2021

The night was July 30, 2017. It was an ordinary night; my mom cooked a tasty meal with the bread that I longed for and the veggies I avoided. My sister was not eating because when Rebecca was born, she suffered a birth injury that caused her disability. Rebecca was handicapped and spent her life in a wheelchair because of a series of mistakes by the doctor. While giving birth, my mom lost so much blood she almost died. Luckily, both of them survived and made it home. Even though my sister could not walk or see, we loved her and made her a central part of our family, our life. Rebecca was not a part of meals though because she was fed through a tube in her stomach. That night, the rest of the family finished dinner, then we all went to bed like every other day.

I woke up to a piercing scream, "SHE'S GONE!" Thoughts started to flood my 7-year-old mind thinking, "Did someone kidnap her? Did she go missing?" What I saw when I went to her room was more horrifying than anything I could have imagined. I walked into Rebecca's room and saw my mother clasping my sister's limp, lifeless body. I didn't comprehend it then. All I saw was my mom crying profusely and my dad trying to be strong while still breaking down. My middle sister broke down before she could even open the door when she saw my mom holding Rebecca. She fell to the ground and just cried. Once she came inside we all went to my oldest sister's room and we all broke down and let all of our tears out until we could cry no longer.

Everything changed after that: a new normal. I miss the little things like holding her on the couch. I would always push her wheelchair into the church and after Sunday school earnestly search for her, waiting to be able to push her wheelchair back to the car and go home. I loved helping her and loved her with every ounce of my essence. When she would have a therapist come over, I would always sing to her and help. I even left a recording of me singing so she could still hear me when I had to go to school. My mom says it was because she loved the sound of my voice, and I loved the sound of hers. No matter how many seizures she had, no matter how much she cried, she was my favorite sister and will always be.

In my old and new normal, having Rebecca as a sister from birth to death was a gift. I wouldn't trade having her as a sister for anything. It taught me that everyone in this world has worth no matter if you have a disability or not; life is short and you need to show everyone love.

Acknowledgments

Every step along this journey, the Lord provided me with encouragement and support from those who love Him and love me. This book has been on my heart since I was in elementary school. There's nothing quite like revisiting the traumatic parts of your life and putting them on paper, but I knew the Lord would use it to both heal parts of my heart and hopefully help others. I'm most grateful through this process for my family; they've been patient with me as I've asked them to revisit these dark days and help me craft Rebecca's story as best as we can. Enduring this together will always bond us deeply, and I'm eternally grateful for that.

After I graduated college and before I started my job, my parents gifted me time away with one of my best friends to focus on writing this book. They've always pushed me towards the bold acts of obedience and faith the Lord has put in front of me; what an honor it is to have godly parents who sacrificially love and disciple me. I'm grateful for that time writing in a fancy treehouse on a lake in Missouri, and I'm thankful I shared that time with Jill. She talked me through the beginning stages of this book, asking me questions and shedding tears alongside me as we read through my childhood prayer journals. Thank you, Jill, for sticking close to me in the grief, heaviness, and healing of remembering.

As I prayed through how to articulate Rebecca's story, what details to share, and what lessons to focus on, I've had a solid team of family and forever friends offering their wisdom, time, feedback, and encouragement. Mom, Dad, Elizabeth, Charlotte, Nana, Cassie, Elle, Haley, Jana, Jill, Kaley, Kelci, Lauren, Reese, Riley, Savannah, Sidney, Victoria: Thank you for the time each of you gave to help this book come to be. When I was tempted to believe that I should just give up, you each reminded me of the ways Rebecca's life has served as an encouragement to you and that her story must be shared for the glory of God. Thank you for letting me talk through each little detail multiple times, reading every draft, and always praying for me.

Creating this physical book would not have been possible without some of my artistically talented friends. The cover artwork was adapted from my sister Elizabeth's drawings etched into Rebecca's tombstone. Taking my handwriting and Elizabeth's drawings, Caroline Cummins beautifully crafted the cover design. Erin Campbell meticulously formatted the interior of the book. Thank you to these creative geniuses for sharing your God-given gifts to help get this book into people's hands.

I'm in awe of the abundance of spiritual mentors God has placed in my life that intentionally poured wisdom into me since I was a young girl. Thank you to every Sunday school teacher, small group leader, friend's mom, church volunteer, pastor, pastor's wife, camp leader, and mentor who took the time to teach me about trusting Jesus. Thank you for the wisdom you've shared with me through your words and shown me through your actions. Thank you for inviting me into your lives and teaching me what it looks like to follow Jesus in the good and the bad times. So much of the wisdom you poured into me has spilled onto these pages. I'm grateful for the way the body of believers through the churches I've been a member of have served and sharpened me while giving me opportunities to do the same for others.

Above all these blessings, what I most want to acknowledge my gratitude for is God choosing me as Rebecca's oldest sister. It's a gift I could never earn and an honor I'll never live up to. It is a privelage to steward her story and share it with you. Thank you for reading.

Notes & Scriptures

INTRODUCTION

1   Petrie, Donald. *Miss Congeniality.* Warner Brothers, 2000.

CHAPTER ONE: THE BIRTH OF FEAR

1   2 Timothy 2:4
2   Psalm 23:6b
3   Romans 8:38-39

CHAPTER TWO: THE REALITY OF THE GOSPEL

1   James; Genesis 3:1-6; Romans 12:1-2
2   Romans 12:1-2
3   John 15:5
4   1 Corinthians 6:19-20
5   Matthew 3:13-17
6   2 Corinthians 5:7
7   1 Corinthians 15:57
8   Hebrews 4:16
9   John 16:33

CHAPTER THREE: THIS DOESN'T FEEL GOOD

1   Philippians 4:11
2   Hebrews 12:1-2
3   2 Corinthians 10:5b
4   Philippians 4:4-9
5   Romans 8:28
6   Isaiah 26:3
7   Psalm 27:13-14 NKJV
8   Hebrews 13:8
9   Psalm 19:14 NIV
10   Matthew 14:22-33
11   Hebrews 11:1
12   Proverbs 16:9
13   Ephesians 2:10
14   Psalm 139:16
15   Deuteronomy 31:8
16   Colossians 1:17
17   Hebrews 10:23
18   Story, Laura. "Blessings." Blessings. INO Records, 2011.
19   James 1:2-4
20   Hebrews 4:13
21   1 Timothy 6:6
22   Psalm 46:1
23   Boom, Corrie Ten. "Corrie Ten Boom Quotes." *Goodreads*, www.goodreads.com/author/quotes/102203.Corrie_ten_Boom.

CHAPTER FOUR: DOES PAIN HAVE A PURPOSE?

1   Mark 2:17
2   1 Corinthians 12
3   2 Corinthians 1:3-4
4   Colossians 3:1
5   Ephesians 2:10

CHAPTER FIVE: THE SOVEREIGNTY OF GOD

1   Colossians 1:17
2   1 Peter 5:7
3   Bridges, Jerry. *Trusting God.* NavPress, 2016, p. 7.
4   Romans 8:28
5   Lamentations 3:37-38
6   Psalm 103:8
7   Luke 23:44
8   Genesis 50:20
9   Psalm 25:10
10   2 Corinthians 5:7
11   Ecclesiastes 3:11
12   Malachi 3:6
13   Romans 6:10
14   Psalm 119:90

CHAPTER SIX: TRUSTWORTHY WISDOM

1   Genesis 1:1
2   Hebrews 10:35 NLT
3   Malachi 3:6; Hebrews 13:8
4   1 Peter 1:25
5   2 Timothy 3:16
6   1 Thessalonians 5:24
7   Numbers 23:19
8   "Definition of Wholehearted." *www.dictionary.com,*
      www.dictionary.com/browse/wholehearted.
9   Psalm 86:11
10   Proverbs 3:5-6
11   1 Peter 1:22
12   Ephesians 4:1-3
13   1 Corinthians 15:58
14   1 Samuel 16:7

15   Colossians 3:17

16   2 Corinthians 5:7

17   Russo, Joe. *Captain America: The Winter Soldier.* Marvel Studios, 2014.

18   Hebrews 4:12

19   Psalm 119:105

20   Isaiah 41:10

21   Gruenewald, Bobby. *YouVersion Bible.* Life.Church, Version 9.2, 2023. *Apple App Store*, https://apps.apple.com/us/app/bible/id282935706.

22   Philippians 4:6-7

23   James 1:17

24   1 Corinthians 10:13

25   Psalm 46:1

26   1 Corinthians 14:33

27   Psalm 119

28   Willard, Dallas. *A Life Without Lack.* Thomas Nelson, 2019, p. XVI.

29   Romans 8:6

30   Isaiah 26:3-4

31   John 10:10

32   Proverbs 9:10

33   James 1:5

34   2 Timothy 3:16-17

35   Isaiah 49:46

CHAPTER SEVEN: THE POWER OF PRAYER

1   Luke 8:40-56

2   Deuteronomy 32:4

3   Hebrews 4:14-16

4   1 Corinthians 6:19

5   John 14:16

6   John 14:26

7   Hebrews 4:12

8   Romans 8:26-27

9   Psalm 56:8; Luke 12:7

10   1 Peter 5:8

11   James 4:8; Matthew 5:4

12   Romans 8:6

13   Matthew 6:8

14   Matthew 19:26

15   1 John 1:9

16   Psalm 139:2,16

17   Matthew 6:10; Luke 22:42

18   1 Thessalonians 5:17

19   Perry, Jackie Hill [@jackiehillperry]. "On Prayer." *Instagram*, 24 May 2022, https://www.instagram.com/p/Cd8CH5OuznN/?hl=en.

20   1 Peter 5:8

21   John 8:44

22   John 10:27-29

23   2 Corinthians 2:11

24   2 Corinthians 11:3

25   James 4:7

26   Ephesians 6:10-18

27   Ephesians 6:11-13

28   Ephesians 6:18

29   John 8:44

30   John 14:6

31   John 8:31-32

32   James 5:16b

33   Joshua 1:8

34   Ephesians 4:1-3

35   Psalm 37:3-6

CHAPTER EIGHT: THE PEACE OF CHRIST

1   Proverbs 31:25
2   Burpo, Todd and Lynn Vincent. *Heaven is for Real.* Thomas Nelson, 2010.
3   Matthew 24:36
4   Deuteronomy 31:6-8
5   Philippians 4:7
6   Rosman, Mark. *A Cinderella Story.* Warner Brothers, 2004.
7   Psalm 3:3
8   Psalm 139:5
9   Matthew 11:28
10   Psalm 90:4; 2 Peter 3:8

CHAPTER NINE: THE FREEDOM OF FORGIVENESS

1   James 1:17
2   Romans 3:23
3   Ephesians 2:8-9
4   1 John 1:9
5   1 Thessalonians 4:3
6   Romans 8:38-39
7   Matthew 18:15
8   Ephesians 6:12
9   Lawrence, Francis. *The Hunger Games: Catching Fire.* Lionsgate, 2013.
10   John 16:33
11   Matthew 6:5-13
12   Matthew 5:44
13   Luke 23:34
14   Jeremiah 31:34
15   Ephesians 4:32
16   Romans 5:8
17   Romans 12:18

18   2 Corinthians 12:9-10

19   James 5:16

20   Psalm 51:1,3-4,7,10-12,17

21   1 Samuel 13:14; Acts 13:22

22   Matthew 11:28-29 NIV

23   Ortlund, Dane. *Gentle and Lowly: The Heart of Christ for Sinners and Sufferers.* Crossway Books, 2021, pp. 19, 20, 24.

24   James 4:8

25   Jeremiah 32:17

26   1 John 4:18

27   James 1:17; 1 Chronicles 16:34

28   Psalm 119:68

29   Isaiah 55:8-9

CHAPTER TEN: FAITHFULNESS

1   Hebrews 11:1

2   2 Timothy 2:13

3   Ephesians 4:13

4   Psalm 1:3

5   John 4:13b-14

6   Ephesians 2:10

7   John 15:4-5

8   Galatians 5:22-23

9   John 15:2

10   Ephesians 4:1-3

11   Ephesians 2:8-9a

12   1 Samuel 16:7

13   John 13:35

14   Matthew 28:19-20

15   Pokluda, Jonathan. "Family Matters: Discipleship." *Harris Creek Baptist Church*, 23 Aug. 2021. Sermon.

16   Luke 22:42

17   James 4:8

18   Hebrews 6:19
19   Matthew 11:28

CHAPTER ELEVEN: PROCLAIM HIS GLORY

1   Galatians 2:20
2   Romans 5:6-11
3   John 3:16
4   Hebrews 4:14-16
5   Romans 5:1-5
6   Romans 10:13b
7   2 Corinthians 5:17-21

CHAPTER TWELVE: ETERNAL HOPE

1   Proverbs 31:10,25-30

About the Author

KATHERINE GATTI is a sister, daughter, and friend who loves Jesus. She grew up in Bossier City, Louisiana, surrounded by family and rooted in faith. Katherine loves to write in journals, online, and now in books. After graduating from Texas Christian University's business school in 2022, Katherine remained in Fort Worth, Texas, to begin her career in Marketing.

WEBSITE: KatherineGatti.com
Click on "Events" to inquire about having Katherine speak at your event.

INSTAGRAM: @KatherineGatti

FACEBOOK: Facebook.com/KatherineGattiAuthor